The Practical Encyclopedia of

THE
MARINE
AQUARIUM

Above: *Tomato Clowns* (Amphiprion frenatus) *at home in their sea anemone.*

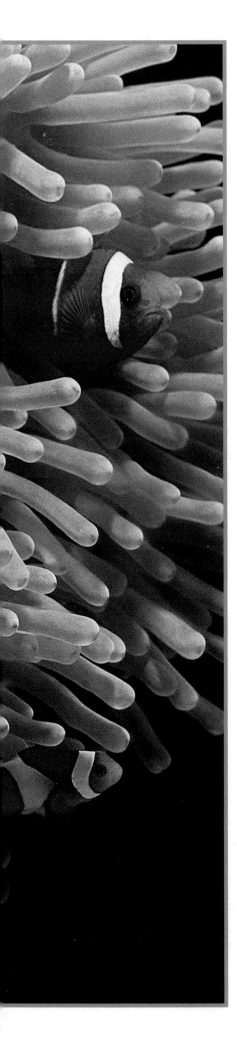

Red Sea

The Practical Encyclopedia of

THE
MARINE
AQUARIUM

Colin Grist
(Part One: Practical Section)

Dick Mills
(Part Two: Species Guide)

Consultants
Neil Marks

Specialist adviser
Andrew Caine

INTERPET PUBLISHING

© 2002 Interpet Publishing
Vincent Lane, Dorking, Surrey,
RH4 3YX, UK.
ISBN: 1-84286-071-2

Credits:
Edited and designed: Ideas into Print,
New Ash Green, Longfield, Kent DA3
8JD, UK and Stonecastle Graphics,
Old Chapel Studio, Tonbridge,
Kent TN12 9LS, UK.

Production management:
Consortium, Poslingford,
Suffolk CO10 8RA, UK.

Print production:
C.S. Graphics, Singapore.

Printed and bound in China

The authors

Colin Grist has worked professionally in the aquatic industry for more than 30 years and is currently at the New England Aquarium, Boston, USA. He has written numerous articles and papers for publications around the world and contributed to several books. He has also lectured extensively on aquarium and aquatic conservation topics throughout the UK, Europe, the USA and Mexico, and coordinates a conservation project in Cameroon, West Africa.

Dick Mills, author of many aquarium books, is a former editor of The Aquarist and Pondkeeper magazine and also a Vice-President of the Federation of British Aquatic Societies. He has kept aquarium and pond fish continuously for the last 40 years, but also finds time to travel, when – as if by accident – he always manages to come across a public aquarium or two.

Below: (Lysmata debelius). *These boldly marked shrimps are beautiful and hardy but shy. Provide a peaceful aquarium with moderate lighting conditions to make them feel secure.*

Contents

Part One: Practical Section

A complete guide to setting up a marine aquarium, from selecting and furnishing a tank to choosing and introducing compatible fishes, their feeding, routine maintenance, breeding and health care.

Part Two: Species Guide

This part of the book is divided into three main sections: tropical marine fishes, tropical invertebrates, and coldwater fishes and invertebrates.

Tropical invertebrates 186-193
A practical introduction to these fascinating creatures – from crabs to sea anemones – with basic advice on how to keep them in the aquarium.

Coldwater fishes and invertebrates 194-199
A brief survey of temperate species suitable for display in a marine aquarium.

Above: This 275-litre (60-gallon) reef aquarium houses a fine display of invertebrates and fishes.

Part One

Practical section

Marine fishes, particularly the tropical species, have to be seen to be believed. With the realization that these vivid and striking fishes exist in a multitude of shapes and sizes in the wild, comes the urge to encapsulate part of this marine world in the aquarium. Newcomers to fishkeeping might think this an impossible dream, but developments over the past twenty years would prove them wrong.

Unlike their freshwater counterparts, which are bred in captivity and have become adapted to aquarium conditions, most tropical marine fishes are brought directly from the wild. As a result, most fish undergo a long and stressful journey from their native waters to your aquarium. With correct handling, they will arrive in good condition, ready to be acclimatised to their new home.

In the sea, and in particular around coral reefs, the water conditions are extremely stable. Once these beautiful creatures are installed in the aquarium, the fishkeeper assumes a vital role. This entails learning about the conditions the fish require and how to provide these ideal conditions on a long-term basis. Over the years, research has resulted in the development of reliable systems and equipment for keeping marine fishes. These advances, together with a greater understanding of the fishes' requirements, mean that we can embark on the splendid hobby of marine fishkeeping with much more confidence than did the early pioneers.

Chapter 1: Why keep marines?

Why keep a marine aquarium? There are many answers to this question: it is a rewarding challenge; it helps develop a better understanding of natural habitats and their ecology and biology; it can instigate a keen interest in conservation, and it can be generally educational by indirectly helping to teach us about geography and various other subjects. Of course, all these considerations can also be applied to keeping a freshwater aquarium, but it is the diversity of species, their characters and personalities, curious appearances and stunning colours that draws our interest to marine fishes and invertebrates. Many have quite distinctive lifestyles, coexisting in association with other animals. For example, some clownfishes have a close symbiotic relationship with certain anemones. The possibility of housing fishes and invertebrates in the same aquarium is an added attraction and one that is not easily achieved in a freshwater aquarium.

Marine fishkeeping also raises other interesting questions: why are juvenile fishes often a totally different colour and pattern to adults of the same species? Why is it the male seahorse that undergoes pregnancy? Why are the fishes' colours so intense? We already have the answers to some of these questions, but others remain a mystery. Perhaps it will be you who finds out the truth behind a perplexing puzzle.

Meeting the challenge
Do not underestimate the challenge of keeping marine fishes; generally speaking, it is a more complex undertaking than maintaining most freshwater aquariums, and demands a certain amount of dedication, which can be time consuming. It is not just a case of setting up the tank and regarding it as a living ornament in your lounge. This is not to say that freshwater aquarists are not dedicated, but it is much easier to set up a freshwater aquarium without having had any previous experience. In fact, it is a positive advantage, although not essential, to have been a freshwater aquarist before moving on to marines. Many aspects of freshwater and marine fishkeeping are similar. For example, the basic principles of filtration apply to both. However, certain aspects of marine fishkeeping have no direct equivalent in the freshwater world, and new skills must be learned from scratch.

The main challenge arises from the fact that marine environments, and coral reefs in particular, are more environmentally stable than most freshwater situations. Coral reefs are so stable that even minute environmental changes can take decades to take effect, whereas in the marine aquarium these same types of changes can happen within a few hours. It is easy to understand that coral reef animals have no mechanism for dealing with such rapid changes, hence the need to work hard at maintaining water quality in the captive environment. Freshwater habitats tend to be very small compared to seas and oceans, are more easily affected by the weather and seasons and are also easier to pollute. Therefore, freshwater organisms have generally evolved into tougher animals, the downside being that there are many critically endangered species and habitats and a faster rate of extinction compared to the situation in tropical marine environments.

The availability of marine fishes and invertebrates has improved with an increase in the numbers of aquarium stores stocking them. Collecting and shipping techniques have generally improved over recent years, with many fisherfolk returning to more traditional methods to catch their fishes. A trend towards sustainable harvesting is giving the industry a better image and is ensuring the livelihood of many fishing villages for the foreseeable future. As the industry develops, it is actually helping to put a value on the reefs that encourages the fisherfolk to manage them sensitively and is ultimately helping to secure their future.

Over time, our knowledge of the reproductive behaviour of marine species has improved to an extent that many species of coral reef animals can now be successfully bred in captivity. Hobbyists and professionals alike have contributed to this knowledge base. Some of the most popular species have been bred in commercial numbers and are now available to marine aquarists. However, there is still much to be learned and the hobbyist is well placed to take on such challenges and help to improve the knowledge base further.

Successful captive breeding programmes will help ensure the future of many species as a kind of 'safety-net' in case of severe habitat degradation in the wild – even though we all hope global damage to this extent will never occur. However, it will always be necessary to import wild stock in order to maintain genetic integrity. In other words, new blood is important to ensure that captive-bred animals are genetically as close as possible to their wild relatives and that there is some element of random selection as would be found in nature. (See page 52-55 for more on breeding marine fishes.)

The systems
In a domestic-size freshwater aquarium, it is possible to establish a natural biological equilibrium using only 'organic' elements, i.e. keeping the correct number of aquatic plants and fishes to create a biologically balanced aquarium. Although not totally

Below: A shoal of wreckfish (Pseudanthias squamipinnis) *on a Red Sea reef. These vibrant and constantly active fish are widely distributed across the tropical oceans. In the wild, males have harems of about 30 females. In spacious aquariums, it is best to keep one male with at least 11 females.*

Stocking levels

Experienced freshwater aquarists will already be familiar with the theory that the number of fishes that can be comfortably held in a tank of any given volume depends on three things; the amount of dissolved oxygen in the water and its replenishment rate capability, the temperature of the water and what sort of fishes you are keeping. Warm water holds less dissolved oxygen than cold water. However, the whole complex problem can be conveniently calculated by using one of two methods illustrated opposite, or a combination of both, to make the calculation. Work on the principal that biological filter beds with a volume of one-fifth of the volume of water in the system are generally sufficient.

Use water quality tests to decide when it is safe to introduce new specimens into the aquarium, ideally only introducing one at any given time. This progressive technique will allow your filter to adjust to the extra loading on the system, which occurs each time you add a new animal. It is a good idea to measure the dissolved oxygen level of the water on a regular basis. This should be in the region of 80-90% saturation; a tendency to drop below this range is a good indication that stocking levels are too high. Consult your dealer if in doubt, but usually a little forethought and common sense will prove effective. These are good husbandry guidelines for a newly set-up aquarium, but with increasing experience and new technology the parameters could be altered.

Fish length and water surface

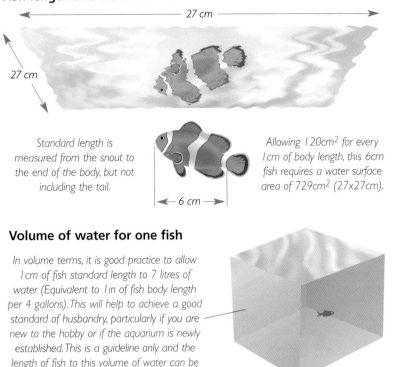

27 cm

27 cm

Standard length is measured from the snout to the end of the body, but not including the tail.

← 6 cm →

Allowing 120cm² for every 1cm of body length, this 6cm fish requires a water surface area of 729cm² (27x27cm).

Volume of water for one fish

In volume terms, it is good practice to allow 1cm of fish standard length to 7 litres of water (Equivalent to 1in of fish body length per 4 gallons). This will help to achieve a good standard of husbandry, particularly if you are new to the hobby or if the aquarium is newly established. This is a guideline only and the length of fish to this volume of water can be increased to a degree with experience.

Above: Reef aquariums can play host to a wide range of fish and invertebrates. Here, a clownfish, damselfish and angelfish share their aquarium home with other tropical reef fishes and a selection of soft corals and anemones. Sustaining such a community demands high standards of fishkeeping.

impossible, it is extremely difficult to achieve a similar equilibrium in the marine aquarium; in attempting to do so, you would first need to combine many years of experience in marine aquarium keeping with an enormous amount of research into reef ecology and biology.

In the sea, the 'waste disposal' problem is solved by the sheer vastness of the water, wave action and the activity of filter-feeding animals, such as sponges, sea squirts and fan worms, etc. At the same time, there is massive bacterial activity on the equally large surface area of rocks, corals and the seabed that serves to 'purify' the water. An aquarium designed to function in exactly the same way would be so large, that it would be beyond the scope of the average fishkeeper. Furthermore,

such an aquarium would be very susceptible to 'explosive pollution' if its subjects were overfed or a decaying body were to go undetected.

Conversely, logic might suppose that a constantly monitored, automatically controlled, smaller marine aquarium is possible in this 'hi-tech' day and age. This may be true to some extent, albeit at a proportionately large financial cost, but, while theoretically everything may be under control, there are always seemingly unpredictable factors to be

considered when keeping live animals in captivity that tend to upset even the best laid plans. Speculation suggests that the animals within such a system could become 'over-protected' by the technological aids and lose their natural resistance to disease should any be inadvertently introduced into the aquarium, or the fishes removed to other, less 'sanitary' quarters. A further drawback with this type of aquarium is that it may not be possible to keep filter-feeding animals, as their food is removed most effectively from the water by the constant action of very powerful filter systems. Efficient removal of vital minerals from the water may also preclude the growth of marine algae.

Marine fishkeeping has in general developed a middle path between these two extremes. An understanding of the natural cleansing processes that occur within the ocean has led to the development of relatively low-cost solutions to the equivalent problems in the aquarium. Modern filtration systems – particularly those based on bacterial activity – use natural methods of processing wastes and this is the key to the increasing popularity and success rate of marine fishkeeping around the world.

Complete aquarium set-ups based around efficient, but in essence 'natural' filter systems are discussed in a later chapter. However, armed with a basic understanding of water management, there is no reason why you should not be able to build up an aquarium system from separate components. In fact, this often proves more satisfying, and probably better suits the needs and finances of the average hobbyist. At the very least, doing things 'bit by bit' offers the opportunity to absorb some knowledge along the way. If you buy everything all at once in a single package, you may not need to find out or even understand how and why the system works because it is a simple case of filling with water and plugging in. The problem is that if the system develops a fault and fails, you may not be equipped with the essential know-how required to put it right.

Coral reef fishes

For most aquarists embarking on marine aquarium keeping, it is the brightly coloured fishes that provide inspiration. This is admittedly the major area of interest for hobbyists and accordingly takes up a substantial part of this book. The techniques of marine aquarium husbandry are usually learned while keeping a fish-only aquarium and are highly valuable when considering the inclusion of other animals.

Coral reef invertebrates

A wide range of reef invertebrate life can be kept in captivity, and this is a rapidly growing area of marine aquarium keeping. Suitable species include shrimps, sea anemones, living corals, clams, starfishes and tubeworms, which all do a great job in helping to create a most naturalistic captive environment. A piece of so-called 'living rock' may have tiny polyps or fan worms living on it, along with many other representative life-forms that will further help create the illusion of having a tiny portion of natural reef in your tank. If you research and carefully choose the invertebrates you wish to keep, you will find many of them will happily coexist with fishes. Indeed many fishes and invertebrates have naturally close associations in nature, as we shall see in later sections.

Alternatively, you may wish to establish an invertebrate-only aquarium, allowing you to study the life-styles of these creatures without the worry of problems caused by predatory fishes. Most tropical invertebrates are every bit as colourful as the fishes and will reward the patient observer with intriguing behaviour patterns.

Coldwater marine fishes and invertebrates

It would not be fair to assume the above selection of tropical marine life presents the whole picture. Fishes and

Right: The coldwater marine aquarium lacks the brilliant colours of the tropical tank but compensates in other ways; invertebrates are relatively easy to collect and keep. Anemones varying in size, shape and colour are ideal.

Above: This strange-looking creature is a nudibranch, or sea slug. These shell-less, brilliantly coloured molluscs bear a tuft of naked gills and spend their time moving slowly over coral and rock surfaces in search of the algae on which they feed.

Below: This overhead view of the giant green sea anemone (Anthopleura xanthogrammica) reveals the central mouth and ring of tentacles – a body plan anemones share with corals and jellyfishes. Symbiotic algae produce the green colour.

invertebrates from coldwater and temperate water regions can also be kept in captivity, sometimes with fewer demands. One advantage of tackling this aspect of marine fishkeeping is that, very often, collecting your own specimens is not only free, but also usually a very enjoyable activity – depending on how near you live to suitable collecting sites. Be aware of laws and regulations, as many coastal areas are nature reserves and it may not be legal to collect from such locations.

Exploring your local seashore can be a useful lesson in conservation and it is likely you will want to do your best to preserve these natural habitats. With this in mind, always take care to replace any rocks you have moved as they maybe home to animals you are not interested in collecting. Always take litter away and dispose of it in the correct manner. Also, only collect animals you are sure you can look after throughout their normal lifespan. It is no longer regarded acceptable to return fishes back into the wild if they grow too large for your aquarium, as there are very serious concerns about the risk of introducing unnatural diseases etc, into the natural habitat by doing this.

Rockpool animals naturally live in conditions that are ever-changing and therefore they tend to be very hardy and ideally suited to the rigours of captivity. However, during hot summer months, the temperature may rise too high for all but the hardiest of rock pool creatures. They can be kept at relatively low cost, but they are generally not as colourful as their tropical relatives.

The colder and more stable conditions found off-shore mean that keeping animals from such locations is a bit more demanding and will probably require the addition of an expensive chilling system. (See page 15 for details of temperature control).

Reaping the rewards

Whatever form of marine fishkeeping you decide to involve yourself in, the rewards are really quite self-evident. You will enjoy a great sense of achievement. Even when things go wrong, you will learn by your mistakes and feel satisfied when you have solved your problems. There is still much to learn about the marine environment and you, as an aquarist, are ideally placed to observe a tiny bit of nature, all of which has relevance in science and conservation. Recording your observations puts you in the enviable position of being able to disseminate information for the benefit of others. At the very least you can sit, watch and enjoy the fascinating and curious lifestyles of your aquarium subjects.

Is marine fishkeeping expensive?

At first, it may look as if marine fishkeeping is relatively expensive, but closer examination shows that there is only a small premium to be paid for the privilege of 'going marine'. Marine fishes may individually be more expensive than their freshwater counterparts, but this is because when they are shipped, they must be packed singly, whereas many freshwater fishes can be packed together in large groups. This means that, where marine fishes are concerned, you are mostly paying the freight costs for the water your fishes are shipped in. On the other hand, it is possible, and often desirable, to keep many more specimens in a freshwater aquarium of a given size than you can marines, so the cost for animals can quite easily even out.

The basic equipment requirements are the same for both marine and freshwater aquariums, but at the setting up stage you will need to use a marine substrate that is generally a bit more expensive, plus you will need the essential saltwater that adds a bit of extra expense. Also you may want, or even need, to include additional lighting and it is likely you will want to install extra devices, such as a protein skimmer. The extra items that are not required for freshwater fishkeeping add to the initial cost, but bear in mind that marine fishes are generally much longer-lived than freshwater fishes, and therefore need replacing less often, so on balance the costs need not be too different when spread over time.

Of course, the above refers to a basic system, but there is no limit to the amount you can spend and there are plenty of opportunities to do so. You may want to go for a fish-only system with basic habitat structures and simple economical lighting. Such a system is relatively inexpensive and will cost much the same as an equivalent-sized, freshwater aquarium. Or you may opt for one of the so-called 'total-systems' that has everything necessary, plus extras, which will cost more. Maybe you have a particular interest in hard corals and clams, which are usually extremely expensive, draining your finances dramatically and, in fact, costing you more in animal purchases than it did to set-up your aquarium with all its apparatus. Potentially, the 'reef aquarium', packed with living rock and hundreds of invertebrates, plus the dedicated equipment and water treatments often used in conjunction with them, can be the most expensive option. The choice is yours, but one thing you must never do is try to cut corners in order to save money. This will almost certainly result in failure and is therefore absolute false economy.

Chapter 2: Selecting a tank

There are a number of constraints that require careful consideration when choosing a suitable aquarium tank for marine use. A little forethought is required when deciding the size, shape and design of the tank, as well as the materials to be used in its construction.

Tank construction

Saltwater is highly corrosive and abrasive, which means the chosen tank must not include any metal in its construction, or any other material that could release toxins into the water. This also applies to all associated equipment used to maintain the aquarium. Even some plastics can present a problem, as seawater can strip potentially dangerous surface chemicals off items such as pipe work. Food-grade materials are safe to use, but to be certain it is always best to use equipment manufactured especially for the aquarium hobby. Fortunately, all-glass and acrylic aquarium tanks are readily available and are totally safe for marine fishkeeping.

If it absolutely necessary to use equipment with metal parts, such as some aquarium hoods, you must apply three or four coats of protective polypropylene varnish before use. Saltwater spray can also be damaging to objects close to the aquarium, so these will require protection also. Always check that the varnish is safe for pets.

Hobbyists can choose from a wide variety of shapes and sizes of commercially available tanks, although the rectangular style is the most common. This long, shallow, 'letter-box' design may not always be the most aesthetically appealing, so tank manufacturers have become more adventurous and creative, although not all their designs are practical for some areas of marine fishkeeping

Selecting tank size and shape

When considering the size of an aquarium, remember the principal that 'large is good, but bigger is better'. The larger the water volume, the more inherently stable it can be in terms of water quality. The same rule applies to the filtration area if it is to be included in the tank. So, although it is possible to establish a marine aquarium in a relatively small tank, always opt for the largest you can accommodate and afford.

Regarding shape, it is important to remember that tall, narrow tanks have less surface area than wide, shallow ones. Marine fishes and invertebrates require a high level of oxygen (O_2), which can only be absorbed into the water at its surface. Potentially dangerous carbon dioxide (CO_2) is also dissipated into the atmosphere at the water surface. So, the larger the surface area is, the more efficient this gas exchange will be. Inefficient gas exchange will mean that the system can support fewer animals. Always bear this in mind when deciding the shape of your tank. It is no accident that the standard, rectangular aquarium remains the most practical and popular.

Unusual shapes are commercially available both in glass and acrylic, although there is greater variety in the latter due to its more flexible properties. Cylinders, corner units and hexagonal tanks are just a few that may appeal and are suitable, providing you consider the rules of gas exchange. One shape that offers interesting viewing aspects along with an acceptable surface area in relation to depth is the cube.

Water is heavy and aquariums are expected to contain a remarkable weight. Both glass and acrylic are very strong materials and, providing the aquarium is well constructed, are ideally suited for the job, although each has its advantages and disadvantages. The final choice will be a matter of personal preference. Glass is more brittle than acrylic and therefore more likely to break if not looked after correctly, but it does not scratch as easily as acrylic, which may require special polishing from time to time. Acrylic has superior light-transmitting properties that give a much clearer view and it is less reflective than most types of glass, especially where thicker materials are necessary. Glass is still somewhat cheaper than acrylic.

If you intend to upgrade your system with new accessories at a later date, make sure it is capable of accommodating these new items. For example, a protein skimmer often requires extra 'headroom' in a tank; a fact that could be easily overlooked when deciding on the initial system. Similarly, extra room above the tank could be required if lighting is to be upgraded.

As a starting point, choose a tank no smaller than 90cm long x 30cm wide x 40cm high (36x12x16in). A tank this size will hold approximately 114 litres (25 gallons) of water. This has a good surface area and will allow for a number of small fishes or invertebrates, or a compatible mix of fishes and invertebrates, to establish themselves within their own space. As long as each fish has a space it can retreat to, it will not feel threatened and will settle more easily, and generally be more visible.

Space for territories

Another consideration is the territoriality of some species. In the relatively confined space of an aquarium, many fishes will not tolerate others of the same species, or even close relatives. An example would be angelfishes, particularly those in the genus *Pomacanthus*, that will aggressively fight with other angelfishes and sometimes with similarly shaped

A tank measuring 90x30x45cm (36x12x18in) is an ideal minimum size for a marine aquarium and has been used in the set-up sequence featured on pages 34-39.

Right: *A large coral reef aquarium built into a wall provides a stunning display. The support and filtration systems are hidden behind the wall panels, but are accessible for regular maintenance – a vital consideration, particularly for such an impressive aquarium.*

species. This often happens because there is not enough space for more than one fish to establish a territory, and the least dominant fishes are continually encroaching on the most dominant individual's space. Even small species, such as many damsels, are so territorial, particularly when they are guarding a nest site, that they will attack virtually any other fish in the aquarium. In many species, the males are intolerant of each other and will fight relentlessly, often to the death.

The same can also apply to many invertebrates, especially crustaceans. Even aggression amongst corals is known. Researching the natural history

Buying a tank

When buying any type of tank, it is worth checking the following points:

• Regardless of material, all edges should be smooth to avoid risk of injury.
• Check for cracks, splinters and other blemishes that could weaken the material.
• Makes sure all sides of the tank have been cut accurately so that all edges are flush without undesirable overhangs.
• In a glass aquarium, the silicone beading used to bond the sides together should be smooth and neat without any bubbles or air pockets.
• In acrylic tanks, it is important that the bonded seams do not have any bubbles or air pockets.

of the species you intend to keep and reading material by experienced fishkeepers will help you to determine which species you can and cannot keep together in one aquarium.

Siting the tank

When a tank measuring 90x30x40cm (36x12x16in) is filled with decorative material, substrate and water, it will weigh about 114kg (250lb) and thus become an immovable object. You must therefore consider where the tank will be situated before you set it up.

Because it is so heavy, site the tank on a firm base, which is in turn evenly supported on a strong floor. Try to arrange an even distribution of weight across floor joists. The aquarium stand should have a solid, perfectly flat top on which to place the tank – particularly where all-glass tanks are concerned. You can cushion the tank against any unevenness in the stand with a material such as expanded polystyrene, cork or special foam sheets available at aquarium dealers. Remember, however, that any such underlay will only compensate for minor irregularities; any major twist or warp in the supporting surface will stress a filled tank and result in breakage. The same principles apply if you decide to install the tank into a dividing wall, or onto a shelf or cabinet.

The aquarium will need lighting equipment and pumps and, if it is to house tropical marines, heating apparatus, so be sure to site the tank near to an electricity supply. Also bear

in mind that water and electricity do not mix, so plugs and sockets must be a safe distance from splashing, or protected in some other way. Ideally, the electricity supply should be above and away from the water surface level.

It is not a good idea to site the aquarium close to a window because, even though it may be a tropical setup, sunshine through glass can seriously overheat the water, making accurate temperature control very difficult. Putting the tank in a bright conservatory or sunroom can cause similar problems. Obviously this situation would be even more critical where coldwater or temperate fishes are concerned. Avoid placing the aquarium too close to radiators for the same reason. Also, excessive light falling on the tank could encourage unwanted growths of algae. Should you wish to grow any of the popular macro algae, it is best to use artificial lighting systems, over which you have control.

To avoid disturbances from external sources, try to place the aquarium away from anything that may cause stressful vibrations in the tank, such as doors opening and shutting. Conversely, some aquarium equipment may be noisy, so consider other members of the household who may enjoy watching TV, or are trying to sleep on the other side of a partitioning wall.

Wherever the aquarium is situated, always make sure there is room for the correct installation of the equipment you want to use and that there is good access for maintenance.

Chapter 3: Temperature control

The water in a marine aquarium must be maintained at a reasonably constant temperature if fishes and invertebrates from tropical coral reefs are to survive. Animals collected from your local coast can be maintained at the temperatures that occur naturally where you live. In some places, measures to cool down the tropical aquarium may be required, particularly during summer months.

Types of heating equipment

Various forms of heating have been developed over the years. However, the most popular method of heating aquarium water is by means of small, individual electric immersion heaters combined with a thermostat control, commonly known as heaterstats. These units are generally protected inside a glass sleeve, although you can also buy more rugged types made from materials such as titanium. Some external, canister-style power filters also incorporate a heating system, but be sure to check these out carefully as most are only safe for use in freshwater systems because the elements and thermostat connections could corrode in saltwater. Undergravel heating cables controlled by an external thermostat are also available.

Heating equipment may also be incorporated within the water treatment compartment (or sump) of a built-in 'total system'. This can make more efficient use of your heater, as it is heating a smaller body of water at any one time. For larger systems there are

Adjust the temperature setting with this dial.

Adjust the air intake with this control cap.

Filtered, heated water returns here.

The outer casing contains filter foam and an activated carbon sachet.

Adjust the water flow rate by turning this dial.

Water is drawn through slots in these side panels.

The heater is housed in this central casing.

Heater-thermostats are available calibrated in °C or °F, or both scales side by side.

Left: *Combined heater-thermostats are easy to adjust by turning the knob at the top until you reach the desired temperature. Some units have a light to indicate whether it is on or off. Make sure you can see it. Always keep a spare heater-thermostat handy in case of failures.*

heating elements housed in a sleeve that can be plumbed directly in the pipework of the water circulation system.

In large fish rooms it would probably be more efficient to heat the space around the tanks. Gas central heating and thermostatically controlled fan heaters are good for the job, as are fuel-burning heaters. However, bear in mind that any form of fuel-burning system must have good ventilation to keep up the oxygen supply to it and to the air around the tanks and also to vent off fumes, which could be harmful to aquarium animals.

To measure the temperature, you can use any type of aquarium thermometer, as they all tend to be made either from glass or a suitable plastic. You can also choose from a variety of digital electronic thermometers designed for aquarium use.

Controlling and conserving heat

In a standard aquarium heaterstat, the built-in thermostat controls the supply of electricity to the heating element by sensing the temperature of the water. This sensing is achieved by means of a bimetallic strip that bends and straightens, making and breaking contact as the temperature changes, or by microchip circuitry. Microchip thermostats are normally a separate unit from the heating element and temperature control is achieved by a

What size heaterstat?

Allow about 10 watts per 4.54 litres (1 gallon) of water content. Our 90x30x38cm (36x15x12in) aquarium has an approximate volume of 110 litres (24 gallons) and would therefore require 240 watts of heat. A smaller-sized heater would be sufficient if the room is permanently heated. Following the guidelines described above, a single 250-watt heater should suffice, but two separate 150-watt heaters would be better and afford some margin for error or heater failure.

probe in the water that sends a message back to the thermostat, which in turn regulates the power to the heating element. Large, ready-built complete systems often use these high-tech thermostats, but they are not so widely used in the average home aquarium.

For most tropical marine aquariums, the ideal temperature is around 75°F (24°C). The familiar heaterstats are usually factory preset to this temperature, but can be adjusted to a few degrees above and below this level if necessary.

External thermostat units can be either analogue or digital. Analogue units are set manually, but digital models allow you to programme a variety of temperature parameters and often have automatic features, such as emitting an alarm if the temperature gets too high or too low. Some include a display that records the maximum and minimum temperature reached in a time period, as well as showing the current temperature. Such digital units can offer the degree of control and accuracy that will provide extra protection for aquarium subjects and peace of mind for you, the aquarist.

Computerized aquarium systems that can control temperature along with a variety of water quality testing features from a single unit are also available. Such equipment often includes software and connecting cables to link with a personal computer, allowing you to plot trends and store other information.

To avoid stressing the fishes, always adjust the water temperature very slowly and gradually, particularly if you are lowering it. Fishes are less tolerant of a sudden drop in temperature than they are of a rise, and such adjustments could trigger a disease problem. Allow time to elapse between each small adjustment before rechecking the temperature and making any further changes. Once the water has reached the required temperature, a relatively small amount of electricity is needed to maintain it at that level. The larger the aquarium is, the slower the rate of heat loss from it.

Any type of heater must be able to maintain the desired water temperature without having to run constantly; for example, in a 136-litre (30-gallon) aquarium in a normally heated room you should allow 2 watts per litre of heating (about 10 watts per gallon).

Left: A typical aquarium chiller. Such devices contain a compact refrigeration unit that cools the incoming water to a preset temperature. The inflow and outflow pipe connectors are clearly visible at the front.

Below: Here, a stone crab (Cancer pagurus) *is pictured with a beautiful sea anemone* (Urticina eques). *Both these hardy animals are suitable for a coldwater aquarium, where they will add colour and interest.*

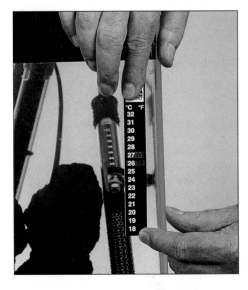

Above: Various types of thermometers are available for aquarium use, including easy-to-read liquid crystal types that stick to the outside surface of the tank. A digital model is shown being used on page 38.

Most aquarium heaters are manufactured in standard ratings, usually in steps of 50 or 100 watts. If you are using heaters inside the tank, it is more efficient to split the total heat requirements between two heaterstat units positioned at opposite ends of the tank. This will help maintain an even temperature distribution throughout the aquarium. It will also safeguard against sudden drops in temperature if one heater fails, as it is less likely that two will malfunction at the same time.

Some external thermostats are fitted to the aquarium with metal clips. Remember the dire warnings about the dangers of metal in contact with saltwater and the resulting toxic effect on aquarium inhabitants, so make sure all fastening clips are waterproof. Better still, use the more advanced microchip thermostats that can be placed anywhere within reach of the aquarium because they operate with a remote sensing probe.

To conserve heat and reduce costs, particularly in cold climates, you can insulate the room where the aquarium is situated, or even the tank itself. Heat rises in water, as it does in air, so fitting a condensation tray over the tank (even a 'double-glazed' one) will go a long way to reduce heat loss through the top of the tank. Of course an aquarium hood will help even further.

Cooling the water

In some situations, particularly in tropical countries, it may prove necessary to cool down your marine aquarium. This could be particularly important if you want to keep live corals, which do not do well in prolonged higher-than-normal temperatures. Water pumps and lighting produce heat and could take temperatures too high. In such cases you will need to install a chilling unit into the system. There are a number of such devices on the market for various applications, but it is far better to invest in one designed and manufactured specifically for marine aquariums. These chillers are never cheap; do not be tempted to risk an undersized unit in order to save money, because you will discover that this can be a false economy. Consult your dealer or the manufacturer to make sure you obtain the correct size and type of chiller.

Chapter 4: *Lighting the tank*

Not surprisingly, sunlight is more intense on a coral reef than over a tropical jungle river, where vegetation and debris dredged up in the water flow filter out much of the light. It therefore follows that the lighting requirements of an anemone or leather coral are very different from those of an Amazonian discus fish or Asian *Aponogeton* plant.

Lighting in a fish-only aquarium is really down to personal taste. Two fluorescent tubes will usually suffice, with perhaps a third, blue lamp for night viewing. However, if there are invertebrates in the tank, lighting becomes far more important. Many corals, anemones and molluscs rely on algae known as zooxanthellae for food. As well as good water quality, the main requirement of zooxanthellae and macro algae, such as caulerpa, is high intensity light at the correct wavelength. In fish-only systems with relatively low light intensities, zooxanthellae will not grow. In a reef aquarium, the correct lighting is therefore of paramount importance and this usually means using metal-halide lamps.

There are two key elements that together contribute to the suitability of a particular tube or lamp for a given marine aquarium setup. Understanding these factors will help you to choose the best lighting system for a fish-only tank or a reef aquarium with invertebrates.

Light intensity

There is a common misconception that the intensity of aquarium lighting is measured in watts, whereas in fact wattage is the amount of power required to make a lamp work and is standard amongst most fluorescent tubes. For example, a 60cm (24in) tube is usually 18-20 watts, a 120cm (48in) tube is usually 36-40 watts, and so on.

So if the power into a lamp is measured in watts, how do we refer to the intensity, or brightness, of a light source? The answer is in 'lumens', which are measured with a lumen meter. (You may also see light intensity quoted in terms of lux, see the panel opposite for more details.)

The intensity of a lamp is usually indicated on the packaging. Most fluorescent tubes rarely exceed 5,000-6,000 lumens, and some are far lower. On the other hand, metal-halide lamps commonly emit in excess of 10,000 lumens, so it is easy to see that you would need many fluorescent tubes to replicate a three-lamp metal-halide unit.

Light intensity also depends on the efficiency of the lamp and it is difficult to achieve high levels of light intensity

Below: This view of Lhuru island in the Maldives emphasises how important clear water and high lighting levels are to the continuing health of the coral. As the level of the sea rises, the corals are dying off.

with fluorescent tubes. This is especially true in deeper tanks, where the light from most tubes fades very quickly. However bright any type of lamp may be, if it cannot penetrate through the upper water layers of an aquarium and provide the correct intensity for reef animals it is obviously of little use in a reef aquarium. A lux meter can measure whether clams, corals and other light-sensitive invertebrates are receiving the correct intensity of light, giving a reading of the light intensity at a particular point in the aquarium. If you buy a good-quality aquarium tube or

Above: Shining a beam of white light into a glass prism produces a very clear spectrum of colours, from violet, through blue, green, yellow to red. The prism literally 'splits' the beam to reveal the colours that make it up.

lamp, the manufacturer will have done the hard work for you.

Another factor to bear in mind is that without sufficiently high light intensity, the aquarium may attract low-light algae, such as dark green and red varieties, that can smother corals and inhibit the growth of zooxanthellae. Furthermore, not only do you need

Light intensity

Sunlight over a reef

The average recorded sunlight over a reef is 20,000 lux at a depth of 10-15m (33-50ft).

Metal-halide lamps

A 150-watt metal-halide lamp produces 10,000 lumens.

Fluorescent tubes

A 25-watt white triphosphor tube produces about 1,600 lumens.

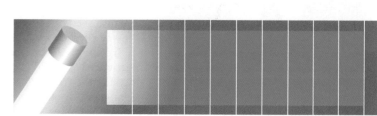

Above: Sunlight appears to 'dapple' the water and corals on a reef. This effect can be recreated with the right lighting. Bear in mind that that intensity falls rapidly with increasing distance from the light source. For example, each 1cm (0.4in) increase in distance from the lamp is equivalent to a 1m (39in) depth increase in the sea.

enough light output, it must also be of the correct 'colour'.

Colour temperature

Any type of lamp, whether metal-halide or fluorescent, appears to give off light in a particular colour. In fact, the colour we perceive is made up of many different colours, each with their own spectral wavelengths. This is called the 'colour temperature' of the lamp and is measured in degrees Kelvin (°K). The higher the Kelvin rating, the more white and 'cool' the light appears. A low Kelvin rating produces a 'warm' appearance, usually predominantly red or yellow, but why should this be and why is it vital to understand?

As we see in a rainbow, light is made up of a spectrum of colours ranging from violet to red. Seawater is an efficient light filter, and different colours are filtered out at different depths. The first to go is red light, which penetrates only the very upper layers of the reef. This is followed by orange and yellow, both of which are also filtered out in the upper layers of the water. The most penetrative light colours are green and blue. This is why many fish that appear bright red in an aquarium, and are easy prey in shallow water, are actually rendered almost black in deeper water, as anyone who has dived off a reef will

Colour temperature explained

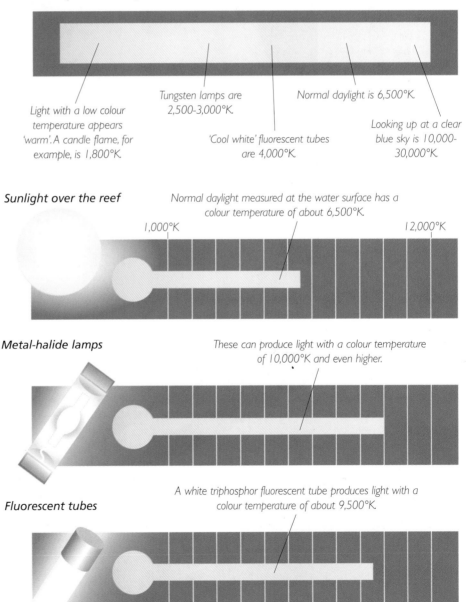

Light with a low colour temperature appears 'warm'. A candle flame, for example, is 1,800°K.

Tungsten lamps are 2,500-3,000°K.

'Cool white' fluorescent tubes are 4,000°K.

Normal daylight is 6,500°K.

Looking up at a clear blue sky is 10,000-30,000°K.

Sunlight over the reef

Normal daylight measured at the water surface has a colour temperature of about 6,500°K.

1,000°K   12,000°K

Metal-halide lamps

These can produce light with a colour temperature of 10,000°K and even higher.

Fluorescent tubes

A white triphosphor fluorescent tube produces light with a colour temperature of about 9,500°K.

Spectral power distributions

Light is made up of many wavelengths and the balance of these produced by a light source affects its overall 'colour'. It is possible to measure which wavelengths are present and at what strengths. This is called its spectral power distribution. The graphs shown below compare the output of three light sources set against the sun's complete spectrum. Wavelengths are in nanometres (nm) – billionths of a metre.

White triphosphor fluorescent tube

These curves show that this type of lamp produces light at a wide range of wavelengths, providing bright illumination for all creatures in the aquarium. (The vertical scale reflects comparative output.)

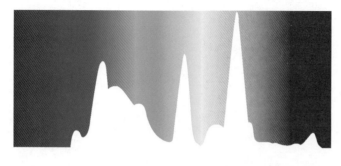

Metal-halide lamp

In common with the lamp above, this has a wide output with high levels at 400-480 nm (good for zooxanthellae) and 550 nm (to simulate sunlight). The volume of the curves here indicates a bright lamp.

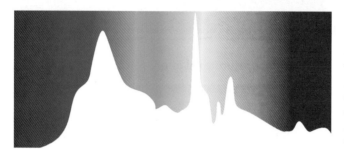

Blue actinic 03 fluorescent tube

This tube is 'strong' in the blue area of the spectrum, especially in the so-called 'actinic' range peaking at 420nm, which is vital for zooxanthellae to thrive. It also supplies some UV for a fluorescent effect.

Below: Using a reflector with fluorescent lighting will greatly enhance the efficiency of the tube by reflecting as much light as possible down into the tank.

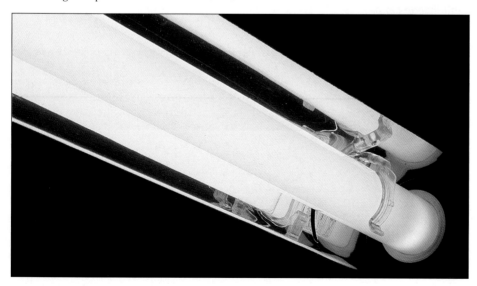

have noticed. For example, a fire shrimp that is bought for its vivid red coloration in the aquarium, actually blends into the dark background in its natural environment.

The output of the various wavelengths of light (and therefore the strength of light in the different colour 'bands') produced by a lamp is also referred to as its spectral power distribution. You will usually see coloured graphs and diagrams on lamp packaging to reflect this.

Fluorescent lighting

The fishkeeping hobby has come a long way since the early days, when tungsten (incandescent) lighting was the norm. The first fluorescent lamps were not designed with the fishkeeper in mind; more often than not they originated from office lighting or, as in the case of Gro-Lux tubes, from the horticulture industry.

The first major breakthrough in fluorescent lighting for aquariums came with the advent of the triphosphor lamp, which concentrates its light output in the key areas of the spectrum essential for invertebrate and macro algae growth. The spectral distribution of the lamp allows for the fact that various colours are filtered out at varying rates in seawater and compensates accordingly.

Furthermore, the lamp retains its spectral qualities until the end of its life. This is particularly important if you are using fluorescents for invertebrate aquariums, as most lamps lose part of their spectrum over a short period of time, while still emitting light. To the human eye they do not appear to have changed at all, but the deteriorating health of any corals in the aquarium often indicates a reduction in the effectiveness of the lamp.

In addition to using triphosphor tubes, many aquarists use blue ones designed specifically for night viewing. Actinic blue tubes (which may be more expensive) produce ultraviolet light, essential to many types of invertebrate, as well as an attractive blue colour for night viewing. When selecting actinic tubes, be sure to buy the 03 type, which gives off a more suitable wavelength than the similar 05 actinic tube.

The efficiency of fluorescent tubes can be greatly enhanced by using polished aluminium reflectors in the hood of the aquarium. They reflect light from the rear and top of the lid back towards the tank, increasing the effectiveness of a light by up to 50%.

Metal-halide lighting

There have been significant advances in our understanding of the light intensities and colour spectrums required by corals, and it is widely accepted now that metal-halide lamps are essential in order to maintain many coral species.

Unlike fluorescent tubes, metal-halide lamps offer a range of high-intensity outputs with hardly any size difference. The most common halide lamps are 150 watts and 250 watts, although 400 watt lamps are now available for very deep aquariums.

In addition to the high-intensity output they afford, metal-halide lamps are now available at Kelvin temperatures far better suited to the reef aquarium than used to be the case. It is now common practice to use lighting with a temperature of between 10,000 and 13,000°K. These high-Kelvin lamps create a beautiful rippling effect in the aquarium and greatly enhance the appearance of the inhabitants, as well as supplying the correct light needs for zooxanthellae to flourish.

Metal-halide lamps are usually suspended from the ceiling or a wall bracket, at least 30cm (12in) from the surface of the aquarium, as they give off a tremendous amount of heat. The other disadvantage is their high cost, although the price of lamps and units is falling all the time.

Before you decide to keep hard corals, clams and other invertebrates that require high light levels, assess whether you are prepared to invest in the correct lighting. If the answer is 'no' then consider keeping a fish-only aquarium until funds are available to buy metal-halides. Never buy delicate corals without having the correct lighting in place to maintain them and allow them to grow.

The photoperiod

The final piece in the lighting jigsaw is the length of time the lighting is left on, known as the 'photoperiod'. There are no hard and fast rules about this, as every aquarium differs slightly in its requirements. Once again, the best way is to learn from nature and try to replicate life on the reef in your aquarium.

Around the equator, the period of sunlight is about 12 hours each day, whereas in tropical latitudes (up to about 20° north and south of the Equator), full sunlight is only experienced between about 9am to 3pm (i.e. six hours). As a starting point, if you are using fluorescent tubes, try

setting your lighting period to about 12 hours. A blue lamp or one of the less bright lamps should come on one to two hours before the main lighting and go off one to two hours after it has been turned off. This will create a rudimentary feeling of dusk and dawn and avoids stressing nervous fish.

If you are using metal-halide lamps, try starting with a photoperiod of about

eight hours, again with blue lamps that come on before the main lights and remain on after the halides have been turned off for the day.

The latest and most sophisticated artificial lighting combines metal-halide with fluorescent lighting units. It includes a programmable timer and a special 'moonlight' lamp that matches the cycle of the moon!

Right: Metal halide lamps and blue actinic tubes over a reef aquarium. Combining lights allows you to create separate day and night lighting effects, as well as highlight a specific 'hot' area for invertebrate life.

Chapter 5: Water–simulating the real thing

A shroud of mystery has surrounded marine fishkeeping as a hobby ever since it began. Many people are still fearful of attempting what, to them, appears to be nigh impossible, and the main problem seems to be maintaining the necessary water quality. To quote Stephen Spotte, one of the leading exponents of water management techniques, success depends on 'how well you control the inevitable changes taking place in seawater ....the water, you see, is everything. It's as simple as that'. You can deduce from this that we are waterkeepers as much as fishkeepers. In fact, you could almost say that if the water is well looked after, the fishes will look after themselves.

Natural seawater

As 71% of the Earth's surface is covered by seawater, you might expect it to be one of the most convenient commodities to obtain. Unfortunately, it is not often suitable for the domestic marine aquarium, for several reasons.

For most aquarists it is totally impractical to make regular trips to the coast to collect and transport large quantities of natural seawater, even if the sea is within easy reach. Secondly, relatively few marine aquarists have the luxury of living in the tropics and being able to collect local water. For most, collecting cooler local water and converting it to 'tropical water' can present a number of problems. Warming up natural seawater could cause plankton either to die off, creating potentially toxic conditions, or rapidly multiply and use up vital oxygen. In addition, coral reef fishes are unlikely to have the natural means to fight off disease pathogens that occur in water from other parts of the world. Should you wish to establish an aquarium to house fishes from your local shores, then it is acceptable, but not always convenient, to use seawater from the same locality.

Another important point to consider is the difficulty of finding a source of unpolluted natural water. The increasing volume of seagoing commercial traffic and effluent from industrial activity around the world means that coastal waters are not likely to be entirely pure, to say the least! It is clear from this that using natural seawater can generally create more problems than it is worth.

Synthetic seawater

The best way of providing suitable water for the marine aquarium is to use an artificial mix that is carefully balanced and combined with good quality tapwater so that the final composition approximates as closely as possible to natural seawater. These commercially available mixes of dry salts, minerals and essential trace elements are sterile and should be manufactured from scientific-grade materials, so that there is no risk of inadvertently introducing diseases and other problems into the aquarium. Also, because you only purchase the dry mix and add it to freshwater when needed, it is very convenient in terms of carrying and storing.

Modern mixes are so exact in their formula and manufacturing process that you no longer need to use up an entire package at once in order to produce a given volume of water with the desired specific gravity (or density) and correct chemical composition. These days you can use up part of a package and still be sure of obtaining the correct chemical composition regardless of what specific gravity you wish to attain. (Reseal partly used bags and store in a cool, dry place.) This offers a great deal of flexibility and is an ideal solution for preparing small amounts of seawater for partial water changes. This is the medium your fishes and invertebrates have to live in, so quality is essential.

The composition of seawater

Seawater is not simply a solution of sodium chloride; it also contains sulphates, magnesium, calcium and potassium, plus many trace elements in very small amounts. The very best synthetic seawater mixes are indistinguishable from natural seawater.

Below: *With their huge mass, the oceans provide very stable water conditions. This feature, and the intolerance of many marine species to changes in water conditions, are key challenges for the marine aquarist.*

Chloride 55%

Sodium 30.5%

Sulphate 7.5%

Magnesium 3.5%

Calcium 1%

Potassium 1%

Bicarbonate 0.5%

Other chemicals and trace elements 1%

Above: Seawater contains a high level of dissolved salts, and marine life is adapted to thrive in this salty environment. Keeping marine creatures successfully in a tank is made easier today by using synthetic mixes that reflect the natural balance of the sea.

Preparing synthetic seawater

To start with, you must carefully follow the manufacturer's directions. It is best to prepare the synthetic seawater in advance of setting up the aquarium so that it is ready to use. It is very important that the salts have dissolved fully before use to avoid ending up with an incorrect specific gravity. You may find the dissolve time differs from one brand to another, but in any case, you must keep regular checks on the specific gravity by using a marine aquarium hydrometer throughout the operation. It is always best, and quicker, to dissolve smaller amounts of the salt mix at a time, rather than a large heap, and to provide strong aeration. During the initial setting up, you can carry out the mixing directly in the aquarium, as there will be no animals in it, of course. However, all subsequent mixes will have to be prepared in a separate container. As always, ensure that the receptacle in which you mix the salt is made from non-corrodible materials.

The following guidelines will help you achieve the best results.

1 It is normal for water authorities to treat domestic tapwater in order to make it safe for humans. Unfortunately, the chemicals used are not safe for aquatic animals. Chloramines are commonly used for this purpose. The more traditional use of chlorine was relatively easy to deal with, as vigorous aeration would dissipate it into the atmosphere. This is not so easy with chloramines. Fortunately, on the other hand, aquarium treatments are now available to remove these and help make tapwater safe.

In some areas there is a risk of fertilizers, such as phosphates and nitrates, getting into water supplies from farms, particularly after heavy rainstorms. Water authorities usually do their best to deal with this problem, but there is evidence that some quantities do get into the system. Also, many cities still have lead piping in their water supply systems, so phosphorous is added to stabilize the lead. All these chemicals are undesirable in the aquarium because, being fertilizers, they are very effective at promoting undesirable hair algae and certain slime bacteria.

If you are unlucky and find these harmful chemicals in your water supply, then you will have to invest in nitrate- and phosphate-removing resins, or a reverse osmosis unit, which will filter out, albeit very slowly, a wide variety of chemicals and minerals. Activated carbon is also useful for removing chlorine and several other chemicals from water. It should go without saying that all tapwater must be treated before it is used to make synthetic seawater, whether it is for a complete fill or just for topping up with freshwater after evaporation loss, once the aquarium is fully functional.

2 As already stressed, only use glass, plastic or other non-metallic containers for preparing seawater. Polythene or polypropylene containers made for use with food or home brewing are good, but beware of any made from recycled plastics, such as refuse bins, as these may release harmful toxins over time.

Fill the container with the required amount of water and mark a line on the outside to indicate the depth of water. This will help you be accurate when making further mixes in the future, and save you time.

3 Ideally, make up the seawater 24-48 hours in advance to allow for complete dissolving. Add the dry salt mixture to the water a small amount at a time, apply vigorous aeration and keep a regular check on the specific gravity. The salts usually dissolve better in warm water and, as marine aquarium hydrometers are calibrated for use at around 75°F (24°C) water temperature, you will be more accurate if you can place an aquarium heater into the mixing container. This also means the water will be at the correct temperature when it is added to the aquarium.

4 Once you have the mixed water in the aquarium, turn on pumps, filters and heaters to be absolutely certain of a thorough mix at the desired temperature and, after a few hours, make a final specific gravity test. If all is correct, leave the aquarium running to continue with the maturation process before introducing any livestock.

5 It is very difficult to assess the exact volume of water in an aquarium that is already furnished with rocks and other forms of habitat, so measure the amount of water used when filling the aquarium for the first time and make a note of it for future reference. This information may one day be very useful in calculating, for example, the exact amount of medication required to treat a disease outbreak.

Specific gravity

You will have noticed this mentioned several times already. To clarify, it is simply the ratio of the density of any liquid compared to that of distilled water, which has a specific gravity of 1. Seawater is greater in density and contains far more dissolved minerals, so its specific gravity (S.G.) is higher than 1. (The concentration of total solids dissolved in a specified amount of water can also be expressed in terms of salinity, i.e. grams/litre. The table shows the relationship between specific gravity and salinity.)

The salinity of seawater varies from one location to another. For instance, the Red Sea is more saline than the

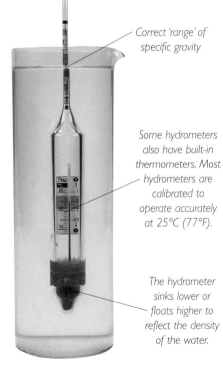

Correct 'range' of specific gravity

Some hydrometers also have built-in thermometers. Most hydrometers are calibrated to operate accurately at 25°C (77°F).

The hydrometer sinks lower or floats higher to reflect the density of the water.

Above: The correct S.G. is indicated when the chosen value coincides with the miniscus (water surface level). It is easy to see in the coloured section on the stem.

Osmoregulation in marine fishes

As part of their regulation of osmotic balance, marine fish must drink water to replace that lost from the body. This creates a salt overload that must be eliminated via the kidneys and gills.

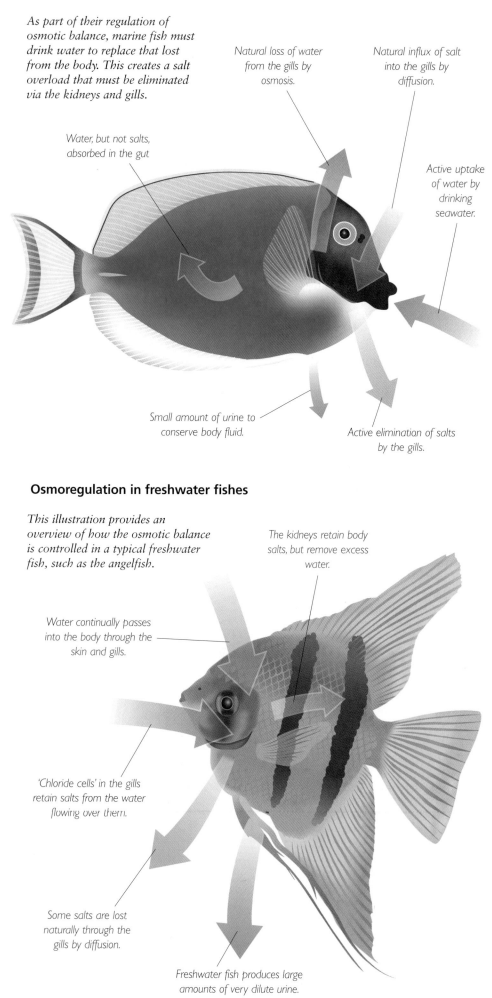

Natural loss of water from the gills by osmosis.

Natural influx of salt into the gills by diffusion.

Water, but not salts, absorbed in the gut

Active uptake of water by drinking seawater.

Small amount of urine to conserve body fluid.

Active elimination of salts by the gills.

Osmoregulation in freshwater fishes

This illustration provides an overview of how the osmotic balance is controlled in a typical freshwater fish, such as the angelfish.

The kidneys retain body salts, but remove excess water.

Water continually passes into the body through the skin and gills.

'Chloride cells' in the gills retain salts from the water flowing over them.

Some salts are lost naturally through the gills by diffusion.

Freshwater fish produces large amounts of very dilute urine.

open ocean because it is non-tidal and has a high rate of evaporation. The Dead Sea is the most extreme example, as it has the highest salinity of any sea anywhere in the world and no fishes can live in it at all.

The salinity/specific gravity of water has an effect on the fishes living in it, and here we come to one of the fundamental differences between freshwater and seawater fishes in terms of their basic biology.

A freshwater fish is surrounded by water that is less dense than its body fluids. Due to a phenomenon known as osmosis, water is absorbed into the body and the fish must excrete water constantly so that it does not burst. The marine fish faces the opposite situation, in that it constantly loses water to its surroundings and must therefore drink copious amounts of water and excrete only salts.

Variations of S.G. can occur in the aquarium as a result of evaporation. Only pure water is lost during this process, so evaporation losses must only be made good with freshwater and not a prepared salt mix. To top up evaporation loss with saltwater will result in the aquarium water becoming progressively more dense, and dangerously so if this incorrect practice is continued on a regular basis. Cover glasses (or condensation trays) will prevent water loss through evaporation, as well as helping to conserve heat.

The control of salinity can be utilized as an aid to disease prevention. Many disease pathogens, particularly external crustaceans and protozoans, cannot survive in low salinities and it has become common practice to maintain marine aquariums at a specific gravity of 1.022, and in some cases as low as 1.018. Most fishes can tolerate these levels and actually seem to benefit from them because of less demanding osmotic pressure. However, many invertebrates will not do well below

S.G. and salinity

Specific gravity varies with temperature. When mixing salt, always take the water temperature into account; the warmer the water in the aquarium, the more salt will be required.

15°C	Salinity	25°C
1.022	30 gm/l	1.020
1.023	32 gm/l	1.022
1.025	34 gm/l	1.023
1.027	36 gm/l	1.025

Left: Tapwater is treated with chemicals such as chloramine to make it safe for drinking. These are harmful to marine creatures and should be removed.

1.022. If you think about it, the crustaceans you keep as tank subjects are close relatives of the crustacean parasites you are trying to prevent by reducing the salinity, so it stands to reason a low specific gravity will not be to their liking.

The pH of water

The pH of water is a measure of its acidity or alkalinity. It is measured on a logarithmic scale; values below 7 are acidic while values above 7 are alkaline (7 being the neutral value). Seawater has a higher pH than most freshwater and domestic tapwater and should be maintained at 8.3. If you are keeping a temperate marine aquarium, then 7.9 is acceptable in many cases. A falling pH usually indicates an increase in carbon dioxide production because of a build-up of organic debris over time, and that the water's buffering capabilities (its ability to resist pH changes) is declining. Regular tank maintenance and partial water changes will go a long way to keeping the pH stable.

Sudden changes in pH are dangerous to fishes and many invertebrates, especially if the trend is upwards. In most cases it is the change in pH that fishes experience when they are moved from one aquarium to another without sufficient time to acclimatize that causes severe stress and often death. When introducing a new fish, it is vital to check the pH of both the water the fish is in and the water it is being moved into and, if necessary, make several checks in between until equalization has been achieved.

Monitoring water quality

Coral reefs are amongst the cleanest and most stable environments in the world and the fishes and invertebrates that live on them thrive on it accordingly. It follows that these same animals are naturally intolerant of environmental change and poor water quality. The environmental pressures on the relatively small body of water contained within an aquarium are enormous and perfect conditions are difficult to maintain without care and dedication. In the main this is because stocking levels are higher pro rata than found in the wild and the resulting metabolic waste matter has a profound impact on water quality. Consequently, elaborate filtration systems have been progressively developed over the years to help maintain the kind of water quality that coral reef organisms would experience in nature.

Regular monitoring of water quality is essential. This is particularly so when the aquarium is first established, because the various initial biological processes are very unstable, making conditions impossible to support fishes and other marine animals. A clear understanding of the nitrogen cycle is essential here. In simple terms, this naturally occurring process involves the breakdown of the extremely poisonous metabolic by-product ammonia (NH_3) into less dangerous but still toxic nitrite (NO_2), which in turn is broken down into relatively harmless nitrate (NO_3). In the natural environment, nitrate is absorbed by plants as a primary nutrient and incorporated into plant tissue. This is eaten by herbivorous animals that are themselves eaten by carnivorous animals. And so this conversion cycle of nitrogen-containing compounds keeps turning. (See page 24 for details of the nitrogen cycle and how biological filtration systems control levels of these waste materials.)

So, in addition to regularly measuring pH and specific gravity, you should be keeping a close check on ammonia, nitrite and, to a lesser degree, nitrate levels in your aquarium. Nutrients in the water supply from agriculture can also be monitored. Although these nutrients, such as phosphates and nitrates, naturally occur in minute quantities in seawater, excessive amounts are definitely unwelcome. Testing the alkalinity will provide an indication of your water's buffering capabilities. All these tests will help you evaluate the efficiency of your filtration system and to determine your schedule for carrying out partial water changes. In addition, the regular measurement of dissolved oxygen will be very useful, especially as an indicator to whether you are overstocking your aquarium with livestock.

Outside of essential monitoring, there are also tests available for other reasons. For example, should you decide to use ozone in your system then, it will be useful to test for residual ozone and for redox potential (see page 30 for more details). Another example is testing for copper in your aquarium water when using it as a treatment for certain parasitic infections. It is important to maintain the correct level throughout the course of treatment and, as it is difficult to calculate the volume of water in a furnished tank accurately, using a test kit will allow you to determine the correct dosage without knowing that volume.

Water testing is vital as an aid to good management in order to keep conditions as stable as possible. Since modern technology has provided the means to monitor water quality, it would be foolish, and false economy, to ignore these facilities.

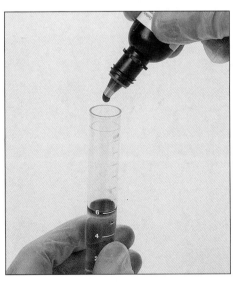

Right: The final stage of testing the pH of tank water, showing a correct reading of between 8.0 and 8.4. When you compare the sample colour against the card, follow the directions; not all tests are the same.

Left: Test the water regularly to monitor the pH level, which in a marine tank should remain fairly stable. Some tests involve adding chemicals to a measured sample and comparing the colour change to a printed chart.

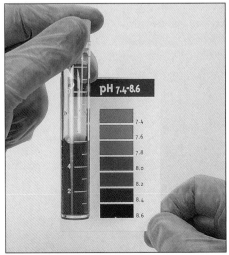

Chapter 6: Filtration systems

As we stated right at the outset, the key to successful marine fishkeeping is maintaining good water quality. Here, we look in detail at aquarium filtration systems and how they help to provide healthy conditions for a wide range of marine creatures.

The nitrogen cycle

The nitrogen cycle is an extremely important biological process on the reef – and in all ecosystems, for that matter. It is an important purification system, but it is more than that, because it is also the source of primary food production, without which nothing on earth would survive. Disturbances to this process caused by pollution from human waste and chemicals are putting a serious question mark over the future of our world, because in many places not even the vast exchange of ocean water is capable of diluting these substances. Likewise, nothing will survive in the aquarium without proper utilisation of the processes within the nitrogen cycle.

The nitrogen cycle is basically the removal of nitrogenous compounds that gradually build up in the aquarium water, starting with free ammonia (NH_3) and ionized ammonia (NH_4^+). Fishes and invertebrates produce ammonia as a waste product from their metabolic processes. This is added to the ammonia produced by bacteria 'working on' other waste materials in the aquarium, such as uneaten food and faeces. Ammonia is highly toxic to fishes and invertebrates; if it is not removed, or converted into other less harmful substances, your aquarium subjects will soon perish. Fortunately, in Nature's Grand Plan, a substance that is poison to one living organism is food for another and, thus, there is a natural way of dealing with ammonia removal.

Aerobic (oxygen-loving) bacteria, such as *Nitrosomonas* species, convert ammonia to nitrite (NO_2), a slightly less toxic substance, but one that is still dangerous to fishes and invertebrates. A second group of bacteria, such as *Nitrobacter* species, transform the nitrite to nitrate (NO_3), which is a much safer substance but one that can still cause some problems if allowed to build up too much. It is not fully

How the nitrogen cycle works

Nitrogen is recycled in the natural world through the digestion of nitrogen-containing proteins by animals and the action of bacteria in the environment. Here is how the cycle works in the marine world.

Fish and other marine creatures digest and metabolise protein as part of their varied diets.

Nitrates are absorbed by plants, such as algae, as a fertilizer.

Nitrite is converted into nitrate by another group of bacteria called Nitrobacter.

Ammonia is converted by Nitrosomonas bacteria into nitrite. These bacteria thrive in oxygenated conditions in the substrate and on the surface of rocks.

The main waste product of protein digestion is ammonia. Fish excrete this in urine and directly from the gills. Ammonia also builds up as faeces, plant matter and uneaten food decay.

NATURE

Mechanical filtration Sediments and detritus become trapped in certain areas of the reef structure, where animals will feed on it and break it down to a form that other organisms and bacteria can utilise. Sand plays a very important role in the process of trapping detritus. Sea cucumbers, worms and many other organisms associate themselves with the sand bed environment and feed off the materials that settle there. New sand is continuously created by boring worms and by parrotfishes that bite off chunks of coral rock and grind it up to extract algae. The resulting sand falls to the seabed.

Gaseous exchange Oxygen is taken in from the atmosphere at the water surface (or air to water interface). Waves help the process by increasing the surface area and allowing more oxygen to be absorbed. Oxygen is distributed through the water column by wave action and currents Carbon dioxide gas is released into the atmosphere at the air to water interface.

Water movement The back and forth swell of the sea combined with currents and countercurrents, creates powerful movement. This is important because it cleanses the reef structure, prevents sediments from settling, particularly on delicate corals, and delivers food to filter-feeding animals.

Biological filtration All solid surfaces throughout the porous structure of the reef provide space for bacteria to colonise. Nitrifying bacteria feed on the ammonia waste from marine organisms and convert it first into nitrite and then into nitrate. Denitrifying bacteria convert nitrate into nitrogen gas. All these bacteria are part of the 'nitrogen cycle'. Huge populations of sponges, sea squirts and clams filter the water directly and contribute greatly to its clarity.

AQUARIUM

Mechanical filtration Most aquariums cannot sustain the level of natural organisms necessary to deal with sediments and other debris. Water must be passed through a suitable filter medium, such as sponge or floss, to filter out fine solid materials.

Gaseous exchange As in nature, gas exchange occurs at the water surface. You can improve its efficiency in the aquarium by using a protein skimmer, which bubbles copious amounts of air through the water, and ensures good water circulation within the aquarium.

Water movement Small submersible pumps, such as powerheads, can be used to create currents in the aquarium. This will help distribute oxygen and prevent debris from accumulating in one place. Timers and wavemakers can introduce a random pattern to the water currents.

Biological filtration All solid surfaces within the aquarium provide space for bacterial colonisation, including porous material used to create habitats. In most cases, special biological filtration units that harbour beneficial bacteria are situated outside the aquarium.

Protein skimming is a filtration process unique to aquariums that relies on the natural affinity of dissolved organic solids to stick to the surface of air bubbles in water.

NATURE

Chemical filtration Certain bacteria and other organisms are capable of utilising organic chemicals and are effective in removing such substances from the water. The calcareous coral rock is also able to adsorb certain chemicals. Water exchange also serves to dilute harmful chemicals.

Sterilisation Natural ultraviolet radiation from the sun helps to reduce the pathogen and suspended algae spore count in the open sea, although it is really only effective in very shallow water. Tropical electric storms produce ozone that, in combination with surf, is a useful sterilisation agent. High-energy surf itself has sterilising properties.

Alkalinity and pH The vast expanses of calcareous material (coral rock), good oxygenation and the buffering power of the oceans' saltwater ensure that alkalinity and pH levels remain constant.

AQUARIUM

Chemical filtration Since the aquarium cannot benefit from the massive water exchange found in nature, regular partial water changes are necessary to dilute the accumulation of undesirable chemicals. Activated carbon and other chemically active media are used to remove dissolved pollutants.

Sterilisation Ozone and ultraviolet light radiation produced by special equipment can help to reduce, or eliminate, disease pathogens and algae spores in the aquarium.

Alkalinity and pH In the aquarium, various natural processes act to reduce the pH, alkalinity and calcium levels. For example, a general build-up of carbon dioxide produced from metabolic functions and the breakdown of organic waste will in time cause a lowering of pH. Ageing water, along with increasing levels of of dissolved organic carbons, have a profound effect on its buffering capabilities and reduce alkalinity and calcium levels. Quite often there is a relationship between pH, alkalinity and calcium levels, and shifts in their concentration can occur at the same time. However, a drop in pH, for example, does not always mean there will be a drop in alkalinity at the same time. Good oxygenation, regular water changes and the frequent addition of calcium, either chemically or with a calcium reactor, will help to maintain desirable levels.

Marine fish will only flourish in the aquarium if you provide them with the best possible water conditions.

understood to what level nitrate can cause problems for aquarium subjects, although it seems to be detrimental to delicate fish species and some invertebrates. The important thing is that nitrate does not occur on the natural coral reef other than in the smallest quantities, so we should not make compromises but strive to keep it to an absolute minimum in the aquarium. Nitrate is a primary nutrient for algae and the mainstay of primary food production right at the beginning of the food chain from which all other living organisms benefit.

It is worth noting that many species of undesirable algae may flourish with the presence of excess nitrates, as well as phosphates.

By the process of denitrification, anaerobic, or oxygen-hating, bacteria convert nitrate into free atmospheric nitrogen, which is naturally vented from the aquarium. The conditions that allow this are often found in porous material such as 'living rock', where pockets of oxygen-deficient water can be trapped, promoting the growth of anaerobic bacteria. The same thing can happen in the bottom levels of substrate, but here the gases can get trapped, including potentially dangerous sulphur (the gas with a pungent smell like bad eggs). However, herein lies a paradox, since if we are to provide ideal conditions for the complete removal of nitrogenous compounds, then it appears we must provide two sets of conditions for opposite types of bacteria.

Filtration systems

The purpose of the aquarium filtration system is to remove as much 'dirt' from the water as possible. As well as visible dirt and sediments stirred up by the actions of fishes and other tank inhabitants, the water will contain invisible dissolved nitrogenous and other organic compounds (waste products and their decomposition) and certain chemicals, such as phenols, that discolour the water, all of which must be removed.

Many types of filters are used in the aquarium hobby, ranging from simple air-operated box filters to highly sophisticated water purification systems. Filters vary not only in their design but in their mode of operation; some provide simple mechanical straining, while others exert a chemical or biological influence on the water flowing through them. Some filter designs perform all three functions.

In addition to these 'standard' filter types, many of which find a ready application in both freshwater and marine aquariums, certain water treatment systems are used more or less exclusively for marines. These include algae scrubbers, protein skimmers, ozonizers and ultraviolet sterilizers. We shall discuss the operation and merits of these water treatment methods later in this section. First we will look at the options open to the marine aquarist among the standard types of filters.

Biological filtration

Biological filtration is by far the most important type of filtration; without it, keeping a marine aquarium just would not be viable. All the biological processes that occur in the aquarium also exist in the wild, but the natural marine environment also benefits from the cleansing action of the sea, which disperses and dilutes nutrients and other potentially harmful chemicals. In the closed confines of an aquarium, fishkeepers must provide an efficient system to purify the water. By making use of the nitrogen cycle, biological filtration provides a natural means of removing ammonia-based wastes from the aquarium.

Certain bacteria that live on virtually any solid surface (although they are more positively attracted to calcareous material) perform biological filtration. Passing oxygenated water over these bacteria helps to maintain an efficient population. To improve this efficiency further, all sorts of filters have been designed that either draw, push or percolate water through a variety of media, such as gravel, sand, open-cell sponge and plastic balls, etc. The more surface area available for bacteria to colonize, the greater the quantity of water that can be filtered. The main aim is to provide the right conditions for aerobic bacteria to thrive.

Providing the necessary oxygen-rich environment for *Nitrosomonas* and *Nitrobacter* bacteria is easy. Agitating the water increases its surface area, boosting the oxygen saturation. As the water travels around the aquarium's circulatory system, the oxygen content is depleted by living organisms within the tank, including the aerobic bacteria. When it is returned to the tank from the filters, the water is relatively low in oxygen and renewed agitation will help to disperse carbon dioxide (CO_2) and absorb fresh oxygen to continue the cycle. If this were to stop, the colonies of beneficial bacteria would die and the water would rapidly become polluted.

In a newly set-up aquarium, bacterial colonies in the biological filter will take time to become established and, until the colony has 'matured', there will be

A fluidized bed filter

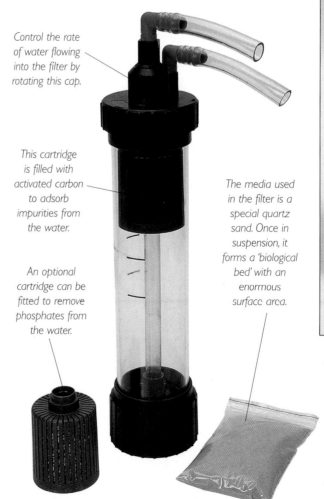

Control the rate of water flowing into the filter by rotating this cap.

This cartridge is filled with activated carbon to adsorb impurities from the water.

An optional cartridge can be fitted to remove phosphates from the water.

The media used in the filter is a special quartz sand. Once in suspension, it forms a 'biological bed' with an enormous surface area.

Above: *When in operation, the sand's moving biological bed is held in suspension (the two lines show the upper and lower levels of the medium). A valve in the unit prevents sand siphoning back into the pump if the power fails.*

little control over the rise of ammonia and nitrite levels. At this stage the aquarium is unable to support fishes and invertebrates.

Nitrosomonas and *Nitrobacter* colonies do not appear from nowhere; conditions have to be right for them. For example, there must be some ammonia present. There are many additives available that will provide food for the bacteria and help get the process underway, otherwise it could take many months for anything to happen. Adding some 'living rock' will also speed up the process, because it will have its own bacterial colonies. Make sure there are no animals living on the rock that would succumb to ammonia poisoning. Another method is to 'seed' the filters with material from an established aquarium.

It has been a common practice to use relatively tough fishes such as damselfishes to provide the necessary ammonia in order to 'kick-start' the nitrifying bacteria colonies. However, this is a serious act of cruelty and if the fishes actually survive the ordeal it is only due to extremely good luck.

Patience is definitely a virtue and, in fact, essential if you are to establish a marine aquarium successfully. Careful monitoring of ammonia and nitrite levels will indicate when it is safe to introduce the first inhabitants, and from then on regular nitrite testing will tell you whether your aquarium water continues to be safe or not. Remember that you must build up the full population capacity of the tank over a reasonably long period of time, ideally several months, so that the filter bed can keep in step with the increasing levels of waste materials it has to deal with.

The inevitable build-up of nitrate is best kept under control by carrying out regular partial water changes. If your mains tapwater supply contains a high level of nitrate, then treating it with nitrate-reducing resins will be particularly useful. Some modern 'total systems' include hi-tech modules for creating the ideal conditions for both aerobic and anaerobic bacteria.

Fluidized bed sand filters

The most significant recent development in biological filtration for the average domestic marine aquarium is the fluidized bed sand filter. This is a vertical tube containing a layer of fine, evenly sized and shaped quartz sand. A controlled flow of water from the aquarium is injected into the base of the tube and forces the sand into a steady tumbling motion, hence the term fluidized bed. As the sand remains in suspension and completely surrounded

The plenum system

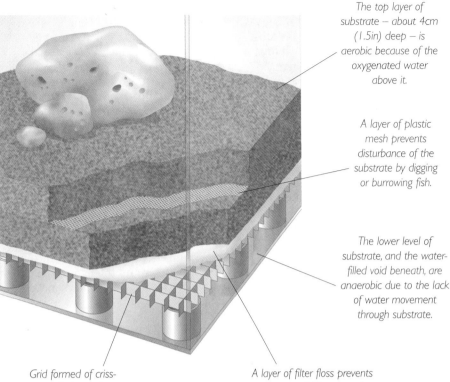

The top layer of substrate – about 4cm (1.5in) deep – is aerobic because of the oxygenated water above it.

A layer of plastic mesh prevents disturbance of the substrate by digging or burrowing fish.

The lower level of substrate, and the water-filled void beneath, are anaerobic due to the lack of water movement through substrate.

Grid formed of criss-crossed plastic slats.

A layer of filter floss prevents substrate trickling through 'egg-crate' grid.

by water, it means that the entire surface of each particle is available for colonisation by bacteria, allowing an enormous area for biological activity and great efficiency. Water returns to the aquarium from the top of the tube. As these sealed units are fitted inline in the water circulation system, they can be placed anywhere around the aquarium without the risk of floods. Another great advantage is, because of their efficiency, their physical size is small compared to other filter designs.

Trickle filters

Also popular are the so-called 'total systems' that use plastic balls as the biological filtration medium. These are often referred to as trickle filters because water from the aquarium literally trickles in a thin layer over the plastic surfaces, providing highly oxygenated water to the bacteria. One downside to this system is that it can become extremely active in nitrate production because of the large populations of bacteria it can support. Trickle filters are not necessarily always part of a 'total system' and can be stand-alone units.

'Total systems' can also include mechanical and chemical filtration modules, heaters, protein skimmers and all manner of ancillary equipment, all conveniently fitted in a sump, which is most popularly housed in a cabinet beneath the aquarium.

Wet/dry filters

In some trickle systems, the filter material is partly submerged in water and these are commonly known as wet/dry filters. Water still percolates through the upper section of the medium in the usual fashion, but the submerged section can provide areas of still water and, in time, anaerobic conditions can occur to allow some denitrification to take place.

The plenum

This is basically a porous plate that fits tightly to the tank's sides about 2.5cm (1in) off the base. It is covered with a layer of 'live' sand approximately 5cm (2in) thick, or in many cases two layers of different-sized gravel and sand, separated by a mesh screen to prevent mixing. The sand is called 'live' because this biological filter works by culturing all manner of sand-dwelling organisms that would be found in such a situation in nature. Small sandhopper shrimps and other minute crustaceans, along with a variety of worm species and all the various bacteria, will maintain a healthy substrate.

With the plenum arrangement, good water movement and oxygenation occur above the substrate, whereas a stagnant state is created below, with no oxygen or water movement. Little water actually passes through the substrate from one condition to the other, but nutrients and chemicals are

27

drawn over the substrate material in a state of flux, causing very efficient reduction of all unwanted elements.

The plenum is most commonly used in 'natural systems' where as little, if any, filtration equipment is used to maintain biological equilibrium. However, they are occasionally included in wet/dry filter systems.

Mechanical filtration

During mechanical filtration, particulate matter is removed from the aquarium water by straining it through a suitable material. The most common materials are open-cell foam (other foams can be toxic), filter floss or matting made from Dacron, spun nylon or some other man-made fibre.

Mechanical filters of any type will only remove particles that are suspended in the water column and therefore are transported to the medium; particles trapped in the substrate or rocks cannot be removed by this method. Strong water movement and, if possible, alternating currents will go a long way in preventing sediments from settling. However, regular gentle stirring of the substrate will always be necessary to bring debris into suspension so that mechanical filters can do their job.

Power filters utilize one or more types of filter media. The internal submersible types normally contain a foam block and also provide extra beneficial water movement. On the other hand, the larger external canister types usually contain two or more materials, as well as creating extra water movement. Some models of external canister filter have separate compartments where the first in line will contain, for example, small ceramic tubes that act as a prefilter to trap large particles, while the next compartment contains foam or matting to collect the finer particles. Another compartment could be used for chemical filtration.

In 'total systems' that are normally incorporated into a sump below the aquarium, water is percolated through a mat prefilter and then an open-cell foam block to facilitate mechanical filtration.

Diatom filters use diatomaceous earth as the medium to filter out the smallest of particles to create excellent water clarity. This diatomaceous earth is an extremely fine powder that provides an ideal barrier for preventing very fine particulate matter from passing through. Such filters are so effective that they can clog very quickly and

therefore require regular maintenance. The most popular type is an external canister, usually made of clear glass, and powered by an integral water pump.

Protein skimmers remove organic compounds (proteins) that dissolve in seawater and therefore cannot be extracted by physical straining. In a protein skimmer (also known as a foam fractionator) air is bubbled into a water column whose uppermost surface is open to the atmosphere. These dissolved organic compounds attach themselves to the air bubbles and rise to the water surface forming a protein-laden foam. The foam is then forced up into a collection cup, where it collapses into a dark brown liquid (skimmate) that can be flushed to waste. There are many types of protein skimmer available, employing different techniques for introducing the air into the water flow (airstone, venturi or turbo air injectors) with varying water/air flow paths (co-current, counter-current or triple-pass). For a protein skimmer to be efficient, a large quantity of small air bubbles must be kept in turbulent contact with the water for as long as possible, producing a concentrated skimmate. Protein

An external canister filter

Shut-off taps allow you to disconnect the filter without water spillage.

These plastic tubes carry water to and from the aquarium.

The electric water pump is housed in the top part of the filter.

The incoming water passes upwards through the filter media, packed in a plastic basket inside the canister. Water flow must be maintained at all times to prevent the media turning anaerobic (without oxygen), as would occur within a short time following any failure of the power supply.

An advanced protein skimmer

This advanced skimmer maximizes the contact time between the tank water and a constant stream of fine air bubbles. Protein wastes stick to the bubble surfaces and can be collected and removed as the bubbles collapse.

Collection cup in which the protein-laden foam collapses.

A pipe can be connected to this port to drain off the protein waste.

Cleaned water returns to the tank over this cascade.

Optional basket for chemical or biological filtration media.

Reaction chamber in which the water and air bubbles remain in close contact.

Optional surface skimmer attachment on the inlet pipe.

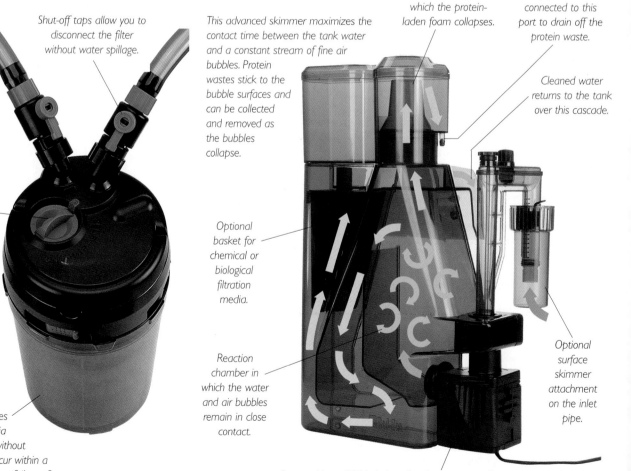

Pump with an 18-blade impeller that generates fine air bubbles in the incoming air/water flow.

skimming can be enhanced by injecting ozone instead of air into the water flow.

Chemical filtration
Filter media that remove chemicals can play a vital role in filtration.

Activated carbon Over time, dissolved organic carbons (DOC) and phenols, etc. build up and give the water that tired and aged yellow look. The traditional way of removing them from aquarium water is by means of activated carbon, which adsorbs these elements onto its surface. Activated carbon is basically wood carbon that is 'activated' by being baked at a high temperature to open up tiny pores in the particles and to make the surface of the carbon more 'attractive' to certain substances. Only highly activated carbon is suitable for use in the marine aquarium because of standard carbon's tendency to lower pH rapidly. Carbon also clogs quickly, which can result in concentrated leaching of all the substances it has adsorbed back into the water, with potentially dangerous consequences. For this reason, it must be replaced with a fresh batch every four to six weeks. Activated carbon is most commonly used in a canister filter or, as in the case of 'total systems', contained in a filter bag in the sump.

By their very nature, any types of chemical filtration must be taken out of action whenever the aquarium needs to be dosed with medicines and certain other water treatments.

Living rock as a natural filter
Using living rock as a means of filtering water is becoming increasingly popular. As we have seen, living rock is populated by aerobic bacteria, and probably even by anaerobic bacteria. In addition, there may also be organisms such as sea squirts and sponges that are very efficient filter-feeders and excellent water conditioners. There may also be a variety of algae growing on the rocks. Good water flow amongst the rocks will mean they can become effective biological filters.

Algae as natural filters
Being plants, algae will take up nutrients from the water and, along with light, use them in the photosynthesis process. The removal of nitrates and phosphates by this method is particularly useful. Algae scrubbers are external units used for culturing macro-algae to absorb unwanted nutrients, including carbon dioxide, and to produce oxygen. Water from the aquarium is passed through the scrubber continuously. The algae must be harvested on a regular basis in order to remove such nutrients from the system completely and to provide space for fresh growth. If harvesting is not carried out, the algae culture could crash, causing all the nutrients to be put back into the system in potentially dangerous concentrations. These systems require plenty of light to function efficiently. When working well they are very effective, as can be seen at one very large public aquarium in Australia, where algae scrubbers are the main form of filtration.

The most popular way of using algae for this purpose is to grow them in the display aquarium. However, they must still be harvested regularly for the same reasons given above.

On a healthy coral reef, algae are not immediately evident, due to the continuous grazing of herbivorous animals. For example, the *Caulerpa* species that often grow very long in a marine aquarium are usually only seen as short stumps on the wild reef. If you prefer this kind of algae-free appearance, then an external algae scrubber in a sump or a tray above the tank would be the best approach.

Do not attempt to use these 'natural' methods as the sole form of filtration for your display marine aquarium unless you are a very experienced marine aquarist with a complete understanding of all the biological processes. As we have seen, overall conditions in the aquarium are not entirely as they are 'in nature'.

Other types of water purification
The above types of filtration will enable you to maintain a well-balanced aquarium. However, you may wish to go one step further in achieving superb water quality or, perhaps, you intend to keep certain animals that demand more exacting water conditions. Here we look at some items of equipment designed to help you make such improvements.

Reverse osmosis filter
If you have concerns about the quality of your tapwater, then a reverse osmosis (RO) unit will help. This is a very efficient means of removing all manner of salts and minerals and even metals from your mains water supply. It works by forcing water through a membrane in order to remove the various substances. Due to its high efficiency, the membranes can quickly clog and must be replaced regularly. This makes RO units quite expensive to operate over time, as the membranes are not cheap. The other downside is that only a portion of the water finds its way through the membrane, while 80-90% goes to waste. However, this wasted water is treated by a carbon block cartridge within another chamber on the unit and can be used for other purposes, even making a good cup of coffee. Try not to waste water unnecessarily. The upside is that you can have water for topping up that is so pure it is close to distilled quality.

How reverse osmosis works

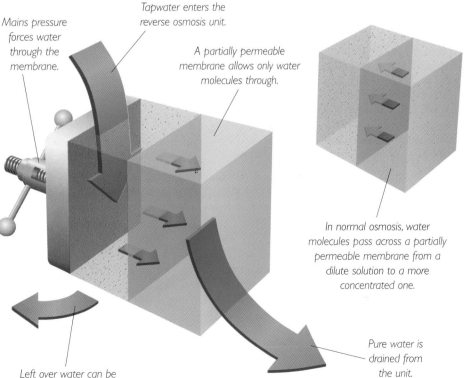

Tapwater enters the reverse osmosis unit.

Mains pressure forces water through the membrane.

A partially permeable membrane allows only water molecules through.

In normal osmosis, water molecules pass across a partially permeable membrane from a dilute solution to a more concentrated one.

Left over water can be used on the garden.

Pure water is drained from the unit.

How a UV sterilizer works

The aquarium water can be sterilized by passing it through a UV unit. The water hose connectors are translucent so that you can see the 'glow' of the UV lamp when in operation, a safety measure to make sure you do not open the unit and damage your eyesight.

Water flows though this outer glass tube.

The fluorescent tube in the middle produces ultraviolet light with a wavelength of 253.7 nm. This UVC is harmful to living tissue.

This quartz sleeve encases the tube but allows UV light to pass through.

Ultraviolet light sterilisation

Ultraviolet (UV) light is capable of eliminating algae spores and bacteria that are freely suspended in the water and sometimes cause cloudiness. A germicidal-grade lamp can also destroy disease pathogens, but is only effective on pathogens with a free-swimming stage that may find their way through the UV unit, so do not rely on it for total disease control. Bear in mind that UV light is dangerous to the eyes, so NEVER look directly at the lamp without eye protection.

The UV sterilizer consists of a UV lamp fitted inside a sealed clear quartz sleeve, mounted within a water jacket. Aquarium water fed into the outer jacket is sterilized as it flows from one end to another. The efficiency of sterilisation depends, among other factors, on the length of time the water is exposed to the UV light. The effectiveness of the lamp can be optimized by prefiltering the water mechanically before passing it through the sterilizer. This prevents organic material and suspended matter from obscuring the quartz sleeve and thus lessening the effect of the UV rays. Even so, the lamp has a definite useful lifespan; used continually, most lamps will require replacement every six months. After this period, the lamp may still appear to be functioning, but in fact the UV light is no longer able to penetrate the quartz sleeve.

Using ozone

Ozone (O_3) is an unstable form of oxygen (O_2). The extra atom of oxygen readily separates from the molecule and oxidizes toxins and other compounds in the aquarium water. This oxidising action makes ozone an effective disinfectant; it will kill bacteria, disease pathogens, algae spores and other free-swimming microorganisms that come into close contact with the gas. Ozone is used by many large public aquariums as part of their overall water quality management systems.

Ozone is formed by passing air (ideally dried) over an electrical discharge in a device known as an ozonizer, converting some of the oxygen in the air to ozone. The ozonized air is then passed through a special water/ozone contact chamber or a protein skimmer. Providing this is made from ozone-resistant materials, it makes an ideal ozone reactor. Since ozone is harmful to the aquarium inhabitants, it must only be applied in a separate vessel, never directly into the aquarium. Ozone-treated water should be passed through a carbon filter before being returned to the aquarium in order to remove any residual ozone or any harmful byproducts of excessive ozonisation. It is advisable to use an ozonizer together with a redox (or ORP – oxidation, reduction potential) controller. A probe in the aquarium monitors ozone concentration in terms of the redox potential of the water and switches on the ozonizer only when the water conditions require it.

As you might imagine, ozone is a dangerous gas and must be used with the utmost care. Always follow the manufacturer's instructions to the letter. Ozone is also capable of damaging a wide range of materials, such as rubber piping and pump diaphragms, and excessive levels can also make plastics turn brittle.

Ozone and protein skimming

Froth carrying organic waste overflows into a collecting cup.

The waste can be drained from the base of the cup through this tube.

A check valve prevents water siphoning back into the ozonizer. Renew it regularly.

This probe hanging in the tank measures the redox potential of the water and regulates the amount of ozone produced by the ozonizer.

Ozone passes into the water flow through the venturi device located here.

The ozone generator uses a high-energy electrical discharge to bond an extra atom to oxygen molecules to create ozone (O_3).

Nitrate and phosphate filters

As we have seen, there are several ways of eradicating nitrates and phosphates. In anaerobic conditions, certain bacteria can use nitrate, and algal filters use nitrate and phosphate as important nutrients. Wherever there is an excess of these substances, another way is to run either tapwater or aquarium water through a canister filled with special resins. Some are designed specifically for nitrate and others for phosphate. These resins often require dangerous chemicals to recharge them, so in a domestic situation it is best just to replace the resins once they are spent.

Another word of warning regarding the high efficiency of some resins: they can sometimes act so fast that the result is an extremely rapid change in environmental conditions, which could put your aquarium subjects into a state of shock. We know that some polyp animals, such as corals, turn white after losing their symbiotic algae due to the use of some resins. Exercise extreme caution when using these materials.

Calcium reactors

A calcium reactor is not a filter, but it is included here because it is normally used in tandem with a filter system. Invertebrates need calcium carbonate in order to grow their skeletons or shells, and regularly take these elements out of the water. As water ages and its calcium buffering capabilities diminish, the pH has a tendency to drop. This can cause metabolic problems for fishes and invertebrates, such as respiration difficulties. Therefore, it is important to maintain the correct pH (8.3 for reef animals). A calcium reactor can help to achieve this. The apparatus is usually a sealed container made from, say, acrylic, and filled with calcareous material such as aragonite. Aquarium water is delivered to the unit fairly slowly via a bypass system from the main filtration. The system is injected with carbon dioxide because its acidic nature slowly dissolves the more alkaline aragonite and thus charges the water with calcium. The carbon dioxide is used up in the process, so there is little risk of excess building up in the aquarium.

Another way of maintaining hardness and alkalinity is to drip-feed calcium water into the aquarium. Some total systems have automatic dosing equipment fitted to the filter sump for this purpose.

Bear in mind that regular partial water changes will do a great deal to help maintain pH, etc. If your mains tapwater is of good quality, nitrate and phosphate levels will be kept low.

Nutrients, minerals, trace elements

Bear in mind that some types of filters – protein skimmers, ozone and UV sterilizers – are capable of either removing or completely destroying certain nutrients, as well as important minerals and trace elements in the water. Furthermore, the metabolism of organisms will make use of all these substances, causing a depletion in the aquarium water. This is another good reason for regular water changes, but it is also likely that you will need to add specially prepared supplements. These are readily available and there is a wide variety to deal with different situations,

Calcium reactors and complete systems

Above: For invertebrates it is essential to maintain the correct hardness, alkalinity and pH levels. A calcium reactor such as this (shown without media) will provide a simple means to do this.

Below: Complete systems provide a convenient way to house the filtration and other water management devices in one unit that you can hide away in the cabinet.

Biological filtration unit

Mechanical filtration

Protein skimmer

such as iodine, strontium and even vitamin deficiencies. It is not always easy to test for such deficiencies, so regular dosing is a necessary part of your routine tank maintenance.

Water movement

Water movement plays an essential role in the good management of the marine environment, as it distributes vital oxygen and helps to prevent stagnant areas where detritus can build up. Equally important is its effect on metabolism. All solid objects in water, including living organisms, are surrounded by a layer of stagnant water, almost like a membrane. In water with a strong flow, this 'membrane' is very thin, whereas in still water, this stagnant layer thickens and can impede metabolic processes. Strong currents can be created in the aquarium by adding extra pumps; small powerheads are ideal for this purpose. Randomly alternating currents can be achieved by using two or more powerheads controlled by a wavemaker, or by a series of timers, to simulate wave action on a natural reef. The result is that the aquarium water is thoroughly oxygenated and detritus is kept in suspension so that the filters can draw it out, thus maintaining the good health of the aquarium's inhabitants.

Using filters with medication

The treatment of disease in the marine aquarium can be complicated by the presence of sophisticated filtration

systems. Activated carbon will adsorb many medications, and protein skimmers are also effective in removing such substances. In these circumstances, it is useful to have a separate hospital tank to which infected animals can be transferred for treatment. If several animals are infected simultaneously, or you are worried about stressing the animals too much by moving them, you will have to treat them in the main aquarium and turn off the chemical filtration for the duration. In any case, do remember that invertebrates in general are intolerant of many chemicals, including copper, so read the instructions carefully to make sure that the medications you use are safe with these animals.

Filter-feeding animals

Many invertebrates are filter-feeders that require their food to remain in suspension. Some filters will draw this food out of the water column quicker than the animals can feed on it completely. In these cases, you may have to turn off the filtration for a while, which is not always ideal. Alternatively, you could spend time individually targeting the relevant animals at feeding time by delivering food directly to them via, say, a drinking straw or pipette. Alternating surge currents often have the effect of keeping such foods in suspension for a longer period before it is drawn out by filters and, therefore, may be a better solution to the problem.

Chapter 7: *Creating habitats*

Newcomers to marine fishkeeping may be forgiven for thinking that decorating the tank with substrate and rocks, etc. is done solely for aesthetic purposes. However, in modern marine aquariums, these items play an integral role in maintaining water quality and providing the fishes and invertebrates with habitat to live in or on. Generally speaking, these materials require thorough cleaning, or curing, before use and must be prepared well in advance of setting up the tank.

When you come to decorate the aquarium, always work from the bottom up. First put in the rockwork or living rock directly on the tank base and then build up the substrate on top. An obvious statement perhaps, but if you intend to use biological filters, such as a plenum, that are often situated below the substrate, then you have to make sure these are fitted before any other work is carried out.

The substrate

In the case of a tropical marine aquarium, coral sand and gravel are the only real choices if you wish to establish a 'natural' look. Where temperate systems are concerned, you could use soft beach sand, gravel or small pebbles, or a combination of these materials.

Sand on the reef is mostly produced by animals such as boring worms and parrotfishes, which crunch up coral to extract tiny organisms and algae. Their crunching activities are so thorough that they eventually excrete fine sand that falls to the seabed. Coral gravel is created by wave action, whereby the coral is broken and the fragments are slowly worn down. In nature, myriad organisms, such as worms and crustaceans, some microscopic, live in the sand and keep it clean and aerated to a certain depth. In the aquarium, too, these organisms can become very useful when the sand is allowed to become 'live'.

Choosing rocks

Apart from deciding how to set out the tank, you must choose the correct materials to put into it. Once again, remember the importance of water quality control and choose from the wide range of calcareous and inert substances available. Fortunately, there is no difficulty in obtaining materials such as lava rock, ocean rock and so-called 'live rock' for use in the tropical marine aquarium. Where temperate or coldwater marine tanks are concerned, you could use a wider variety, such as sandstone, granite, some slates (grey is safe) and limestone. Whichever you decide on, you must examine the pieces before use to make sure there is no evidence of metallic-ore veins in the rock. Ores have occasionally been found in tufa and volcanic lava rock, in particular.

How you design the habitat in your aquarium is largely a matter of taste, but it is worth taking a bit of time to consider the needs of the animals you want to keep. Fishes certainly need somewhere to go at night, unless they are nocturnal and the reverse applies. Shrimps and other crustaceans require overhang ledges to get under, and some fishes, such as lionfishes, often hang upside-down under ledges. Territorial animals, as the name implies, must be able to establish their own territories, whilst cruising species, such as triggerfishes, batfishes and angelfishes, need a reasonable amount of open space. By including caves, crevices, ledges and arches along with plenty of swimming space, you will be able to cater for a wide range of needs.

Living rock

The term 'living rock' refers to rock that has been collected from the wild and kept damp whilst in transit, so that any organisms attached to it will, hopefully, remain alive. The pieces popularly regarded as the best quality are generally coated in pink coralline

Above: The surface of a piece of living rock. Notice the macro-algae, pink encrusting calcareous algae and small polyp animals. Such a rock will also support a range of tiny crustaceans and worms.

algae. This rock is the ideal medium for building habitat and the bonus is it may bring with it an array of invertebrate life, algae and on rare occasions, the odd small fish, or a young growth of coral. Often eggs and larvae will be hidden within holes and crevices, and eventually emerge as a pleasant surprise to the aquarist. Of course, it can work the other way round, and undesirable animals, such as certain types of predatory crab or mantis shrimps, appear as if from nowhere.

Living rock is expensive because it is heavy and costs a lot to ship, so filling the entire aquarium with it could be prohibitive. If this is the case you could build a base of, say, ocean rock and

Rocks for a marine aquarium

Calcareous oceanic rock will help to maintain pH levels in the aquarium.

This ocean rock has been smoothed off and will provide an excellent footing for algal growth.

Below: Coral gravel and sand (shown here) are the most suitable and easily available substrates for a marine aquarium. They not only look right but also help to maintain a stable pH and high buffering capacity.

Below: Models of corals moulded in resin are incredibly lifelike and will soon take on the patina of realism as they become covered in algae and detritus in a marine aquarium. They are the only choice if we are to conserve the real thing in the wild.

Although it looks garish out of water, this simulated tree coral will soon lose its harsh appearance and add colour and interest to any display.

This synthetic seafan looks surprisingly realistic, and its elegant sweeping form will contrast well with more upright shapes.

then strategically place choice pieces of live rock around the structure. If you choose rock with a similar appearance to living rock, with time, the two types of rock will start to blend in with each other as algae and invertebrates spread themselves around the aquarium.

Good-quality living rock has excellent qualities for helping achieve and maintain optimum water conditions, so much so that some very experienced marine aquarists use it as the only form of filtration and water conditioning in their aquariums. However, this type of rock needs to be properly looked after right from the time it is collected, otherwise organisms will start to die. If this happens, you may end up with a nasty, foul-smelling lump that requires some urgent curing before it is placed in the aquarium. In this event, keep the rock in a separate, well-aerated container of saltwater at the correct temperature and specific gravity, preferably with filtration. Check it every day and if you find any decaying patches on the rock, scrub them away thoroughly with a small, stiff brush. Only when the decay has halted and there is no longer a nasty smell can you introduce it into the tank. Fortunately, the majority of living rock is either of good condition or the collectors and importers have already cured it before sale, but always check.

Collecting living rock is becoming more controlled in certain countries and may be banned in future, so some enterprising collectors and dealers now seed other types of rock in aquaculture-style systems and 'grow' them on until they look just right for sale.

Coral

Living hard corals (also called stony corals), the reef-building corals, are controlled by C.I.T.E.S. (Convention for the International Trade in Endangered Species) but licenses to import them can be obtained. Clams (*Tridacna* spp.) are also controlled, but soft corals, anemones and other polyp animals are not. Commercial coral propagation farms now exist and it is far more appropriate to buy pieces that have originated from such sources whenever possible. Many aquarists have successfully propagated their own corals and swapping pieces with fellow enthusiasts is quite common. You can also obtain artificial coral 'skeletons' moulded in resin that soon take on a more realistic appearance in the tank.

Adding corals and related animals to the marine aquarium will help create a stunning and realistic environment, and is not as difficult to achieve as it was some years ago. However, hard corals are still not for the inexperienced and you should begin with other, tougher, related polyp animals. One thing you must always keep in mind is that certain species of fishes will eat corals

Above: Caulerpa prolifera, the most common species of macro-algae in the genus. It has flat, lobe-shaped leaves and usually grows on rocks, but it may extend through the tank with its creeping stem.

and other invertebrates, even those found on living rock, so some forethought will be required when considering what mix of animals you wish to keep.

Marine algae

Some authorities have had the notion that coral reefs should more accurately be called algae reefs, as the sheer mass of algae on a reef is quite enormous. Apart from the more recognisable types of macro-algae that grow on one substrate or another, there are the zooxanthellae that live within the tissues of corals, particularly hard corals, and clams. It is because of these algae that corals can only survive in areas of very strong sunlight. Like other plants, zooxanthellae need light to photosynthesize.

By including macro-algae in the reef aquarium, you can provide the plant element that many aquarists miss if they have moved from keeping a freshwater aquarium to setting up a marine tank. Macro-algae can be not only attractive, but also very useful for marine fishes that like to graze, such as herbivorous surgeonfishes. The algae derive much of their nourishment from waste products in the aquarium water, but you may have to supplement their needs by adding trace elements, fertilizers and even extra carbon dioxide, which is perhaps the most important nutrient for plants. One drawback of achieving a lush growth is that it may suddenly 'crash', releasing toxins into the aquarium water as it dies back. To avoid this, harvest your algae periodically. Macro-algae, especially some of those in the genus *Caulerpa*, are capable of rapidly taking over the tank, as their daily growth rate is quite phenomenal when conditions are right.

Below: It is fairly unusual to encounter red algae as an aquarium decoration. This striking specimen is growing attached to a piece of rock and provides an excellent focal point in the display tank.

Chapter 8: Setting up the aquarium

In this chapter we consider the stages involved in setting up a basic marine aquarium using separate pieces of equipment to achieve the three main types of filtration, i.e. biological, mechanical and chemical, along with heating and lighting. (This so-called customized system differs from a total system that incorporates integral filters, heating and lighting and which is purchased as a single unit. Total systems may also include a variety of water management aids, such as a protein skimmer, calcium reactor, UV sterilizer and denitrifying unit.) Our customized aquarium includes some 'living rock' and a compatible selection of fishes and invertebrates (shown being added in the next chapter).

Our setup will feature an externally fitted fluidized bed sand filter for biological filtration, an external protein skimmer for removing organic and chemical waste, and an external power sponge filter to help remove particles in suspension and to improve water movement. As some of the equipment is to be situated outside of the tank, make sure there will be room on the stand (or along the back panel of the tank) to accommodate them. Lighting will be provided by fluorescent lamps and for heating we will use two small thermofilters without their foam-filled filter 'jackets' in place. For decoration, we will have a coral sand substrate and a seascape built up using pieces of 'living rock'. Some hardy polyp animals will be included along with other invertebrates and, of course, some fishes. This system is easy to set up and is not too expensive, but it will provide the means of managing good water quality and a wide variety of animals. Even if you choose to install a more sophisticated system, you will find that much of the practical information is still relevant.

Advanced preparation

It is useful, as discussed earlier, to prepare your saltwater mixture in advance of setting up the aquarium. If 'living rock' is to be immediately introduced at the setup stage then it will not be appropriate to make the initial saltwater mix directly in the tank. However, if 'living rock' can be introduced a few days later then it will probably be more convenient to mix the saltwater in the aquarium. Remember that subsequent water changes must be made with water that has been prepared in another container. Also make sure any rockwork you plan to use in the display (not the 'living rock') and substrate are sufficiently cleaned before the designated setting-up time.

Preparing the site and tank

It is a good idea to make a checklist of items you will be requiring and the jobs you will have to carry out. Use the list to make sure that everything is at hand before you start setting up. Choose a site for your tank that is near to an electric power point and easily accessible, not only during the setting-up stage, but also for maintenance afterwards. For safety sake, fit an RCD circuit breaker. Make sure your work area is free of clutter.

Just to recap on a couple of points already made. Make sure your tank stand or cabinet is strong enough to take the weight of your aquarium when it is full of water and, likewise the floor must also be strong enough. If possible make sure the whole system is supported directly on floor joists as opposed to inbetween them.

Good commercially-made aquariums should have been pre-tested for leaks. However, if you have any doubts test the tank by placing it on a suitable strong, flat surface somewhere outside your house. Fill it with water and should you find a leak, return the tank to the shop where you bought it.

If you are happy with your tank then you can start the setting up. Remember to locate your aquarium away from bright sunlight and heating radiators.

Siting the aquarium

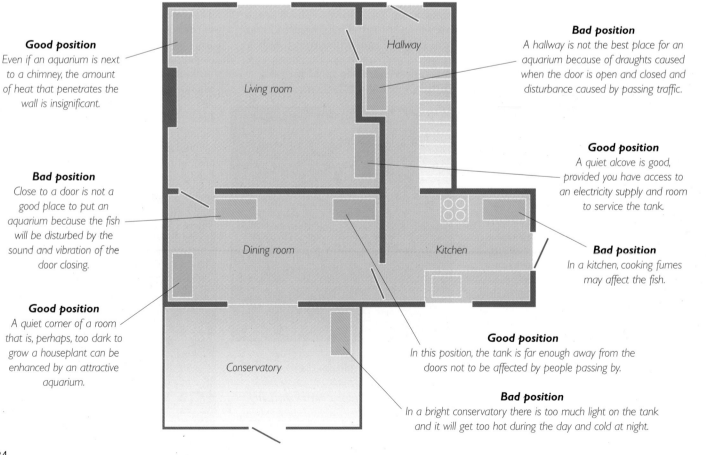

Good position
Even if an aquarium is next to a chimney, the amount of heat that penetrates the wall is insignificant.

Bad position
Close to a door is not a good place to put an aquarium because the fish will be disturbed by the sound and vibration of the door closing.

Good position
A quiet corner of a room that is, perhaps, too dark to grow a houseplant can be enhanced by an attractive aquarium.

Hallway

Living room

Dining room

Kitchen

Conservatory

Bad position
A hallway is not the best place for an aquarium because of draughts caused when the door is open and closed and disturbance caused by passing traffic.

Good position
A quiet alcove is good, provided you have access to an electricity supply and room to service the tank.

Bad position
In a kitchen, cooking fumes may affect the fish.

Good position
In this position, the tank is far enough away from the doors not to be affected by people passing by.

Bad position
In a bright conservatory there is too much light on the tank and it will get too hot during the day and cold at night.

Installing the technical equipment

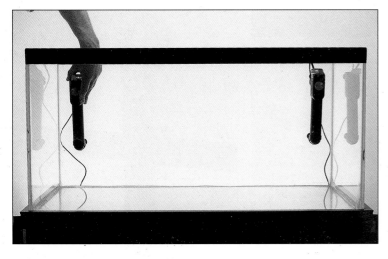

1 *In all but the smallest of aquariums, it is best to use two heaters placed at opposite ends of the tank to ensure even heat distribution and as a safeguard against heater failure.*

2 *Place the return pipe from the external power filter at one end of the tank and try to arrange it so that it can easily be hidden by your habitat.*

3 *Place the inlet filter pipe at the opposite end of the tank from the return pipe to provide the most efficient water circulation.*

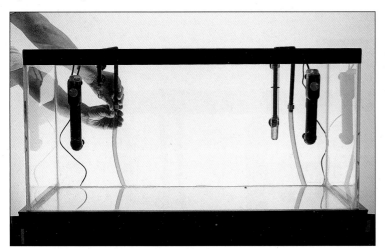

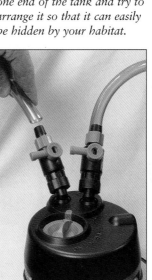

4 *Connect hoses to the external power filter. Take care to fit these securely so that they do not come apart when the filter is running under full pressure – otherwise water in the tank ends up on the floor!*

5 *Connect the hoses to the external filter securely, making sure they are not tangled and, if necessary, mark them IN and OUT.*

6 *If you choose to place your aquarium on a cabinet, then it is easy to hide away external equipment such as this power filter.*

Also make sure there is plenty of room to accommodate the different pieces of equipment around the outside of the tank. Place a sheet of expanded polystyrene equal to the area of the aquarium's base on top of the stand or cabinet to help support the tank evenly. Then sit the tank on top of that.

Installing pumps, filters and heater
Now is the time to arrange where you are going to place any pumps required for running the fluidized bed sand filter and skimmer, as well as the external power filter and heater units. Do not plug any equipment into the electricity supply at this stage. Pumps need to be positioned at the back of the tank where they can be easily connected to the apparatus, whilst the intake and

return pipes for the external power filter can be placed at opposite ends along the back wall of the tank. Position the heater units on the back glass near the corners using the suckers supplied with them, making sure that the element does not get covered by any substrate and that there will be good water flow around them.

Place the fluidized bed filter and skimmer wherever is convenient, although, if possible, situate them at opposite ends of the tank. Some models will need to be stood on top the aquarium stand, whilst others have attachments for hanging on the side or back glass of the tank (as here). Fluidized bed sand filters are usually pressurized so they can be sited anywhere providing the hoses are long

enough and the associated pump is powerful enough to maintain the correct throughput of water through the unit. Protein skimmers are not pressurized, however, and must be placed so that the correct operating water level is no lower than that of the aquarium, otherwise they will overflow. Connect up to the pumps by following the maker's instructions carefully.

The habitat
In this setup the habitat will be serving two purposes, one to provide cover and territory for the inhabitants and, secondly to hide the equipment you have installed. If you are on a limited budget and cannot afford to create your habitat entirely from 'living rock' then use some cheaper inert rock for

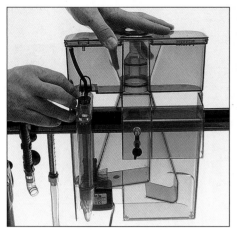

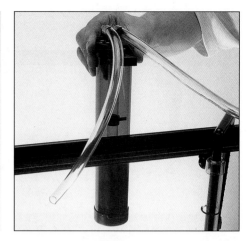

7 There are several designs of protein skimmer available. This one needs to be hung on the back panel of the aquarium. Make sure you provide easy access to such equipment for regular cleaning.

8 This aquarium makes use of a fluidized bed sand filter for biological filtration. This particular unit is driven by a small submersible water pump. Attach this by suckers inside the tank on the back glass.

9 Hang the fluidized bed sand filter on the outside of the back glass and connect it to the internal pump with a hose. Always make sure that the chamber containing the sand is fitted in a truly vertical position.

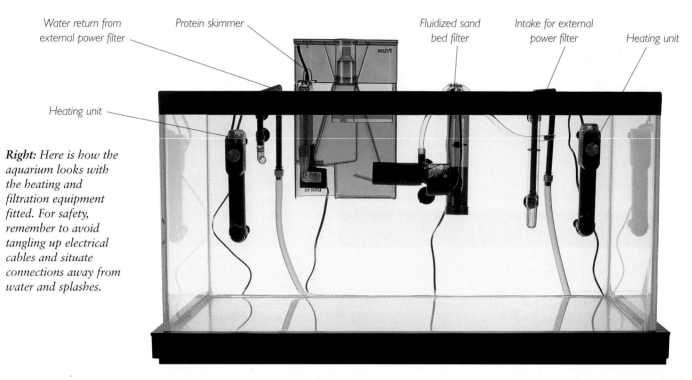

Water return from external power filter

Protein skimmer

Fluidized sand bed filter

Intake for external power filter

Heating unit

Heating unit

Right: *Here is how the aquarium looks with the heating and filtration equipment fitted. For safety, remember to avoid tangling up electrical cables and situate connections away from water and splashes.*

constructing the base features. Check with your aquarium dealer to find out what is available. It is likely that this base rock will require washing before use. It is also a good idea to place each piece in a pan of boiling water for a few minutes at a time to sterilize them before arranging them in the tank.

It will be your own artistic abilities that govern how you arrange your rock, but some knowledge of natural reefs and an idea of what animals you want to keep will help. Be sure to provide plenty of crevices, caves, overhangs and perhaps archways for the inhabitants to take up residence in. Also keep in mind that any pieces of 'living rock' being added later will need sites to fit into.

If you have no budgetary constraints

it is far better to create your habitat from 'living rock' only, as this will improve the water conditioning and natural filtering properties of the tank.

Adding living rock

Providing you have a supply of previously matured saltwater available to hand that has the correct temperature, specific gravity and pH of 8.3, you can introduce your pieces of 'living rock' to complete the habitat. In this case it is important your water is added immediately after placing your rocks and laying the substrate. As this rock includes living organisms it is not good practice to subject it to the harsh environment of new, unmatured saltwater. If you only have newly mixed

saltwater available at the setting up stage, then it is important to wait until the aquarium is fully operational before adding the 'living rock'.

The substrate

The substrate is the next thing to install into the aquarium, and in this case we are using coral sand. Ideally, introduce enough to cover the base of the tank to a depth of about 2.5cm (1in). This is equivalent to about 4.5kg (10lb) per 30cm^2 (1ft^2); any deeper and you will run the risk of anaerobic conditions developing in the lower layers.

It is likely you will need to wash the substrate before use and this is best done in advance of starting the setting-up process. The best, and quickest, way is to wash a small amount at a time in a fine mesh hand net. Hold the net over a bucket and run water through from a tap or hose until all the detritus has been flushed out of the sand. Dispose of the waste by whatever means you have available, but it is advisable to avoid clogging the trap in your sink. When you are happy that all your sand is clean you can spread it over the base of your tank and around your habitat in a manner that ensures the rocks appear to be rising out of the substrate.

Adding the water

If you have already matured the water in another aquarium then it is simply a case of carefully pouring it into the tank. It is a good idea to pour the water onto a rock or into a container placed on the substrate to avoid the sand being moved out of place. You will now need to connect the pumps for the fluidized bed sand filter and protein skimmer to the electricity supply and switch on in order to fill their chambers and start circulation. Carry this out in full accordance with the manufacturer's instructions. The water level in the aquarium will drop a little and will need to be topped up. Now switch on the power filter and the heater.

If you do not have pre-matured water ready you will have to mix a new batch in advance of setting up. When mixing, the temperature should be at the normal aquarium operating level of 24°C (75°F), as the salts will dissolve more readily. A thermometer stuck to the outside of the mixing container is good for making a quick reference, but to be accurate it is best to use a glass thermometer that reads directly from the water. Once you are certain the salts have completely dissolved take a specific gravity reading using a hydrometer. If it is low, add more salts and continue doing this while taking further specific gravity tests, until the S.G. is 1.022-1.023. Remember, once the aquarium is fully operational and has animals living in it, you must never mix saltwater directly in the tank again. Always perform this task in a separate container.

When you are happy all is correct, add the water to the aquarium and connect up the heating and filtration.

Installing the lights

The lighting canopy must be made from non-corrosive and non-toxic materials and be large enough to accommodate

Adding decor to the aquarium

1 Fit a background to the outside of the back glass to hide the equipment. Blue is the best choice, as the colours of fishes and invertebrates stand out well against it. Black can also be used to good effect.

2 Add the first pieces of living rock directly onto the tank floor. Place them carefully so that you can build up a stable display. In this setup we are using high-quality living rock only and have opted not to include any form of base rock or other decor.

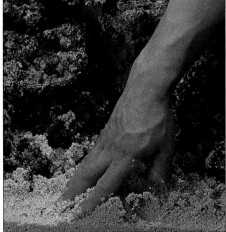

3 Create the habitat in a way to provide plenty of retreats for the inhabitants and to hide pieces of equipment placed internally. However, leave open swimming space for those fishes that require it. It is vital that the rock is not allowed to dry out.

4 The best substrate for this aquarium setup is coral sand. Spread it around the base of the tank and against the rocks to give the appearance of the habitat rising up from within the sand.

Adding water and maturing the tank

1 *Because this setup includes living rock, it is important to add matured saltwater, i.e. from another established aquarium. New saltwater can harm the many tiny invertebrates already living on the rock. Pour the water gently onto the rocks to prevent displacing the sand substrate.*

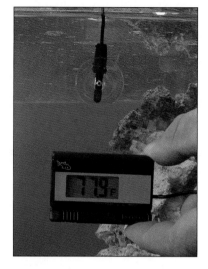

2 *Attach the readout unit of a digital thermometer to the outer glass and place the probe in the water, ideally some distance away from the heating units.*

3 Connect the heating and filtration equipment to the electricity supply and turn them on. However, it is vital that you monitor water quality and do not introduce any livestock until ammonia and nitrite levels have been zero for several days.

two white 10,000°K fluorescent tubes and one blue actinic 03. It is also important that the canopy can have sections cut out of it to allow filter fittings, hoses and cables to be routed through. A wooden hood laminated with plastic, or painted with several coats of polyurethane varnish, is ideal. Any control gear for the lamps must be situated away from water and splashes.

It would be useful to connect the power cables for the lights into a remote control box or power strip with the pumps and heaters so that there is only one cable running to the electricity supply socket. Some controllers have on/off switches incorporated for each of the various appliances connected to them and are protected by cutout functions in case of equipment faults.

Maturing the filters

Even though there are no animals in the aquarium at this stage it is good to have the lights on for the normal photoperiod, i.e. 12 hours per day, as this will help the maturation process, and is essential once the 'living rock' has been introduced.

It is absolutely critical that you do not introduce any more livestock into the aquarium until the filters have matured. This means you must wait and be patient until there is a large enough population of nitrifying bacteria to deal with ammonia and nitrite. As 'living rock' is included in this setup that may have the bacteria already living on it, the process could be faster than in other arrangements. However, you must now make daily tests for ammonia and nitrite levels using aquarium test kits until the readings show clear for both. It is likely you will not see any evidence of ammonia or nitrite right away, but this does not mean the coast is clear, as the levels will build up gradually, with ammonia peaking first. Be patient and wait until you have had several consecutive days of clear readings before considering adding livestock. When you are certain that all is clear make a 20-25% saltwater change to dilute the resulting levels of nitrate.

The coldwater aquarium

More or less the same criteria apply to setting up a coldwater or temperate marine aquarium. The main difference being that a heating system is not required.

Of course, the substrate and habitat will be different to a coral reef setup and will be made up of materials more common to the locations where your choice of fishes and/or invertebrates are naturally found. As suitable animals and some habitat materials for such aquaria are not so commonly found in the aquarium trade, it may be a case of collecting your own. If this is the situation for you, remember to look out for nice pieces of rock with plenty of life on it and treat it as 'living rock'. Be aware though that many species of seaweeds, particularly wracks and kelps, do not do well in small tanks and should be avoided. When collecting, especially during the warmer months, make sure you transport your specimens home in insulated containers to prevent overheating. Provide aeration if you can by investing in a battery-operated airpump. Also, be sure not to transport predator with prey in the same container to reduce the risk of arriving home with less specimens than you collected. For this reason you must research your animals to decide exactly what you will be able to keep together.

Rockpool animals are subjected to frequent changes in temperature and other water conditions due to the to-and-fro movement of the tides and the subsequent exposure to the sun. Therefore, these animals are generally hardy and are most suited to life in the aquarium. However, if your choice is fishes that are found in open water

where conditions are cooler, then you will most likely have to consider incorporating a chiller into your system, which ultimately can make a coldwater marine aquarium far more expensive to set up and run than a tropical one.

Otherwise, you can use exactly the same type of tank, filtration, protein skimmer and lighting as you would for a tropical marine aquarium to establish a successful coldwater marine system.

Alternative options

Should you find the setting-up arrangement described above unsuitable, you could fit the fluidized bed sand filter, protein skimmer and heater units into a sump, which could be hidden inside a cabinet. In this case,

an overflow will have to be fitted from the aquarium to the sump and a pump installed in the sump to return water to the aquarium.

To improve water movement, extra pumps, such as small powerheads, could be installed in the aquarium and hidden behind the habitat. Alternate currents can be achieved by controlling these pumps from an electronic surge unit. Further improvements can be made by directing the flow from one or two pumps directly at the 'living rock'.

You may also want to consider including an UV (ultraviolet light) sterilizer to help maintain excellent water clarity. The UV light disrupts living cells and can be effective against some bacteria and parasites.

Installing the lights

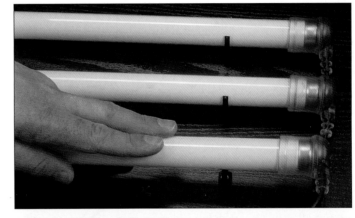

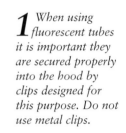

1 *When using fluorescent tubes it is important they are secured properly into the hood by clips designed for this purpose. Do not use metal clips.*

2 *Position the tubes in the hood so that they provide the best light coverage within the aquarium. Place each one as far apart from its neighbouring tube to create the best coverage and to allow for good air circulation between them to prevent overheating.*

Two triphosphor white tubes

One actinic 03 'blue' tube

Chapter 9: Choosing and introducing fishes

Having taken all possible care to set up the tank and provide the ideal conditions, do not ruin your painstaking preparations by choosing unsuitable animals for your aquarium. Several factors must influence your choice; their compatibility, both with their own kind and unrelated species; their feeding requirements; their tolerance of captivity; their appearance and even their cost. It is, therefore, very important to research thoroughly all the species you would like to keep .

Obtaining healthy stock

Observe fishes and invertebrates carefully before buying them. They should be alert and free from any sort of damage. Avoid fishes that look thin, or have pinched stomachs, as they often have trouble recovering. Freshwater fishkeepers are used to seeing their healthy fishes swim with erect fins, but many marine fishes naturally keep their fins down, so this is not necessarily a sign of ill-health. With invertebrates, it is more difficult to tell whether they are in good condition or not. In the case of corals (ideally attached to rock), anemones and other polyp animals, look out for tissue damage or even decay. The same applies to sponges, but with crustaceans and starfishes it is usually a case of making sure all their limbs are intact. Sea urchins should not be showing any signs of shedding their spines. Generally speaking, it is worth avoiding any invertebrates that appear to be shedding unusual mucus-like substances, unless you know for sure that this is a normal trait in that species.

Stressed fishes will often produce excessive skin mucus that usually has the appearance of white slimy patches. Avoid these fish, even though the temptation may be to transfer them to your own tank, where conditions are much better.

Many tropical marine fishes and invertebrates are brilliantly coloured, which is what makes them particularly attractive as aquarium subjects. Make sure their colours are as they should be and avoid specimens with an unnaturally dull appearance or any with poorly defined markings. Cloudy or swollen eyes, ulcerations and abnormal swimming or instability are bad signs. In particular, look out for signs of scratching or unusually high respiration, as these indicate parasite infections or other possible ailments, as well as toxic water conditions.

Some species, particularly those caught directly from the wild, may take a while to start feeding in captivity, so it is worth asking if you can observe them eating before you buy. Most aquarium dealers will not have any problem with this. However, one problem arising from this is the risk of the food being regurgitated or the fish defecating in the transit container on the way home and causing an ammonia problem. If the journey is short the risks may be negligible, but if it takes more than half an hour to get your subjects home, then refrain from transporting them until they have been purged. Once you have seen the animal feed, it is worth leaving a deposit and arranging to collect it the following day. For these reasons it is always worth developing a good relationship and level of trust between yourself and your chosen dealer.

Continually using the same source for your fishes and invertebrates will help to ensure a consistent quality of livestock and service. Listen to the recommendations of other aquarists before trying new dealers. If you obtain specimens from a variety of sources it will often be difficult to trace where a problem may have originated and therefore you will not be able to alert the relevant people, or expect any one source to take responsibility.

The journey home

Once you have obtained your chosen specimens you will be taking them, presumably, on the final stage of their journey from natural habitat to aquarium. Assuming they have survived all the traumas of capture, air travel and several changes of aquarium conditions, you must make sure that their introduction into your aquarium is as stress-free as possible.

The best, and standard, way of transporting most fishes and invertebrates is in plastic bags filled with one-third aquarium water and two-thirds air. If your journey home is a long one, explain the situation to the dealer so that you can arrange for oxygen to be injected into the bag instead of air. If the weather is cold, or very hot, you may be able to buy or borrow an insulating polystyrene shipping box to transport your animals.

Below: When faced with the wide range of fishes to choose from at the aquatic store, you should know what to look for, so that you only buy healthy stock. Avoid buying fish simply because you like the look of them; they might not be compatible.

Above: Once caught from the dealer's tank and bagged up, fish are usually placed into a brown paper bag. Being in dark surroundings usually calms them down and prevents undue stress occurring during the journey home.

Above: Equalize the transport water with that in the aquarium by floating the unopened bags in the tank, preferably with the lights off as this will help the fishes or invertebrates stay calm during this process.

Above: After the bags have floated for 15 minutes you can open them and start gradually mixing in some aquarium water as described in the main text. Doing this will equalise differences in pH, salinity and 'fine tune' the temperature before release.

Whilst in transit, never subject your fish to bright light, but keep them calm in the dark. The plastic bags should be wrapped in paper or kept in a dark paper bag or box. Likewise, do not subject them to sudden movements and vibrations. If travelling in a vehicle, cushion the transit container to prevent excessive vibrations from the engine or uneven road surfaces disturbing the animals.

Introducing the animals
Continue to keep the new animals in dimly lit conditions throughout the introduction process. Unpack the bags and float them in your aquarium for approximately 15 minutes to allow any differences in temperature to equalize. If you have had a long journey, there is a risk that the pH of the water in the transit bags will have dropped. Sudden changes in pH are dangerous to marine animals, so gradually mix the transit water with the aquarium water until equalisation has been achieved. There are two ways to do this. You could open the floating bags and introduce a small amount of aquarium water at a time until the bag is full, making sure it does not sink, then pour two-thirds back into the tank and repeat the process. By the time you have filled the bag a second time, you should find that the pH, S.G. and temperature have all equalized. Nevertheless, you must take some tests to be absolutely certain before releasing the animals.

Alternatively, you could transfer the animals into a receptacle such as a very clean bucket, and then drip-feed water from the aquarium into the bucket via a length of airline with a valve on the end. Continually monitor conditions until equalisation has been achieved

and it is safe to transfer the animals into the aquarium.

To avoid further stress on the fishes and invertebrates you should carefully balance the need to acclimatize them with the length of time it takes to do so. Carefully monitoring respiration will indicate to some degree the level of stress a fish is experiencing, but it is much more difficult to assess with invertebrates.

As living rock actually includes living organisms, it is necessary to acclimatize it to your aquarium in exactly the same way you would fishes and invertebrates. The same also applies to algae.

Quarantining new stock
If you are not certain about the health of new animals, it may be advisable to quarantine them in a tank designed for this purpose before introducing them to the aquarium. Always maintain such a tank to the same standard as your main aquarium. Despite the best intentions, it may be argued (with some degree of logic) that any extra transference of animals from one situation to another can cause stress. The extra quarantining stage may be an example of this and will require that you acclimatize the animals in the usual ways when transferring them. Careful handling of healthy stock from a reputable dealer will reduce the number of occasions where quarantining is necessary.

The first days
After the animals have been successfully introduced into the aquarium, leave them with the lights off, but not in total darkness, for about an hour. After this the lights can be turned on in stages, and it is often a good idea to offer a very tiny amount of food. For many

animals, eating when in a new situation is what is known as a displacement activity and the fact that food is available helps them to settle. Imagine being thrown into a totally new environment and discovering there is no evidence of a food source, you would certainly feel stressed, as the most powerful survival instinct is to eat. Obviously, the presence of healthy living rock will provide a number of suitable food items in the form of microorganisms and algae. However, some fishes may not feed for a couple of days while they are settling in and, in most cases, this will not cause undue harm. The most notable exceptions to this are surgeonfishes and seahorses, which must keep eating virtually constantly.

Whether you are introducing animals to a newly set up aquarium or an established system, add only one fish at a time to avoid overloading the capabilities of the biological filtration. Gradually the bacteria population will catch up with the extra loading and you will be able to make another addition. For corals and other invertebrates, you can count a cluster of polyp animals on a rock as the equivalent of one animal, providing it is not a massive piece. In fact, invertebrates can be added in pairs at weekly intervals.

It is worth bearing in mind that any animals known to exhibit particularly aggressive territorial behaviour are best introduced last of all. If established in the tank any earlier, these animals could mercilessly attack newcomers that are introduced after them.

Compatibility

To avoid unwarranted aggression, choose your aquarium subjects in terms of their compatibility with one another. This will require some research before drawing up your species 'wish list'. If you are not sure, it is best to avoid mixing fishes that have big mouths with ones that are small enough to be swallowed. Conversely, do not include crustaceans with large claws in a community of delicate animals. Employing some forethought and common sense, and providing a variety of habitat features with a good amount of open swimming space will usually ensure that the aquarium inhabitants can find sufficient escape routes and retreats should a skirmish break out.

Lifespans

Our knowledge of marine fishkeeping is increasing all the time, but it is still difficult to give any accurate guidance concerning the projected lifespan of aquatic animals kept in aquarium conditions. Nor has there been a great deal of research into the longevity of the same species in the wild. That said, many species originally thought to live for only, say, a couple of years in captivity have now been found to survive much longer, thanks to advancements in aquarium technology and husbandry. Often in the past, it was fishes in public aquariums that had the longest lifespan, presumably because they fared better in the generally larger systems. Today, however, marine aquarium hobbyists are finding that their species often live as long and occasionally longer than those kept in large exhibits.

Above: A pair of cleaner shrimps. All kinds of invertebrates require the same type of careful treatment as marine fishes when being introduced to the aquarium.

Below: The same approach applies to living rock, algae and corals. Take care not to damage other invertebrates when placing new items into your habitat formation. Place them onto the rockscape in stable position to prevent other tank inhabitants from easily dislodging them.

Above: Avoid placing individual corals and anemones too close to each other and never touch their living tissue with your fingers as you position them, as this may cause serious damage to the animals.

Right: The finished aquarium, including the initial livestock. Only introduce one fish or invertebrate at a time, unless they are small enough to allow more – please use good judgement! Always monitor the water quality before making any further introductions to avoid over burdening the filter system and in turn stressing the animals.

Yellow sailfin tang – a hardy fish ideally suited to this type of aquarium setup.

The living rock habitat supports its own community of living organisms, but also provides retreats for other aquarium subjects and a base for adding live corals, anemones and other sessile creatures.

Compatibility

It is important to consider the compatibility of both the fishes and invertebrates you intend to keep together in the same aquarium. Nature seems cruel when you think about a large predatory fish eating a smaller species, which in turn may eat a yet smaller fish or invertebrate; or the fact that certain invertebrates are quite capable of devouring fishes. Sadly, tank inmates do not necessarily become docile and domesticated in the home aquarium where food is more easily available, so food chain trends continue.

If you are not certain about the normal lifestyle of a species, it is best to use the guideline that if one fish is bigger than the others in the aquarium and has a large mouth, then the chances are that the smaller fishes will be eaten. Groupers, lionfishes, anglerfishes and moray eels are typical of those that fall into this category. Likewise, invertebrates with large claws are potentially going to do some serious damage, and anemones with powerful stinging cells can easily catch slow, weak-swimming fishes, such as seahorses.

Less obvious threats are butterflyfishes that eat the stinging cells of corals, filefishes that often bite out the eyes of less robust species and triggerfishes that have jaws adapted to eating spiny sea urchins. Another consideration is that when a fish that naturally lives in a shoal is kept as an individual, it may change its defence tactic by becoming aggressive and territorial because it can no longer rely on the safety of numbers. The best line of defence against predation in the aquarium is to read about the lifestyles of the animals you are interested in before obtaining them.

To avoid other types of aggression, it is a good idea to learn how to tell sexes apart. In the case of damselfishes, for example, males that have established a nest site will fiercely fight with one another, and other fishes that get too close for that matter, whilst females are happier living together out in the water column. Male damsels often have colour in their fins, but the females' fins are transparent.

Above: *A great mixed community aquarium, home to common clownfishes* (Amphiprion ocellaris), *the majestic Cuban hogfish* (Bodianus pulchellus), *blue damsels* (Chrysiptera springeri) *and the black-tailed humbug damsel* (Dascyllus melanurus), *plus a variety of invertebrates. However, the black-tailed humbug is typical of the damsels that can become aggressive if males establish a nest site in a small aquarium.*

Right: *Needlefishes* (Dunkerocampus pessuliferus) *are peaceful and shy and need a quiet aquarium if they are to thrive. Feed them regularly on plenty of tiny live foods, such as mysis and brineshrimp.*

Chapter 10: *Feeding*

Providing the correct diet for many of the marine species kept in the aquarium was once a major problem, but these days you can choose from a wide variety of foods, and new technology in manufacturing and processing means that most species can be catered for. A greater knowledge of the natural history and biology of invertebrates also means that it is no longer such a difficult task to sustain them in the aquarium. Needless to say, there are still species that are regarded as impossible to feed successfully. For example, several species of marine angelfishes only feed on specific sponges that are not readily available to the aquarist, and although these fishes may accept other types of food, their digestive systems are not designed to deal with them. In such cases, the fishes derive no nourishment and over several weeks, sometimes months even, they will slowly die of starvation. Sometimes a single species can cause confusion because it has developed different feeding strategies according to the location it lives in. For instance, the Regal angelfish, Pygoplites diacanthus, was once believed to be impossible to keep in the aquarium due to its highly specialized feeding habits. However, that was the situation for specimens originating from within its Pacific Ocean range. It was discovered that the Regals living in the Red Sea had naturally developed a more varied diet and were therefore better suited to life in the aquarium.

In recent years the aquarium industry has taken a hard look at its practices and has done much to inform hobbyists and dealers alike of those species regarded as difficult and therefore better off left in the wild, resulting in reduced demand. In general, it is another case of doing some homework to learn as much as you can about the species you would like to keep in an effort to avoid making unnecessary mistakes.

The food pyramid
A clear understanding of the food pyramid, or food chain, and where the species you want to keep are placed within it, will be very useful. It can be very complex but, in essence, there are plants, algae and phytoplankton at the bottom of the pyramid, with herbivorous animals situated above them in the scheme of things and carnivorous animals further up. The apex predators are situated right at the top of the pyramid. The plants are primary providers of nourishment and all species in the pyramid derive some benefits from them. This is because herbivorous animals that are directly nourished by plants are eaten by carnivorous species, allowing them to be indirectly benefited. Finding out where fishes and invertebrates fit into the scheme of things will help you make better informed choices for your aquarium. For example, it is no good mixing most triggerfishes with sea urchins, as urchins are the natural diet of these fishes. Likewise, you will see that groupers and lionfishes are predatory carnivores that will eat virtually any fish, or crustacean in some cases, that they can fit into their enormous mouths.

Furthermore, if you are hoping to establish lush macro-algae growth then you will have to avoid keeping herbivorous species such as surgeonfishes in the same aquarium.

Feeding strategies
Marine fishes and invertebrates employ a wide variety of feeding strategies, and you should take these into careful account for the well-being of your aquarium subjects. Some species will readily take food in the open water column, but many have jaws and teeth modified for grazing algae or tiny microorganisms from the rock surfaces. Parrotfishes have gone one stage further; they actually bite off portions of rock, crush it, extract the algae from it and then excrete it, thus adding fresh sand to the substratum.

Predators usually employ an element of surprise and adopt one of two strategies; either they ambush their prey, as many moray eels do, or, like groupers and lionfishes, they often stalk it.

Plankton is most evident at dusk and animals that feed on such organisms, including polyp animals such as corals, take particular advantage of this. Corals and many other polyp animals derive their main nourishment from the photosynthetic processes of the zooxanthellae algae that live within their tissues, but they will also extend their tentacles in the evening to catch planktonic animals (zooplankton). Filter-feeding invertebrates continually

Flakes and granules

Flake foods fall slowly through the water and are ideal for most midwater and upper water level species.

Mixed flakes satisfy the nutritional needs of most marine fish.

Brineshrimp flakes. Initially, you may have to mix them with live or frozen brineshrimp to tempt the fish.

Granular food. This sinks quickly for the benefit of bottom-dwellers.

Freeze-dried foods

Based on fresh natural foods, most freeze-dried portions can be stuck onto the interior glass panels at any level.

Tablet foods

Freeze-dried krill

Freeze-dried river shrimp

Freeze-dried brineshrimp

The food pyramid

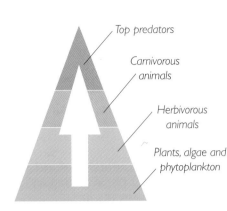

Top predators

Carnivorous animals

Herbivorous animals

Plants, algae and phytoplankton

take in and pump out water in order to extract microorganisms, phytoplankton or sometimes even organic debris as their food source.

Generally speaking, marine fish fit into one of three main feeding groups: the open-water feeders, the grazers, and the specialist feeders. Many species are surprisingly adaptable in the aquarium, but it is still sensible to understand their natural behaviours. In the main, fish in the open-water category are easy to cater for and the grazers are not too difficult either. However, you must pay special attention to the specialist

feeders, which can include predators, filter-feeders, all the polyp animals such as corals and anemones, and even those species with a nocturnal lifestyle that only feed after dark.

Sources of food

Here we examine the advantages and disadvantages of foods available for marine aquarium animals.

Prepared foods

Research continues into suitable foods for use in marine aquariums and the many advances to date ensure there is now a wide variety available for a number of applications.

Dried foods, such as flakes and pellets, are excellent and convenient to use as part of a staple diet for the wide range of species that will readily accept them. They are also first-rate conditioning foods, as they usually contain added vitamins and other beneficial substances that are often missing in frozen foods as a result of processing. Freeze-dried shrimps and worms are also convenient additions to diets. Liquid preparations are also available that provide suspended food particles for filter-feeding animals, but

for more specific requirements you may want to make your own by blending fish, shrimp and perhaps some flake with water in a food processor.

Prepared dried foods have few disadvantages apart from the fact that in general, predators and other specialized feeders will not be interested in them. However, it is important to offer some of the foods listed below in addition to flake food, as in most cases a varied diet will improve the well-being of your animals.

Fresh foods

It would be easy to assume that because marine animals take their food from the sea, obtaining seafoods from a fishmonger would be ideal for aquarium fish. In some cases this is true, as small whole fishes, prawns and cockles, for example, are good fare for carnivorous species. The advantage of these fresh foods is that they will contain their original goodness in terms of vitamins and certain beneficial minerals. On the other hand, their main disadvantage is that they could introduce disease pathogens that infect your animals, particularly if they have come from a location where your fishes and invertebrates do not naturally occur. In this instance, your animals will have little resistance to such ailments. It could be argued that strong, healthy animals should be able to ward off such illnesses, but in reality there is no guarantee.

To reduce the risk of infection from fresh foods, it is worth removing the guts from fish and shrimps, but this also means you are removing some very nutritional items. Soaking fresh seafoods in freshwater for half an hour or so before use, also helps to kill off marine parasites that may be on the food. However, neither of these

Frozen foods

Whole cockle. This natural food is accepted by all marine fishes.

Marine mix is a mixture of various natural marine invertebrate and fish meats.

Krill. A nutritious food for larger fish; break up for small fishes.

Small fish make excellent 'one-gulp' food for larger fishes.

Shrimp. Many wild-caught foods are irradiated to destroy disease pathogens.

Right: Frozen foods are sold in single slabs (break off pieces as required) or in individual push-out 'servings'. Thaw frozen foods before offering them to fish.

Right: This decorated dartfish (Nemateleotris decora) is a midwater feeder and has no problems in capturing food such as this fragment of thawed-out shrimp as it falls through the water.

techniques will offer any form of guarantee, so to be more certain you should boil and then freeze these foodstuffs before offering them to your aquarium subjects.

Frozen foods

Many types of frozen foods are produced commercially, specifically for aquarium use and these can provide the bulk of the diet for many species. Small fishes, squid, krill, mysis and other shrimps, algae, clams, cockles and mussels, worms, plankton and eggs from fishes, crabs and lobsters are all now available in frozen packs from aquarium stores. Generally, these frozen foods have been irradiated with gamma rays to sterilize them and eliminate the risk of introducing diseases. The other important advantage is they can be stored for several months in a freezer and pieces broken off as required.

But, there is a serious disadvantage in that the irradiation and freezing processes destroy important vitamins. If possible, therefore, it will be necessary to add some dried prepared foods to the diet and/or soak the food with liquid supplementary vitamins on a regular basis before feeding it to your animals. Such vitamins should be available from your dealer.

Live foods

There are several different types of live foods available to aquarists, although most are particularly suited to freshwater fishes. Those, such as black worms (*Tubifex*), bloodworms and water fleas (*Daphnia*) that will not live for long in the marine environment should only be fed to marine fishes and invertebrates as long as you are sure they will all be eaten in less than a minute. Otherwise, you run the risk of polluting your aquarium water as the live foods you have offered die off. The likes of black worms originate from freshwater ponds that are often polluted, so they must be kept in good-quality, running water for several days to flush out any potentially toxic substances before you use them as food. Treating them with a general bactericide may also help.

By far the most popular and readily available live foods for marine aquariums are brineshrimp (*Artemia*). Many aquarium stores have regular supplies of adult brineshrimps for sale and these make an excellent and nutritious treat for a large number of species. Brineshrimp eggs are also readily available and are very easy to hatch in a well-aerated saline solution. Special hatcheries can be bought for this purpose, but it is easy to make your own, using any clean container made from non-corrosive and non-toxic materials. The base should be narrower than the top, i.e. a wedge or funnel shape. As the egg cases generally float after hatching, it is much easier to drain the shrimps from the bottom of a container with such a shape. To make life even easier, you can also buy decapsulated brineshrimp eggs. As the name suggests, the outer case has been removed from the eggs. The newly hatched nauplii stages are ideal for filter-feeding invertebrates and planktivorous fishes, such as damselfishes in the genus *Chromis*. They are also a good food for small juvenile fishes. However, since brineshrimps lack calcium, they should not be offered as the sole food to fishes such as seahorses and pipefishes that require quite high levels of calcium in their diet. Mysis shrimps are much better in such circumstances.

Live mysis shrimps have become increasingly available in aquarium stores over recent years. Mysids are small saltwater shrimps, although larger than brineshrimps, and can be found in most parts of the world. You can collect your own from places such as sea walls, where they often congregate in huge numbers, and then keep them alive in their own well-aerated and filtered tank until they are required. To avoid introducing potentially harmful microorganisms with these shrimps, once again it is worth medicating them with a general bactericide suitable for use in a marine aquarium and with crustaceans.

Vegetable foods

As we have seen in the food pyramid, all species derive benefits from eating plants, either directly or indirectly, therefore it is essential that you include vegetable matter in the general marine diet. Culturing algae in the aquarium is probably the best way to provide this food. If this is not practical then you must provide it by other means. Vegetable flake foods are available and make a good alternative, while species such as surgeonfishes and angelfishes often seem happy to take fresh lettuce. Lettuce is largely made up of water, but it is a great source of a large number of vitamins. Spinach is also good, but blanch it first with boiling water or freeze it before use in order to break down its cellulose, which fishes cannot digest. Feed spinach sparingly, however, as its leaves contain small traces of arsenic. Always wash fresh vegetables thoroughly, as they may have agricultural pesticides on them that could prove fatal to your animals.

A balanced diet

Understandably, most of the research on fish nutrition has been centred on species raised in captivity for conservation purposes or on foods for humans – trout bred on fish farms, for example. It seems logical that many of these findings will also apply to other fishes in captivity, including ornamental marine fishes.

Such research has shown how vital it is to provide a diet containing the right balance of carbohydrates, proteins and fats to provide energy and to build body tissue. As we have seen, this has led to the production of high-quality prepared foods for a wide range of fishes, and should influence all our decisions about suitable diets. For example, it is clear that fishes need a ready supply of so-called 'essential' amino acids (the building blocks of proteins) for normal growth and healthy development. These requirements are species dependent and vary with the age of individuals. Deficiency in any particular essential amino acid produces characteristic symptoms, ranging from reduced

Ease of feeding in the aquarium

Group	Easy	Reasonable once feeding	Difficult	Difficult, need livefoods
Angels		●	●	
Basses	●			
Blennies	●	●		
Butterflyfishes	●	●	●	●
Cardinals	●	●		
Catfishes	●			
Clownfishes	●	●		
Damsels	●			
Eels	●			
Filefishes			●	
Gobies	●			
Jawfishes		●		
Lionfishes		●		●
Seahorses			●	●
Squirrelfishes		●		●
Surgeons	●			
Tangs	●			
Triggers		●		
Wrasses	●			

Feeding for groups with multiple entries depends on species.

Vitamin sources in foods

FOOD	VITAMIN
Algae	A, B_{12}, C, E
Beef	A, B_2, B_6, B_{12}, C, K
Crustaceans	A, B_2, B_6, D, K
Daphnia	D, K
Earthworms	D
Egg yolk	A, B_{12}, D, E
Fish meat	B_2, B_6
Fish eggs	C
Fish liver	A, D
Lettuce	A, C, B_2, B_6, B_{12}, C, E, K
Mealworms	D
Mussels	B_2, B_6, B_{12}
Shrimps	D, K
Snails	D
Spinach	A, B_2, B_6, C, E, K
Tubifex	D
Water plants	A, C, K
Wheatgerm	E
Yeast	A, B

growth rate to death, in extreme cases. Although it is possible to add these amino acids to the diet in a 'free' form, many fishes cannot make use of them in this way. The best approach is to provide a varied and well-balanced diet.

Research into nutrition also shows that fishes require highly unsaturated fatty acids to maintain good health. One vital reason for this is that such fats enable the delicate membranes throughout a fish's body to remain flexible and fluid at relatively low temperatures. It is particularly important to prevent fats in fish foods from becoming rancid, i.e. oxidized, as this will cause specific health problems.

It is also important to remember the vital role that minerals and vitamins play in diets. Although needed in only very small amounts, vitamins act as catalysts to activate the nutritional processes. Some vitamins are manufactured in the fish's body, while others must be constantly available in the food. No single type of food provides all the essential vitamins, but all foods contain some vitamins. Thus, there is an added bonus in offering a varied and balanced diet in that a wide range of vitamins will become available. Vitamin groups may be fat soluble (A, D, E and K) or water soluble (B and C). Vitamin B is a collective name for a group of vitamins known by individual names and/or numbers, such as B_1 (Thiamine), B_2 (Riboflavin), B_6 and B_{12}, the last one of which is the very useful vitamin responsible for encouraging animals to eat. The table shows the vitamin content of some foods, although please note that not all those listed are useful for marine aquarium animals.

Feeding methods

The well-tried formula of feeding 'a little and often' is suited to a large number of marine fishes and invertebrates, as many feed in this manner in the wild. There is one proviso to this feeding technique and that is to take the utmost care not to give so much that uneaten food is continually left to pollute the water. Always remove uneaten food as soon as the animals have stopped feeding, either by netting it or siphoning it out. Regular nitrite testing will indicate whether water quality is declining due to uneaten food being left in the aquarium, or if an animal has died unnoticed. This practice will reassure you that the biological filters are working efficiently or alert you to a problem if they are not.

If a newly acquired fish shows no interest in feeding, it may be helpful to add vitamin B_{12} directly to the aquarium water in the hope that the fish will take it in and it will trigger the urge to eat. Suitable vitamin supplements for this purpose are available. Squid has a powerful odour in water and many species may find it irresistible, so it is worth offering small pieces of this to finicky eaters, making sure you remove it again if not taken.

In the case of predators that are normally used to eating living food it may be necessary to 'train' them to take more convenient and safer dead foods. This can be done by impaling a strip of fish, squid or prawn onto the end of a transparent plastic or glass rod with the idea that the fishes see the food but not the rod. By trying to simulate swimming movements, it is often possible to entice such fishes into feeding by this method.

Never forget the needs of any animals with nocturnal feeding habits. However, once nocturnal animals have become used to their aquarium surroundings, they will often adapt to feeding during the daylight hours, making it much easier on the aquarist.

Most free-swimming invertebrates tend to graze continually, scavenge or wait for an opportune moment to feed. However, the sessile (non-moving) species, such as corals and anemones, do not need constant attention where feeding is concerned. Polyp animals that contain photosynthetic zooxanthellae algae derive much nourishment from by-products of photosynthesis. Anemones can be fed small pieces of prawn or fish every couple of weeks, but corals usually only require the occasional feeding of a plankton substitute. If filter feeders, such as fan worms, clams and sponges, are present in the tank, offer a suitable suspension food a couple of times a week, plus regular offerings of newly-hatched brineshrimps. Any corals sharing the same aquarium may also benefit from these feeds.

Should you go on holiday, you must arrange for a totally trustworthy fellow hobbyist, relative or neighbour to look after your aquarium and feed its subjects while you are away. Unlike freshwater aquarium fishes, which can survive for relatively long periods without food providing they are in a healthy condition to start with, the majority of marine aquarium fishes must be fed on a regular basis regardless. Do not use holiday food blocks in the marine aquarium, as they could pollute the water if uneaten because the fishes find them too unfamiliar. It is far better to make up the correct amount for each feed due while you are away and store it in separate packages in a freezer so that whoever is looking after your aquarium does not accidentally overfeed. This person should also be given some basic training in looking after the life-support system of your aquarium and the phone number of a friendly expert or two in case of emergencies.

Left: To prevent green foods becoming stuck in filter inlets, secure them firmly to the aquarium glass using a sucker and clip. Remove and discard any leaves that remain uneaten.

Above: *Fish such as the regal tang* (Paracanthurus hepatus) *require an almost constant supply of green foods such as spinach and algae. They can devour almost a whole lettuce every day.*

Chapter 11: *Regular maintenance*

Being able to see the fruits of your labour is a great pleasure and it is entirely up to you how much time you spend on maintenance. Once your aquarium is completely up and running, the time taken by routine maintenance is relatively small, yet it is something you can still enjoy.

Routine checks

There are several checks that you should make on a regular basis. First and foremost are daily temperature checks, along with a 'head count' of your aquarium subjects. Counting fishes is best done at feeding time, when they tend to be the most visible, although some invertebrates may be more difficult. Over time, you will develop an 'eye' for what is right and wrong, so that you can tell almost instinctively if any animals are more than just missing. Do your best to locate them and immediately remove any that have died. If an animal dies and the cause is unlikely to have been old age, you must try to discover the cause and take action accordingly. Marine fishes and invertebrates are generally sensitive to disturbances and the potential stress they cause, so do your best to use your eyes rather than searching around the tank with your hands. In other words, keep your physical intrusions to an absolute minimum. Some species are capable of jumping, so if an animal is not evident in the aquarium, it is worth looking on the floor, especially if the tank is not covered.

As the aquarium gradually becomes more established, its subjects will settle down into their natural behavioural patterns. If you take time to observe the animals' normal activities, you will soon be able to recognize any irregularities that may be early indications of trouble.

In a fully established aquarium, you should check pH weekly, making sure it remains stable at around 8.3 – but no higher – and no lower than 8.1. If it starts to drop, adjust it by adding buffering materials (see pages 31). The situation may require some water renewal, especially if the pH continues to drop after you have attempted to adjust it. Siphoning off debris from the substrate on a weekly basis will go a long way in preventing a decline in water conditions, especially pH. Most of this debris is likely to be organic, so as it breaks down it will be releasing carbon dioxide into the water and affecting its buffering capabilities.

Take a specific gravity reading once a week and test for ammonia and nitrite levels once every two weeks. It is also a good idea to keep a check on the nitrate and phosphate levels weekly. Fishes generally appear to have a higher tolerance of nitrate than many invertebrates, and experienced marine aquarists have suggested 40 mg/litre is an acceptable upper limit. However, it is always best not to make any compromises and try to keep nitrate levels below 5 mg/litre.

It is important to carry out regular partial water changes. Do not change too much at any one time as it may cause a sudden drift in environmental conditions and cause some stress to the animals. Around 10% change each week is good, although smaller amounts on a daily basis would be more efficient, but far less convenient, for most aquarists. As already discussed elsewhere, never mix new supplies of saltwater directly in the tank once there are living organisms in it. Occasionally, it may be necessary to top up due to evaporation loss. As only water evaporates, leaving the salts behind, you must only top up using freshwater. Always use the best quality freshwater available to you for this purpose.

How your aquarium matures

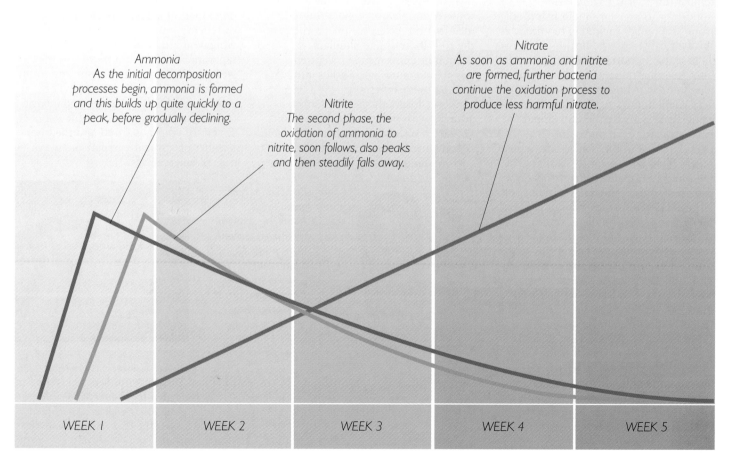

Ammonia
As the initial decomposition processes begin, ammonia is formed and this builds up quite quickly to a peak, before gradually declining.

Nitrite
The second phase, the oxidation of ammonia to nitrite, soon follows, also peaks and then steadily falls away.

Nitrate
As soon as ammonia and nitrite are formed, further bacteria continue the oxidation process to produce less harmful nitrate.

WEEK 1 WEEK 2 WEEK 3 WEEK 4 WEEK 5

Phosphate test

1 Add 5 drops of the phosphate reagent to a 5ml sample of tank water and shake gently to mix.

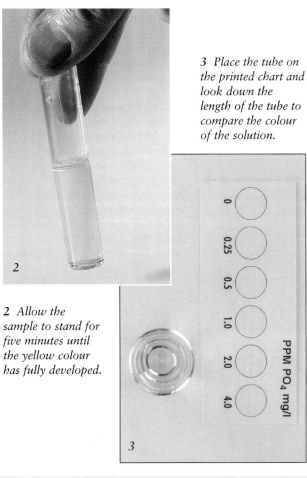

2 Allow the sample to stand for five minutes until the yellow colour has fully developed.

3 Place the tube on the printed chart and look down the length of the tube to compare the colour of the solution.

PPM PO$_4$ mg/l

0
0.25
0.5
1.0
2.0
4.0

Emergency measures

Occasionally things can go wrong. If a heater fails, causing a serious drop in temperature, it is a good idea to float plastic bottles filled with hot water in the aquarium, taking care that the displacement of aquarium water does not overflow. If you own an enamel pan, you could also heat up some aquarium water and return it to the tank very carefully and gradually. In the meantime, either repair the heater or replace it with a new unit – the latter being the most likely course of action.

On the other hand, should your heater's thermostat stick in the 'on' position, causing the temperature to rise, switch off power to the unit and apply extra aeration. In a reverse of the method described above, you could fill plastic bottles with ice in order to reduce the temperature gradually.

Should your electricity supply fail, such as in a power cut, the relatively large body of water in the aquarium can act as a heat reserve and will take a while to cool down. Lagging the tank with insulating material will help if there is concern that the power outage will last a long time. If you have other means of heating water, you could use

Practical tips for a healthy aquarium

Choose healthy stock and quarantine all new additions, provided that you keep the quarantine tank up to the standard of your main tank. Avoid stressing the fish in any way.

Do not hope to keep all the fishes that you like the look of; bear in mind the feeding habits of different species, their compatibility with fish of the same or different species and their eventual mature size.

Do not use any metal objects in the aquarium. Purists even remove the inside half of magnetic algae-scrapers when they are not using them.

Remove uneaten food at the earliest opportunity; any water siphoned off during this process can be filtered through a fine cloth and returned to the aquarium. Acclimatise fish to any new food over a period of time.

Learn to recognise symptoms of impending water problems: frothy, cloudy, yellowing and smelly water are all signs of deteriorating conditions.

Do not neglect regular partial water changes. Changing 20-25% of the water in the aquarium each month is an average guide, but an invertebrate tank may require more frequent changes.

Top up evaporation losses with fresh water.

Make all changes to the water gradually. For example, after siphoning off 20-25% of the tank water for a water change, add the new water slowly over a period of at least half an hour. Remember to turn off powerheads or other motorised filters that may be left 'high and dry' when the water level is low.

Keep cover glasses clean. Salt spray soon renders them opaque, which prevents the full light intensity reaching right down into the water.

Check that the water flow rate from filters remains high. Clean external mechanical filters and replace both the filter medium and activated carbon frequently – at least once a week if necessary. Wash filter media in tank water to avoid killing any bacterial colonies.

You can check the efficiency of activated carbon by adding a few drops of a dye, such as methylene blue, next to the filter inlet. If clear water emerges from the outlet, the carbon is still working; if blue emerges, the carbon needs replacing.

Isolate taps in the hoses to external filters to lessen the risk of spillages when cleaning filters.

After cleaning external power filters, make sure that the hoses are tightly attached – a filter pump will just as easily empty a tank as filter it!

Empty the collecting chambers of protein skimmers regularly.

After a period of time, algae will grow all over the tank. Remove it from the front glass with a non-metal scraper; nylon and plastic scourers are very effective for this purpose. Excess algae scrapings may be fed to fish in less algae-covered tanks. There is no need to remove algae from the remaining panels of the aquarium, as the fish will graze on it. Thin out excessive growths, as a sudden 'algae death' could cause pollution.

When treating fishes with disease remedies, follow the manufacturer's recommendations. Most treatments are designed to be added to the whole aquarium, but remember that copper-based cures will kill most invertebrates in the tank. (Which is one reason why it is more difficult to keep fishes and invertebrates together. A practical ratio would be 80% invertebrates to 20%, or even less, fishes.) If necessary, remove sick fishes and treat them separately from the main tank. Do not mix medications. Sterilise all equipment after use and do not share a net between two tanks.

bottles as described above. It is more critical to keep the filters running and to provide extra aeration. If the nitrifying bacteria die off due to a lack of oxygenated water, you will be back to 'square one', running the serious risk of deadly ammonia build-up. In such an event, one or two battery-powered airpumps would be very valuable investments and could maintain both water movement and the filter system until power is restored.

Back-up systems are worth considering. To avoid disaster from a sticking thermostat, you could connect a second one in line to the power supply. The idea is to set the second thermostat at a couple of degrees higher than the first, so that if the main one sticks, the other one will still turn off the heater and prevent an unwanted temperature increase. Otherwise, you could install two units as a precaution against one failing and causing a temperature drop. A further refinement would be to install a buzzer alarm to announce trouble; battery-operated buzzer alarms are available to indicate power failures.

Look on the bright side

Finally, remember not to look on routine tasks as chores to be avoided; most of them should be part of the pleasurable task of providing your aquarium subjects with the care and attention that they undoubtedly deserve. They will repay you in the best manner possible – with a living picture of beauty and colour that is both entertaining and educational. As a hobbyist, this is your reward.

Testing for ammonia, nitrates and nitrite

Testing the water involves adding chemicals to a measured sample and comparing the colour change to a printed chart. Some tests involve adding two or three chemicals in stages. Allow the correct time period to elapse between adding reagents. Wear protective gloves when using chemicals, as they may cause skin irritation.

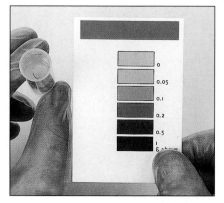

Above: *Any indication of the presence of nitrite does at least mean that the bacteria are doing their job in the conversion process but, like ammonia, nitrite is still very toxic and a zero reading is what you need.*

Above: *When testing for ammonia, the aim is to achieve a reading of zero. Not until this reading is consistently at the lowest possible value, is it safe to introduce any fish into the aquarium. Test the water regularly.*

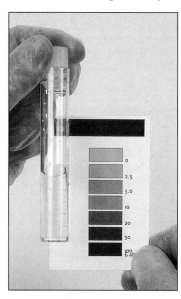

Left: *With some original nitrate already present in the mixing water, readings are likely to be high. Although nitrate can be tolerated by some species, it should not be allowed to exceed 10mg/litre. Here, the reading is very low.*

Dissolved oxygen test

Regularly checking the dissolved oxygen content of aquarium water indicates whether the system is overstocked with animals. Over time, animals grow and certain invertebrates will reproduce and increase the demand for oxygen. Excess waste will result in larger populations of nitrifying bacteria in the filters, which will also add to the demand for oxygen. Use the test shown here to record the oxygen level in mg per litre.

1 Stabilize the oxygen content with the first reagent, then add eight drops of the second (shown here), forming a cloudy precipitate.

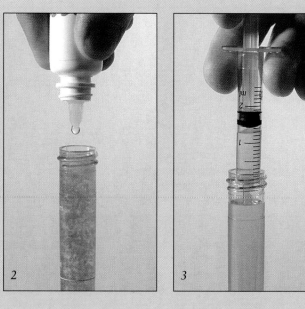

2 Add five drops of the third reagent and mix. The solution turns clear yellow.

3 Use the syringe to remove liquid down to the 10ml mark on the test tube.

A maintenance schedule

Task	Frequency (new tank)	Frequency (old tank)
Check ammonia, nitrite	Every day for a week when first animals added. Then every week up to week 8	Daily for 2/3 days when new animals added. Then monthly or when needed
Check nitrate.	Every week (up to week 8)	Monthly or when needed
Check pH level.	Every week	Every week
Check specific gravity.	Every week (to week 8)	Monthly; after all water changes and when needed
Partial water change (lightly stocked tank) (heavily stocked tank)	Every month Every two weeks	Every month Every two weeks
Empty protein skimmer cup and clean interior of protein skimmer.	As needed	As needed
Clean cover glass/ reflector and remove algae. Check airstones.	As needed	As needed
Rinse/replace filter media. Cut filter sponge in half and clean alternately.	Every month	Every month
Top up evaporation losses with freshwater	As needed	As needed
Check for dead fish, signs of disease, bullying, abnormal behaviour.	Daily	Daily
Check equipment, temperature / flow rate.	Daily	Daily

Carbonate hardness (KH) test

1 Add the KH reagent a drop at a time to a 5ml sample of tank water and gently swirl the tube to mix. Count each drop of reagent.

2 Initially, the sample turns blue.

3 As more reagent is added, the water sample turns yellow. Continue counting the drops added until the yellow colour is stable. Each drop added from the beginning of the test represents 1°dH, which is equivalent to 17.5 mg per litre of carbonate.

4 Pour the 10ml of yellow solution into a small beaker for the next stage of the oxygen test.

5 Add five drops of a fourth reagent to the yellow solution in the beaker, which turns black.

6 - 8 Gently swirl the black solution until it is an even colour. Add the final reagent a drop at a time until the black solution is colourless. Each drop added is equivalent to 0.5mg/litre of oxygen in the sample of tank water.

Chapter 12: Breeding marine fishes

The art of breeding marine fishes and invertebrates in captivity is still regarded as being in its infancy. However, well over 100 species have now been bred in aquarium conditions and some of these are actually available commercially, yet only a few years ago this would have been thought impossible with most species. Successfully breeding and rearing a species must be the ultimate achievement for any marine aquarist. The results of such achievement are very important for the future of the hobby and for conservation. The knowledge gained from such experience will in time help to reduce the demand for wild-caught specimens and help the conservation of natural habitats. Just as importantly, this information could be used to teach those who are currently collecting for the aquarium hobby to set up breeding stations as an alternative means of income should the demand for wild stock diminish. To breed the popular species in their natural countries of origin would be far more cost effective than attempting the same on a commercial level in, say, northern Europe, because the ideal natural seawater would be available, as well as the correct foods, good sunlight and perfect temperature. The infrastructure for packing and shipping already exists and very little else is required, apart from knowledge.

There are tried and tested methods for breeding and rearing some marine species, but there is still a great deal of experimentation to be done for most. Some species may require a more radical approach and perhaps aquarists will need to employ a certain amount of creative license to attain success. For example, one of the earliest successes in breeding and rearing clownfishes back in the 1950s involved offering a combination of foods, including powdered silkworm cocoons, to rear the fry. What on earth made that person think of using silkworm cocoons?

Breeding strategies

Marine fishes and invertebrates employ various methods of reproduction. There are egg-scattering species, egg-depositors, mouthbrooders and even pouchbrooders. Egg-scattering species, which include basslets and angelfishes, are probably the most difficult to deal with, but definitely not impossible, especially where relatively small species are concerned. Clownfishes, damselfishes and gobies are all well known egg-depositors and

Left: A pair of green chromis (Chromis caerulea). As with many other damselfishes, the males, control a harem of females, which they invite to mate by performing elaborate courtship dances.

their breeding behaviour, particularly that of the clowns and damsels, is very similar to that of some freshwater cichlids. The mouthbrooding jawfishes and some cardinalfishes are also similar to many African cichlids. Potentially, it is these marine mouthbrooders that present the easiest opportunities for captive breeding. For example, the fascinating Banggai cardinalfish *(Pterapogon kauderni)*, is currently very popular with marine aquarists and reproduces frequently in the aquarium.

Large species are often not practical contenders for captive breeding due to aggressiveness toward their own kind in confined spaces. Also, fish such as surgeonfishes require something in the region of 4.5m (15ft) of water depth in order to carry out their intricate courtship routines and are unlikely to reproduce in most captive situations.

In the case of invertebrates, some lay, or carry, eggs, while others simply divide in order to multiply. Crustaceans are often cannibalistic right from birth, making them difficult to rear, but corals will multiply readily, providing water conditions are just right. However, in very basic terms, it seems that when dealing with clownfishes and some damsel and cardinalfishes, all that is required is a male and female, and breeding will regularly occur.

Basic requirements for breeding

Firstly, you must thoroughly research the species you wish to try breeding in your aquarium. It is important to find out all you can about the natural history of the species in order to get their habitat and water conditions right, as well as providing the correct types of food, and so on.

In the course of a great number of tropical marine breeding projects, it has been discovered that the special water conditioning power that living rock seems to possess can go a long way to help induce breeding behaviour. In fact,

many of the most successful projects have been carried out with minimal equipment and have relied upon a simple biological filter, such as a fluidized bed sand filter, living rock, a single fluorescent lamp, regular partial water changes and heating where needed. Of course, in most cases, such breeding setups only need to support little more than a pair of fishes, so the biological loading is at a minimum. The important thing is that water quality must be optimum for the species in question if there is to be any chance of breeding them.

Space in the aquarium is important for many species. Obviously, if the species is physically large it will require corresponding amounts of space. Also, some species operate as a harem, where a single male will service a number of females, either in a group, such as in the lyretail anthias *(Pseudanthias squamipinnis)* or the male visits a number of females in turn spread over an area of reef, as in certain species of dwarf angelfish, *Centropyge*. Available space becomes more of a problem when rearing juvenile fishes. Once fry have been produced, it is usually best to attempt rearing them in a separate tank from the parents. As the young fishes grow, it is also possible that you will have to separate them further into even more tanks to prevent overcrowding. If you are this successful, you should have in mind what course of action you will take to maintain such a large number of young fishes and how you will dispose of them if it is not practical to keep them all.

There are several other points worth considering to increase the chances of successful breeding. For instance, the influence of moon phases or season may be particularly important. Temperature, fluctuations in salinity and food availability are also likely triggers for one species or another. As we have seen, a good knowledge of the

Anemonefishes – egglayers

Anemonefishes are amongst the most popular of marine aquarium fishes and, although not the hardiest, they are probably the most likely to breed in a home aquarium. The common clown anemonefish, *Amphiprion ocellaris*, has been bred in captivity over and again since the early 1950s and has fascinated even novice marine fishkeepers with its characteristic breeding behaviour.

Selecting pairs

Finding a true, viable pair of clown anemonefishes is easier than almost any other species. Because they all start life as males, with the largest, most dominant eventually turning into a female, it means you can obtain any two fishes with a very strong likelihood of ending up with a true pair.

Breeding strategy

In nature, clown anemonefishes live in association with any one of three anemone species: *Heteractis magnifica, Stichodactyla gigantea* or *Stichodactyla mertensii*. However, in the aquarium they will occasionally strike up a symbiotic relationship with other anemone species. They normally live in a close-knit group around their anemone, where the female rules over a sexually active male and a number of sexually inactive males that live on the periphery of the anemone. Should the female die, the active male will change into a female and the next attendant male in line will become sexually active. When spawning, they clean an area of rock, usually close to their anemone's trunk, to deposit the eggs. The

male aggressively protects the nest site and cares for the eggs by fanning them to prevent detritus settling. Occasionally the female will help, but generally spends her time on feeding.

The eggs are orange in colour because of the yolk sac they contain. Just before hatching at six to seven days, the large eyes of the embryos are clearly visible. On hatching, which occurs in the evening just after dark, the larvae first drop to the bottom but quickly make their way up into the water column. These larvae remain in the plankton for 8 to 12 days, but then settle near the reef substrate, close to anemones, and begin to develop their juvenile form and colour.

In the aquarium, clown anemonefishes seem to spawn readily without the presence of an anemone or attending males.

Rearing the larvae

The larvae are attracted to light, so soon after hatching they can be collected from the surface by shining a torch to gather them in one place and then very gently scooping them out into a plastic container. Do not use a net. Transfer them into the rearing tank. The larvae are only about 3mm (0.125in) long at this stage and transparent, other than their eyes and a few tiny spots. They still have their yolk sac at this stage.

Ideally, the sides of the rearing tank should be blacked out and there should be a cover with a central hole through which some light can be directed. This will ensure the larvae stay centred and do not crash into the sides of the tank and damage themselves. It may be useful

to add a mild fungicide to the water as a precaution. No substrate is required. Filtration is not essential for the first few days, but should you wish you could use a small air-driven sponge filter with minimal water movement.

The larval fishes rapidly use up their yolk sacs, so other food must be ready and available to them, lest they quickly starve. The rotifer *Brachionus plicatilis* is the most readily available, and most suitable, for rearing larval anemonefishes. To ensure there is plenty to satisfy the larvae, drip-feed the rotifers into the tank at a slow but steady rate. When metamorphosis occurs at 8-12 days – the stage at which the yolk sacs are used up and the larvae begin to look like tiny fish – offer a wider variety of foods. It is at this time that aquarists have the most problems with rearing the fry, and this is believed to be due to nutrition. While continuing to give rotifers, also offer some newly hatched brineshrimp, as well as a mixture of liquidized mysis shrimps and marine flake food. At this time, it is also worth increasing the filtration and water movement a little. At around 20 days, the juveniles will be more recognisable as young anemonefishes and you can wean them off rotifers in favour of more conventional foods. You can now keep them in a more standard marine aquarium setup, but at this stage it may be necessary to transfer some of them into another tank to provide more space for efficient growth.

The above sequence reflects only one breeding strategy for these fish; clown anemonefishes have been bred and reared successfully in a variety of tank arrangements.

A clownfish breeding tank

Install a simple bubble-up sponge filter.

Provide a flat surface such as a piece of slate for the eggs to be laid on.

Remove the adults and slate once the fry are free swimming.

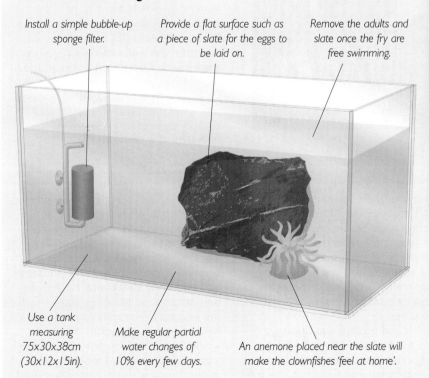

Use a tank measuring 75x30x38cm (30x12x15in).

Make regular partial water changes of 10% every few days.

An anemone placed near the slate will make the clownfishes 'feel at home'.

Above: *A pair of common clownfish* (Amphiprion ocellaris) *guard the eggs they have laid on a tile in their otherwise bare tank. In the wild, they clean a flat rock surface on which to lay their eggs.*

Left: *Ideally, the breeding tank should be as natural as possible to allow the parent fish to settle in. However, you can succeed with a sparsely furnished aquarium as shown here.*

Cardinalfishes – mouthbrooders

Many cardinalfishes are popular with marine aquarists, but there is one that has captured a great deal of interest in recent times – the Emperor, or Banggai, cardinalfish, *Pterapogon kauderni*. This species was only discovered relatively recently and appears to be very restricted in its distribution, being found at only a couple of locations around the Banggai Islands off the coast of Sulawesi in Indonesia. Because of its limited distribution, there has been some concern that collecting for the aquarium hobby will impact on the wild population, so breeding the fish in captivity is a worthy initiative. Fortunately, they reproduce readily in the aquarium and it is hoped that in the near future all specimens offered for sale will be captive bred.

Selecting pairs
It is sometimes possible to acquire proven pairs, but in general it is difficult to be certain of the sexes. It is best to obtain a small group and hope that there is a male and female among them and that pairing occurs.

Breeding strategy
Freshwater aquarists will be familiar with mouthbrooding cichlid species, and these cardinalfishes reproduce in a very similar manner. Eggs are produced and fertilized in the normal way for egglayers, but are then taken into the mouth of the male for incubation. Even after hatching, the juvenile fishes remain in the mouth for protection from predators. Because the juvenile fishes are afforded this extra parental care, they are better equipped to fend for themselves when they become free swimming. Since it is not necessary for these cardinalfishes to invest energy in producing large numbers of egg, their broods are quite small. When

Right: In Banggai cardinalfishes, the male undertakes the mouthbrooding duties of the fertilized eggs. Once hatched, the free-swimming fry can take newly hatched brineshrimp as a first food.

the juveniles emerge from their parent's mouth they are tiny, fully formed replicas of the adults. Banggai cardinals live in association with long-spined sea urchins (*Diadema* sp.) and the newly emerged juveniles head straight for the urchins to spend their early days living amongst the spines for protection.

Rearing
It is not essential to keep sea urchins in order to rear this species successfully, but if they are not available it is advisable to separate the juveniles from the adults, at least until they have grown larger. Some enterprising aquarists use artificial urchins with good results. It has been noted that juvenile Banggai cardinals will sometimes protect themselves in anemones if urchins are not present in the aquarium.

In nature, young Banggai cardinals feed on zooplankton and small bottom-dwelling invertebrates, so newly hatched brineshrimp and very finely chopped mysis shrimps, etc., are good foods for these relatively large juveniles. As they grow, you can offer them larger food particles.

The great thing about breeding this, and similar, species is that the entire operation can be carried out in an aquarium as small as 90 litres (20 gallons). This is due to the very small brood sizes and the fact that you can easily separate adults from juveniles by using a partition that allows a flow-through of aquarium water.

required for a breeding project before you acquire it. Of course, it may be possible to obtain pairs, or groups, that have already proven to be breeders, but such opportunities are still quite rare.

Dealing with offspring
Before embarking on any breeding project for the first time, you must be aware of the specific requirements of the resulting larvae and juveniles. Newly hatched fishes make up a large proportion of natural food for other fishes, so it is easy to understand the importance of rearing them in their own tank. In many species, the parents will eat their young once they have become free swimming, making it difficult to rear the offspring in the tank the eggs were laid in. However, it is equally important that the water the fry are transferred to is identical to that in the breeding tank to prevent shock.

Providing suitable foods for hatchling fishes can sometimes be difficult and time consuming. The majority of marine fish larvae are much smaller than those of freshwater fishes and cannot even cope with newly hatched brineshrimp. As the young fishes grow, however, brineshrimp can become a useful part of the diet later on. In most cases, rotifers are a more suitable first food. Rotifers have to be cultured using certain types of algae for their food. Fortunately, rotifer- and algae-culturing kits, complete with instructions, are now available to make the situation a little easier.

Because marine fish fry are generally so small, they can be easily filtered out by water circulation systems. Strong water movement can also pose the risk of fatal damage to these delicate baby fishes, as they could be easily swept against rocks and other solid objects. In some cases, filtration is not required in the first stages of rearing, but if it is necessary, then small air-driven sponge filters are the most suitable.

Meeting the challenge
So, you want to take the next step towards breeding your own marine fishes! There is an enormous number of species to choose from, most with very little or no information available to help guide you. To start things off, it will be best to gain some experience by working with species that have already been bred successfully in the aquarium. Success is not always achieved at the first attempt, so persevere until you find the best way. The techniques described here are only suggestions that have worked for some aquarists, but there is a great deal yet to learn and easier methods just waiting to be discovered. You may be the one to do it.

natural history of the fishes you wish to breed is extremely useful, and you should adjust the operation of your tank accordingly.

Selecting suitable pairs of fishes
Obtaining a suitable pair to breed from can sometimes be difficult, for a number of reasons. To start with, fishes offered for sale are often juveniles that have completely different coloration and patterns from the mature adults of their species. Secondly, in many species, the sexes have no easily distinguishable features, and thirdly, a large number of

marine fish species change sex during the course of their lifetime. Clearly, you need all the relevant information about your chosen species before you can ensure that you have a true pair. And as we have seen, it may not be a simple case of acquiring just a pair of fishes because some species need to be part of a harem to mate and reproduce successfully.

Health and general condition are also very important when selecting suitable candidates. Conditioning a fish can be achieved over time, but it is still worth fully screening any specimen

Seahorses – pouchbrooders

There is increasing concern for seahorse conservation, which suggests that as many attempts at captive breeding as possible would benefit them. On the other hand, seahorses are so difficult to keep, due to their continuous need for live foods and their susceptibility to various diseases, that only aquarists with a history of breeding other marine species successfully should attempt them. Seahorses do not possess a stomach and therefore have to eat continuously in order to derive any nourishment, devouring thousands of tiny shrimps during the course of a day.

Wild-caught seahorses that mated before capture often release young in the aquarium shortly after being introduced. In these cases, both adults and offspring find it difficult to deal with anything other than large quantities of live foods. However, should any captive-born seahorses survive to reproduce themselves, the subsequent generations seem better able to thrive on a combination of live and frozen foods and are more resistant to diseases.

Seahorses are fascinating and unique fishes, so aquarists are always going to want to keep them. However, the best advice is not to try breeding them until you have first had plenty of experience with other marine species.

Selecting pairs

Whenever possible, only acquire specimens that have been bred and reared in captivity. It is very easy to distinguish males from females, as the males possess a pouch, which causes the body line from the belly to curve smoothly and gradually to the tail. Females, which do not have a pouch, are acutely angled from the belly to the tail. It appears that seahorses are monogamous – i.e. they keep the same partner for life – and it is possible to select a true pair in some species by observing their daily ritual greeting at sunrise.

Breeding strategy

Seahorses are unique in that it is the male that becomes pregnant and gives birth to the young. Breeding can be linked to the lunar cycle and it is known that most, but not all, species perform a ritual greeting at the start of each day. This is believed to help reinforce pair bonding and to help maintain synchronisation between egg production by the female and the male's ability to accept them into his pouch.

The female produces eggs just as in other fishes, but she transfers them to the male's pouch after elaborate courtship. He indicates his readiness to accept the eggs by making muscular contractions of the pouch. Once the eggs are inside and fertilized, the pouch functions in a similar way to a womb, where hormones and calcium are supplied directly to the developing embryos. The hormone

prolactin promotes enzyme activity that breaks down the outer layer of the eggs to produce 'placental fluids'. However, essential nutrients are provided from within the eggs. Development can take 10-42 days, depending on the species and water temperature. When the juvenile seahorses are fully developed they emerge from the pouch as miniature versions of their parents. The female is continually producing eggs and it is likely that another transfer to the male's pouch will occur later on the 'birthday'. The males only produce sperm to fertilize the eggs seasonally, which means that when their partners are not receptive, the females often abort eggs, dropping them onto the substrate.

Rearing the young

Rear young seahorses in their own tank, allowing plenty of space for growth. As they need to feed on a large amount of shrimps, it is understandable that they produce a great deal of waste matter. Because of this, it is best to use a bare tank with no substrate to facilitate regular siphoning of faeces and other detritus. This really has to be done religiously before every feeding session and you must replace the resulting loss of water with a fresh batch of seawater. A simple air-driven sponge filter is all that is required to help maintain water quality. Seahorses need to anchor themselves by wrapping their prehensile tails around a suitable holdfast, so provide, for example, some plastic plants with fine stems and branches or a resin-moulded seafan.

A continual supply of live food is essential for newborn seahorses. Newly hatched brineshrimp can be used, but as they do not provide calcium – and seahorses have a high

calcium requirement – many aquarists feed the brineshrimp a vitamin- and calcium-enriched food before offering them to the developing seahorses.

As is the case with many other marine fishes, it appears that correct nutrition becomes critical when the juveniles are 12 days old. Mysid shrimps are an excellent food for both growing seahorses and adults, so it is vital to encourage the young to take these as soon as possible. At first, offer finely chopped mysids while continuing to offer live brineshrimp. As the seahorses become interested and start taking the mysids from the bottom of the tank, reduce the amount of brineshrimps being offered and, with luck, you will eventually train the juveniles to take only the more beneficial mysid shrimps. Until they are adult and able to take them whole, you can offer growing seahorses larger pieces of shrimp. Remove any uneaten food regularly and to achieve success, offer these creatures at least four feeds a day.

Above: *A parent seahorse with two young in close attendance. Seahorses and their relatives are unique in that it is the males that undergo pregnancy and give birth to their offspring.*

A seahorse breeding tank

A fairly sparse tank setup is fine for breeding seahorses. It is vital to maintain good water quality.

Use a tank measuring 60x30x38cm (24x12x15in).

Cover the filter inlet with foam to prevent fry being sucked into the pipe.

Use an external canister filter containing mature biological filter media.

Make regular partial water changes of 10% every few days.

Place an artificial seafan in the tank for the adults and eventual fry to hang on to.

Chapter 13: Health care

The general health and longevity of animals in the marine aquarium has improved greatly in recent years, and this trend should continue as more is discovered about husbandry. It is likely that poor health and even death are the result of bad water management. Incorrect diet, bad handling and anything that may cause stress could trigger ill-health. Stress is a serious cause of reduced efficiency in the animals' immune system.

In their natural habitats, marine organisms live in extremely stable conditions, but in the comparatively unstable environmental conditions found in the aquarium, they are more likely to succumb to parasitic attacks or microbial diseases. Aquarium subjects are at their most vulnerable when in transit and on first being introduced into a new tank. The stress they experience during this period is often enough to cause illness. However, once completely settled, and providing conditions are at optimum, most species will build up a strong resistance to many ailments.

Minimising the risks

As we have seen, stress is the main catalyst for poor health, and the three main causes of such stress are poor water conditions, poor diet and direct exposure to disease pathogens. We have discussed ways of minimising the stresses of transportation and introduction to a new aquarium, providing the correct diets and maintaining optimum water quality. Now we will look at the procedures for quarantining. If you are not certain that your dealer has sufficiently quarantined animals before sale, you will no doubt find this practice beneficial.

Keeping fishes in a lower than normal salinity can help prevent infections from certain parasites. (More information on this can be found on page 22.)

The value of quarantining

All new aquarium subjects must be screened for diseases and other ailments. Hopefully your dealer has already quarantined them, which will make the screening process easier. If you are absolutely certain that your new purchases are in top condition, you might risk introducing them directly into your main aquarium, but remember, if diseases are inadvertently transferred then all your established animals will be at risk. It is far better to keep your new animals in a separate tank for at least three weeks.

Setting up a quarantine tank

Use a clean tank with no substrate.

Use a heaterstat to maintain the water temperature. Fit a guard to protect fishes that might rest against the heating element.

Intake and return pipes connected to an external filter to maintain water quality.

A clay flowerpot will provide shelter and security.

'Quarantine' actually means 40 days, as this period has been deemed sufficient for pathogens to run their course and allow for effective treatment. While in their quarantine tank your livestock can take time to settle into your particular water conditions and get used to some of your husbandry routines, such as feeding times and so on. Hopefully, the final move into the main aquarium will then be less of an ordeal.

The quarantine tank should be simple. There is no need to include any substrate or habitat other than somewhere for the animals to retreat into for security. A clay flowerpot is good for this purpose. Otherwise, the water quality must be as good as that in your main aquarium, with pH, specific gravity and water temperature exactly the same. As it is unlikely that many animals will be held in quarantine at any one time, there will be little loading on the filter, so a small external canister filter should be able to provide all the biological, mechanical and chemical filtration necessary. If any treatment turns out to be necessary then chemical filtration must not be included.

Organics in the water will often impede the effectiveness of some treatments, so keeping the quarantine tank spotlessly clean is important. Once a quarantine tank has been set up, it is wise to keep it running whether there are subjects in it or not, and to be ready for any eventualities. This means you will have to maintain the bacterial population in the biological filter by ensuring there is a suitable food source.

While your animals are in quarantine take time to check for damage or any lesions that are, or could become, infected. Where fishes are concerned, look for unusual white spots or other blemishes that are obviously not part of their normal markings. The same goes for behaviour; listlessness, lack of interest in food and abnormal swimming can all indicate there is something wrong. You will almost certainly observe higher than normal respiration, but this will not be unusual for the first few hours. If gill rates are still high on the second day, this could indicate a problem. Carrying out such observations is infinitely easier in an uncluttered quarantine tank.

Having said all that, do not regard quarantining as an absolute guarantee against all problems, because the latent effects of stress can sometimes, albeit rarely, take three months or more to manifest themselves.

Recognising ailments

Loss of appetite is a good indication that something is wrong and that further investigation is necessary. Observing feeding habits on a daily basis is very useful. It is another good reason to ask your dealer if you can see the animals you are interested in feeding before you purchase them. When fishes have been caught from the wild with chemicals such as cyanide, irreparable damage can be done to their digestive systems and, although they can look in good health otherwise, they will slowly starve to death.

External parasites are among the easiest ailments to recognise, because they are often clearly visible and the infection is accompanied by vigorous and continual scratching on rocks and substrate. Do not be too alarmed at very occasional scratching because it may only be the fish trying to dislodge a bit of debris it has picked up, or some other minor irritation. Likewise, bacterial infections are generally clearly visible because they generally appear as reddening around the bases of fins and tail, or on a wound. It is the internal ailments that present the most difficulties in identification, although some will offer a visible sign through red ulcerations appearing from beneath the scales. Generally, the only way to tell that there may be something wrong internally is through a change in the animal's behaviour.

Often, internal ailments are recognised too late to do anything about them and the animal dies, or sometimes it is kinder to put it out of its misery humanely. Postmortem examination will be useful in these cases in order to determine whether you need to take any action to protect your other aquarium subjects. To preserve a dead fish for later examination, freezing is the best option. Although freezing can damage tissue, it is best to do so as soon after death as possible, otherwise the processes of decay can change the nature of the body so much that accurate diagnosis becomes impossible.

However, a word of caution is necessary here. Do not be too quick to jump to potentially wrong conclusions, as poor water quality and certain toxic situations can cause similar symptoms to a number of diseases. Some toxic conditions can cause a reddening of the fins and ulcerations and also scratching, whilst sluggish behaviour, lack of appetite, scratching and abnormal swimming could all be symptoms of other water quality problems. Always eliminate water quality from your investigations before deciding on any course of medication for diseases. (See panel on pages 58-59.)

Treating ailments

If disease breaks out in your aquarium you will have to make one of

Right: Mix medications in a little tank water before adding them to the treatment tank. This helps rapid dispersion and also stops fish eating the droplets!

Disposing of fish humanely

At some point in your fishkeeping career, you may find it necessary to dispatch a fish because of illness or old age. If a sick fish is beyond saving, the best thing is to dispose of it humanely. If you can bring yourself to do it, the quickest method is to sever the spinal cord behind the head with a sharp knife. Alternatively, obtain the fish anaesthetic MS222 from a veterinary surgeon or pharmacist and leave the patient in a solution of this for several hours. Never flush a fish down the lavatory, throw it on the floor or place it alive in the freezer. Freezing affects the capillary blood vessels just under the skin, causing the fish great pain before it loses consciousness.

two choices: whether to treat the entire aquarium or to remove the infected individual and treat that one alone. There are other factors to consider as well, such as whether there are invertebrates in the aquarium that cannot tolerate the medications you will be using and, whether the same medications are going to be harmful to the bacteria in the biological filter. Should you opt for transferring individuals into a treatment tank remember that, although conditions should be very similar, proper acclimatisation procedures must still be observed.

Numerous reliable remedies are available for marine aquarium use; they are the result of prolonged research programmes. Be sure to follow the manufacturer's directions for their use to the letter. Copper is a widely used substance for treating an array of parasitic infections, but it does have drawbacks. Firstly, it cannot be used where invertebrates are being kept, and some species of fishes, notably surgeonfishes, sharks and rays, do not tolerate it either. Secondly, its effectiveness can be nullified by certain water treatment additives, which can eliminate non-chelated copper from the water. (Chelated metallic ions are bound with an organic molecule.) The power of copper-based remedies will also be diminished by calcareous materials in the aquarium system; it may be necessary to increase the dose in tanks where coral sand is used, for example. Use a copper test kit to be certain that you are maintaining the correct dosage level during the treatment.

As a general rule, use only one type of medication at a time. Although it is true that some work well – or even better – together, it is also possible that the combination of ingredients can produce a substance that is toxic. If in doubt, ask your dealer for advice. In general though, always restore normal water conditions before beginning another course of medication.

Antibiotics

In some countries antibiotics can only be obtained with a veterinary prescription. Antibiotics can be very effective when correctly used, but they are capable of destroying the beneficial bacteria in your filters and so are better administered in a treatment tank. One particularly effective way of giving antibiotics is with food. You could soak food in the medication for a period before use, but there will always be wastage in terms of the antibiotics washing out when put into the aquarium water. Commercially made medicated foods where the antibiotics are fixed into the food during manufacture are more effective than home-mixed equivalents.

Freshwater baths

Some large public aquariums give freshwater baths to incoming specimens as a routine part of their quarantine protocols. It could be argued that this treatment subjects the animals to stress over and above that caused by capture and transportation. However, it is known to be effective for the control of many parasites, although the level of effectiveness can vary according to different species' tolerance of this kind of treatment. Accordingly, different species are held in freshwater baths for varying lengths of time. For example, a snapper might be able to withstand 10-15 minutes in freshwater, but a butterflyfish may only be able to take 1-2 minutes. Basically, a fish must be removed as soon as it starts showing discomfort and its respiration rate has risen to a level that causes concern. A useful indicator is to approach the fish with your hand and if there is absolutely no response, remove the fish from the bath and return it to normal conditions as quickly as you can.

To avoid sudden shocks when giving marine fish a freshwater bath, make absolutely sure that the temperature and pH of the water the fish is coming out of is the same as the bath and also the eventual display aquarium.

Sterilisers

Exposure to germicidal UV light may eradicate some parasitic organisms, or at least keep their numbers low, but unless the parasites have a free-swimming stage and can actually be drawn through the unit, its effectiveness will be negligible. The same applies to using ozone and even diatomaceous earth filters used for stripping out microscopic matter from the water.

Diseases of invertebrates

The diseases and other ailments of invertebrates are still poorly understood. It is known that parasitic infections occur, as well as bacterial and fungal ones. Recognising these infections is not always easy, but look for excess mucus production, decaying tissue and discoloration, as these may all be indications of health problems. Treatment is not easy either, because without an exact knowledge of the ailments, it is impossible to treat them accordingly. Very short freshwater baths have been tried with varying results, but have been found to be particularly useful for polyp animals attached to rocks, such as corals, before they are introduced into the aquarium for the first time.

Sudden deaths in the aquarium

Every now and then, fishkeepers may experience a setback for which there appears to be no cause or obvious reason. The worst of these is the dreaded 'wipe-out'. This phrase is singularly descriptive: one day all is progressing well and the next everything is dead. So swift is such a disaster that there is little opportunity to spot any signs of the impending catastrophe. Authorities who have made prolonged studies of the phenomenon report that before it occurs, fishes will behave oddly – hiding, breathing differently, apparently hanging in the water, rapidly jerking back and forth or darting erratically around the aquarium. Foam appearing at the water surface has also been observed. Furthermore, it seems that a fish can be removed with some aquarium water and placed in a separate container and survive, while those left in the aquarium die. Sometimes it is only one species, or very closely related species, that are affected. This phenomenon is now referred to as 'toxic tank syndrome' and appears to be caused by the build-up of species-specific toxic proteins. The problem is particularly prevalent with freshwater fishes in aquarium stores, where shipment after shipment of the same species is placed in the same tank for display. Fortunately it can be less of a

Detecting and treating health problems

Symptoms	Cause	Treatment
Gills affected, breathing difficulties, mouth kept open. Fish listless, not eating. Eyes may become cloudy. Triangular spots on body (with apex towards rear of fish).	*Benedenia*, a trematode parasite similar to *Dactylogyrus* gill fluke.	Proprietary remedies and anti-parasite treatments are effective. Follow instructions and check for incompatibility with invertebrates. Consider giving a freshwater bath – with extreme care.
Body swellings that may be either localised or spread over larger areas. Secondary infections may occur if swellings burst. (See also 'dropsy'.)	Bacterial infection – caused by various bacteria. Other bacterial conditions are described below.	Use copper-based remedies and then medicated food. Follow veterinarian's or manufacturer's instructions for use when giving medicated foods.
Opaque areas on the skin, especially on the dorsal surface of the body.	*Chilodonella*, a single-celled parasite that attacks skin around a wound or ulcer. May spread to the gills and cause asphyxia.	Anti-parasite treatments are effective. Requires a host fish, so an uninhabited aquarium will be free of the parasite within about 5 days.
White spots 2mm (0.08in) in diameter appear on body and fins. Fish scratch against rocks. Breathing may become rapid if gills are affected.	*Cryptocaryon irritans*, parasite causing 'salt water itch'. One-celled parasites penetrate the outer layer of skin. Secondary infection may follow.	Copper-based remedies or other anti-parasite remedies are effective; follow instructions carefully. Check for incompatibility with invertebrates.
Thin white slimy faeces. Rear part of body may be swollen.	Diarrhoea. Poor diet, insufficient roughage or rotten, unclean fish meat given as food.	Raise tank temperature to 28°C (82°F). Do not feed for two days then give plenty of roughage foods such as shrimp, water fleas, etc.
Pronounced swellings of body accompanied by erect scales.	'Dropsy' often resulting from a bacterial infection. Similar to dropsy in freshwater fishes.	Consult your veterinarian. If caught in time, the most effective treatment involves giving suitable antibiotics to the affected fish and its contacts.
One or both eyes protrude from the socket. Eye disorders also connected with other ailments.	Exophthalmus or 'pop-eye'. In one eye, the cause may be TB; in both eyes, chronic or acute bacterial infection. Possibly parasites.	No definite remedy, but anti-bacterial and anti-parasite treatments may be effective. Affected fish do not appear too distressed by the condition.
Edges of fins ragged; tissue between rays gradually disintegrates.	Fin rot. Bacterial infection often aggravated by poor water conditions.	Copper-based remedies and antibiotics may be effective if used early, otherwise surgical trimming may be necessary. Improve aquarium conditions.
White tufts of cotton-wool-like or threadlike growths on body. (See also *Chilodonella*.)	*Saprolegnia* fungus. Usually affects fish with mucus deficiencies, open wounds or other skin ailments. Encouraged by excess organic matter in water.	Immediate partial water changes can be effective, as are malachite green remedies, temporary freshwater baths and antibiotic treatment. Wipe away fungal growth.

problem for marine fishes, as protein skimmers seem to be effective in stripping out these toxins, which is another good reason for installing one.

In a newly set-up aquarium where the biological filters are being matured, another cause of sudden 'wipe-outs' can be attributed to the naturally excited and impatient aquarist who decides to introduce several animals as soon as an acceptable nitrite reading has been taken. This action overloads the capabilities of the biological filter system, causing a rapid increase in ammonia levels and the aquarium animals to die. In this case, the phenomenon is known as 'new tank syndrome'. Only ever introduce one animal at a time to avoid this.

It is more difficult to determine the cause of a sudden 'wipe-out' in long-established systems. Apart from the possible reasons already discussed, it is worth investigating the potential of accelerated bacterial activity producing toxic conditions (particularly those involved in the ammonia conversion process). Excessive algae spores could also present problems. Any increase in bacteria populations, possibly as a result of too much organic waste material accumulating, could cause a significant drop in oxygen levels. It should go without saying that such incidents would be seriously detrimental to fishes and invertebrates, and, potentially, the bacteria in your filters. In general, the continuous use of an efficient biological filter allied to protein skimming will prevent such problems arising in the first place.

Right: Lymphocystis *forms unsightly granular growths, as seen on this angelfish. It is possible that the growths can be surgically removed, but with improved water quality they will often disappear without attention.*

Symptoms	Cause	Treatment
Rapid breathing and gaping gills, without other external signs found in *Oodinium* and *Cryptocaryon*.	Gill trematode parasites, such as *Dactylogyrus* and other species. Tiny wormlike 1mm (0.04in) flukes grip with disc of hooks.	A brief formalin bath (3ml per 4.5 litres/gallon of 37% formaldehyde) for 15-30 minutes, followed by treatment as for *Oodinium* and *Cryptocaryon*.
Fish emaciated, although eating normally. Fins ragged, scales raised in groups. Colours fade, eyes may protrude. Balance problems. The symptoms can be very similar to tuberculosis.	*Ichthyosporidium*, an internal fungal disease. Complex infection cycle may involve direct spread of fungal spores or through eating crustaceans carrying spores. Infection spreads through body and damages internal organs.	No effective cure known, but raising the water temperature to 28-30°C (82-86°F) and feeding medicated foods may help.
Cauliflower-like growths appear on the body and fins over a period of several weeks.	*Lymphocystis*, a viral infection. Affected fishes may eventually waste away or recover spontaneously.	Improving conditions often induces self-healing. Treatment of viral infections is always uncertain.
Tiny, dustlike white spots on body and fins. Fish scratch against rocks. Gills may be inflamed. Rapid gill movements, breathing affected.	An infection by the single-celled parasite *Oodinium ocellatum* – known as coral fish disease. Infection cycle involves formation of cysts on tank floor that release new batches of free-swimming parasites.	Proprietary remedies and anti-parasite treatments are effective, but follow the manufacturer's instructions carefully and check for incompatibility with invertebrates, corals etc.
Dull eyes and rapid breathing. Fish dash and whirl about and usually die from exhaustion.	Poisoning by paint fumes, tobacco smoke, metals in water, poisons secreted by other fishes.	Immediate partial water changes, with a total water change as a last resort.
Fish cannot control its position in the water.	Swimbladder trouble, often caused by chilling.	Isolate fish in warmer water. Medicated foods.
Fish emaciated, but may still be eating normally. Fins ragged, scales raised in groups, colours fade, eyes may protrude. Similar to *Ichthyosporidium*. Usually only individual fishes affected, although others may succumb over a longer period.	Tuberculosis. Bacterial infection. Difficult to diagnose accurately because the collective symptoms include some seen in other diseases.	Antibiotics may bring temporary relief. Isolate sick and dying fish; otherwise, cannibalism will occur and may spread the disease to other fishes in the aquarium.
Discoloured skin, loss of appetite, open ulcers, vent and junction of body and fins inflamed.	Ulcer disease, an infection with *Vibrio* bacteria.	Consult your veterinarian, who may treat the affected fish with antibiotics. Also consider using medicated foods.
Wounds	Perhaps caused by bullying in the aquarium, accidental damage or mishandling when transferring fishes, etc.	General antibacterial treatments, antibiotics or medicated foods. Povidone iodine can be applied to the affected area with a cotton bud.

Above: *A shoal of Green Chromis* (Chromis caerulea).

Part Two

Species guide

In this part of the book we present a photographic survey of some of the many species of both tropical and coldwater marine fishes and invertebrates that you may consider keeping.

Which species to include in a book – and which to leave out – is not a simple matter. Apart from the limitations imposed by space and the availability of pictures and information, there is always the question of why some species are included at the expense of other, maybe even more deserving species. Personal preference naturally exerts a subconscious influence, but we have tried to take a wider view by including not only those species that have stood the test of time, but also the more exotic fishes that are known to be delicate. They are available to you, the fishkeeper, and only by encouraging you to persevere in your endeavours (and warning of the possible difficulties) will any progress be made in this rapidly expanding branch of fishkeeping.

Wherever possible, the sizes of the species kept in captivity have been provided to offer some indication of what fishes will be the most suitable for your size aquarium. If your aquarium subjects are given the best water conditions, correct food requirements and space to grow, there is no reason why they should not live full lives and grow to their natural adult size.

If you are thinking of including any of the species in this book in your aquarium, be guided by the amount of information provided; the more information there is, the longer the species has been kept in aquariums and the more likely it is to thrive in captivity. Such species may be considered suitable for the beginner to keep. This is the first step; with experience, you will acquire the confidence to keep some of the less documented species and, maybe, extend the frontiers of knowledge yourself.

TROPICAL
MARINE FISHES

Right: *Although it is fantastically beautiful, the Blue-faced Angelfish (Euxiphipops xanthometapon) is one fish that you should graduate to keeping only after a long period of time; surely you would not want to lose such an attractive fish through your own inexperience?*

Although nearly three-quarters of the earth's surface is covered by salt water, relatively few marine fishes are kept in the aquarium. And of these, by far the most are tropical species. Nevertheless, such is the appeal of this small group of fishes that the marine fishkeeping hobby has flourished and continues to attract more hobbyists around the world.

The most striking tropical marine fishes are native to the coral reefs and coastal waters, where collection is quite easy. Fishes from the deepest waters usually grow too large for the aquarium, and also present too many collection and transportation problems. The majority of suitable fishes come from the Indo-Pacific Oceans, the Caribbean area of the Northern Atlantic Ocean, and the Red Sea.

The water conditions on a tropical reef are extremely stable – the water is well oxygenated and almost completely free from waste products due to the constant cleansing action of the sea. The water is relatively shallow and this means that the fishes are quite used to fairly high light levels. One distinct advantage of simulating these brightly lit conditions in the aquarium is that growths of green algae (usually shunned by freshwater fishkeepers) can be encouraged, much to the appreciation of the fishes, many of which are herbivorous by nature.

Coral reef fishes are extremely territorial, each fish's chosen 'living space' in nature being much larger than that possible in the average indoor aquarium. This makes keeping shoals difficult in many cases because the fishes are intolerant of other members of the same species, although they rarely regard different 'neighbours' as a threat.

These are the challenges facing the tropical marine fishkeeper: maintaining clean, stable conditions; providing enough space; and choosing compatible species. Achieve these successfully and you can then sit back and admire these truly wonderful 'living jewels' of the sea.

Left: *If you could tear yourself away from this beach paradise and don a face mask and snorkel, you could soon be sharing the underwater delights of the fishes' natural home. With patience, a little practical knowledge and plenty of understanding, you can gradually simulate the tropical coral reef in your home aquarium.*

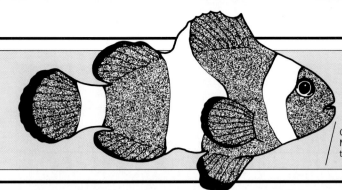

Common Clown (*Amphiprion ocellaris*)
Mature at 80mm (3.2in) and shown as a guide
to the maximum wild size of each species.

Family: ACANTHURIDAE
Surgeons and Tangs

Family characteristics
Members of this Family are characterized by their high profile and laterally compressed, oval bodies. In addition, they have very sharp 'scalpel-like' erectile spines on the caudal peduncle (hence the name 'surgeons'), which are used during inter-territorial disputes and in defence. The dorsal and anal fins are long based and the eyes are set high on the head. The scales often end in a small protruberance, giving a rough feel to the skin. In their natural habitat these fishes may grow up to 400mm (16in), but aquarium specimens usually attain only half the size, if that, of their wild counterparts.

Although there are no drastic colour changes between juveniles and adults in most species, the Caribbean Blue Tang (*Acanthurus coeruleus*) has a yellow juvenile form. Since the adult colour occurs at no predetermined age or size, small fishes can show adult coloration while larger specimens retain their immature colours. When the change occurs, the body is the first area to show the blue adult colour, followed by the caudal fin. Thus, for a period there is an intermediate stage which has a blue body with a yellow caudal fin.

Although external differences between the sexes are normally rare, some darkening of the male's colours during breeding is quite usual. Size is not a reliable indication of the sex of the fishes; sometimes the male is larger, sometimes the female. The pelagic (free floating) eggs that result from the typical ascending spawning actions of two fishes (or a group of fishes) take a long time – possibly months – to pass through the planktonic stage. This means that, although spawning in captivity may occur under favourable conditions, rearing the fry may prove to be much more difficult. (See pages 54-55 for general advice on breeding.)

Diet and feeding
Surgeons and Tangs need to be fed several times each day, especially if there is insufficient algal growth for them to browse upon. In fact, algae are such an important element of their diet that you should not introduce them into an algae-free aquarium.

Young fishes grow very quickly and will starve if denied ready nourishment. Although many species are herbivorous, others will eat small animals too, which means that once they have become accustomed to feeding in captivity they will take many of the established dried, frozen and live foods.

Aquarium behaviour
Surgeons and Tangs live in shoals around the coral reefs of the world. In the aquarium, however, they forsake this gregariousness and will quarrel among themselves, unless you provide a suitably spacious tank. Established species often resent new fishes introduced into the aquarium; smaller fishes may well get off with a warning but similarly sized fishes can suffer attacks. Young specimens, whose scalpels are not as dangerous as those of adults, mount threatening motions against newcomers, but these displays are generally shortlived. Once settled in, they are quite hardy fishes.

Above: **Acanthurus achilles**
Members of the Acanthuridae Family are easily distinguished by their oval shape. Apart from one or two species, many – like this Achilles Tang – are brilliantly coloured, with beautiful body patterns. These fishes graze on growths of algae (the high forehead makes it easy), which constitute a vital part of their diet. Keep them in a well-lit aquarium with an abundant supply of vegetable matter.

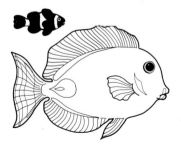

Acanthurus achilles
Achilles Tang; Red-tailed Surgeon
● **Distribution:** Pacific.
● **Length:** 250mm/10in (wild), 180-200mm/7-8in (aquarium).
● **Diet and feeding:** Will accept the usual protein foods, such as gamma-irradiated frozen foods (*Mysis* shrimp, plankton, krill, etc.) and live brineshrimp, plus algae and other greenstuff. Shy grazer.
● **Aquarium behaviour:** Normally peaceful, but very delicate. Compatible with most fish, but may fight at first with other members of its own Family. Do not add to tank until the first fish are established.

The brown body is offset by yellow-red baselines to the dorsal and anal fins. The white marking on the gill cover behind the eye and the dull white patch on the chest are shared by other members of the Family, but the feature that positively identifies this fish is the teardrop-shaped orange-red area on the caudal peduncle, in which the scalpels are set. Young specimens do not have nearly as many red markings as the adult fish.

Acanthurus coeruleus
Blue Tang
● **Distribution:** Western Atlantic.
● **Length:** 300mm/12in (wild), 150mm/6in (aquarium).
● **Diet and feeding:** Mainly algae. Bold grazer.
● **Aquarium behaviour:** Small species may become bullies if established in the aquarium ahead of other fishes, but this tendency generally decreases with time.

Young fishes are yellow with blue markings around the eye. As they age, the fish develop narrow blue lines, the adult fish being darker blue than the 'almost adult' fish. The scalpels on the caudal peduncle are ringed with yellow or white in adult fishes.

A practical reminder
You will get maximum enjoyment from fishkeeping by providing your fishes with the very best conditions. Only then will they be able to repay your efforts with a healthy appearance and long life.

Above right:
Acanthurus coeruleus
The juvenile form of the Blue Tang differs in two significant respects from the adult: firstly, the young fish is bright yellow with blue-rimmed eyes, whereas the adult is blue overall. (Do not confuse the juvenile Blue Tang with Zebrasoma flavescens, *see page 70). Secondly, the strongly territorial nature of the juvenile generally lessens with age and the adult fish becomes more sociable.*

Right: **Acanthurus coeruleus**
As you might expect, the adult Blue Tang is a uniform blue all over (here shown at a sub-adult stage), except for some yellow or white coloration around the scalpels on the caudal peduncle region. It is not possible to say at exactly what age or size a fish will change into adult coloration. As a result, there have been many instances of confusion when fishkeepers have tried to identify different species.

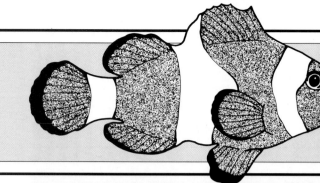

Common Clown (*Amphiprion ocellaris*)
Mature at 80mm (3.2in) and shown as a guide
to the maximum wild size of each species.

Acanthurus glaucopareius

Goldrim Tang; Powder Brown
- **Distribution:** Mainly the Pacific Ocean, but is sometimes found in the eastern Indian Ocean.
- **Length:** 200mm/8in (wild).
- **Diet and feeding:** Algae. Bold grazer.
- **Aquarium behaviour:** Normally peaceful.

It is fairly easy to identify this fish by the white area on the cheeks. Yellow zones along the base of blue-edged dorsal and anal fins may extend into the base of the caudal fin. A yellow vertical bar extends across the caudal fin. Another name for this attractive species is *Acanthurus aliala*.

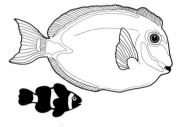

Acanthurus leucosternon

Powder Blue Surgeon
- **Distribution:** Indo-Pacific.
- **Length:** 250mm/10in (wild), 180-200mm/7-8in (aquarium)
- **Diet and feeding:** Protein foods and vegetable matter. Bold grazer.
- **Aquarium behaviour:** Keep only one in the aquarium. Dealers usually segregate juveniles to prevent quarrels developing.

This is a favourite Surgeon among aquarists. The oval-shaped body is a delicate blue; the black of the head is separated from the body by a white area beneath the jawline. The dorsal fin is bright yellow, as is the caudal peduncle. The white-edged black caudal fin carries a vertical white crescent. The female is larger than the male. In common with all Surgeonfishes, it requires plenty of space and well-aerated water.

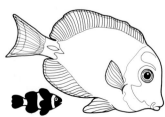

Acanthurus lineatus

Clown Surgeonfish; Blue-lined Surgeonfish; Pyjama Tang
- **Distribution:** Indo-Pacific.
- **Length:** 280mm/11in (wild), rarely above 150mm/6in in the aquarium.
- **Diet and feeding:** Algae. Bold grazer.
- **Aquarium behaviour:** Small specimens can be quarrelsome. Keep only one per tank or, alternatively, try keeping several together on the assumption that there is safety in numbers – rather than a mischievous two or three.

The yellow ground colour of the body is covered with longitudinal dark-edged, light blue lines. The pelvic fins are yellow.

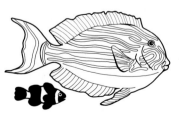

Above: **Acanthurus glaucopareius**
The alternative common names of White-cheeked Surgeon and Lipstick Surgeon (see also Naso lituratus*) are equally apt, for the markings on this fish are extremely fine. There is some justification in defining it as a Powder Brown as the colour patterning is similar to that of the Powder Blue Surgeon. It is fairly easy to keep in the aquarium, being quite peaceful.*

Above right:
Acanthurus leucosternon
One of the most familiar of all Surgeonfishes, the Powder Blue Surgeon is a firm favourite with hobbyists. When first captured and during transportation, dealers keep them separated to prevent fights breaking out. Given room and sufficient vegetable matter, it makes a welcome contribution to the marine collection.

Right: **Acanthurus lineatus**
This is one of the fishes in the Family with a split level of coloration; there is a lighter area to the lower body with decorative parallel longitudinal lines above. Acanthurus sohal (page 68) has a similar body pattern. Like other Surgeonfishes, it appreciates some coral or rockwork to provide welcome sheltering places.

A practical reminder
Select the biggest tank you can afford
(or find room for); a large surface area is
more important than overall capacity.
This will ensure more stable water
conditions, vital to marine fishes.

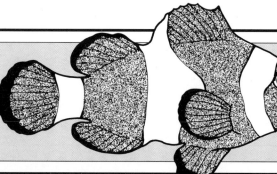

Common Clown (*Amphiprion ocellaris*)
Mature at 80mm (3.2in) and shown as a guide
to the maximum wild size of each species.

Above: **Acanthurus sohal**
*This striking fish is not a common
sight in aquatic dealers' tanks, but
its smart lines make it readily
noticeable when it does appear.*

Acanthurus sohal

Zebra Surgeon; Majestic Surgeon
● **Distribution:** Red Sea.
● **Length:** 250mm/10in (wild),
180mm/7in (aquarium).
● **Diet and feeding:** Algae. Bold
grazer.
● **Aquarium behaviour:** Small
specimens can be quarrelsome;
keep only one per tank.

This smart fish is similar in body
shape to *A.lineatus*. Its blue-
edged, blue-black fins add an
outline to the pale body, and the
scalpels are marked with a vivid
orange stripe. The upper part of
the body and head are covered
with a series of parallel dark lines.
A rare but beautiful fish.

Naso lituratus

Lipstick Tang; Lipstick Surgeon
● **Distribution:** Indo-Pacific.
● **Length:** 500mm/20in (wild),
200mm/8in (aquarium).
● **Diet and feeding:** Protein foods
and greenstuff. Bold grazer.
● **Aquarium behaviour:** Normally
peaceful.

The facial 'make-up' of this fish is
quite remarkable; the lips are red
or orange and a yellow-edged,
dark brown-grey mask covers the
snout and eyes. The front of the
narrow dorsal fin is also bright
yellow. The basic colour of the
dorsal fin varies according to
geographical origin of the fishes;
Hawaiian specimens have a black
dorsal, in those from the Indian
Ocean the dorsal is orange. The
two immovable, forward-pointing
'scalpels' on each side of the
caudal peduncle are set in yellow
patches. The male fish is larger
than the female.

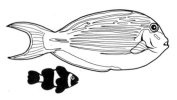

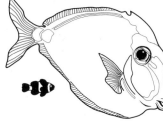

Above: **Naso lituratus**
*The extremely well-defined facial
markings of the Lipstick Tang are
quite remarkable, worthy of any
beautician's salon.*

Right: **Naso lituratus**
*The remainder of the streamlined
fish is no less attractive, with a
lyre-shaped caudal fin and double
scalpels set in vivid patches.*

A practical reminder
The aquarium will be very heavy when completely furnished. Ensure that its foundation is firm and level. You will need an electrical outlet nearby and adequate access for maintenance.

Paracanthurus hepatus
Regal Tang
● **Distribution:** Indo-Pacific.
● **Length:** 250mm/10in (wild), 100-150mm/4-6in (aquarium).
● **Diet and feeding:** Algae. Bold grazer.
● **Aquarium behaviour:** May occasionally be agressive towards members of the same species.

The brilliant blue body has a black 'painter's palette' shape marking, but the most striking feature of this species is the bright yellow wedge section in the caudal fin. The dorsal and anal fins are black-edged, and the pectoral fin is yellow-tipped. This fish was once called *P.theuthis*.

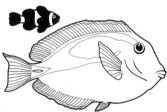

Left: **Paracanthurus hepatus**
This fish's black markings and yellow caudal fin make positive identification very easy.

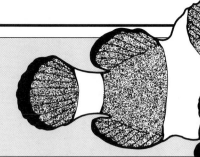

Common Clown (*Amphiprion ocellaris*)
Mature at 80mm (3.2in) and shown as a guide
to the maximum wild size of each species.

Zebrasoma flavescens
Yellow Tang
● **Distribution:** Pacific Ocean.
● **Length:** 200mm/8in (wild),
100-150mm/4-6in (aquarium).
● **Diet and feeding:** Algae. Bold
grazer.
● **Aquarium behaviour:** Highly
territorial. Keep either a single fish
or a group of six or more per tank;
never keep two or three together.

It is unusual to find a marine fish of
a single colour, but the vividness
of the bright yellow makes up for
any lack of pattern. This species
can be distinguished from juvenile
forms of *A. coeruleus* by the
absence of blue around the eyes,
although a more obvious guide is
the difference in shape of the head
and mouth.

Right: **Zebrasoma flavescens**
*Many such Surgeonfish and Tangs
are quarrelsome, but keeping them
in larger numbers may reduce
friction between individuals.*

Below: **Zebrasoma flavescens**
*The long snout of this species
enables it to graze effortlessly on
luxuriant growths of algae.*

A practical reminder
All-glass tanks are best for marine fishes as the salt water cannot damage them. Make sure that the glass is thick enough to withstand the pressure of water in the size of tank recommended.

Below: **Zebrasoma veliferum**
This is an extremely variable species. In this adult, the pale brown vertical stripes extend into the large dorsal and anal fins.

Right: **Zebrasoma veliferum**
A juvenile specimen, with a different body pattern and no facial markings. The typical Tang body shape is clearly visible.

Zebrasoma veliferum
Striped Sailfin Tang
● **Distribution:** Indo-Pacific, Red Sea.
● **Length:** 380mm/15in (wild), 180-200mm/7-8in (aquarium).
● **Diet and feeding:** Protein foods and greenstuff. Bold grazer.
● **Aquarium behaviour:** Normally peaceful, but may be aggressive with large fish. Young specimens do better in captivity.

The main feature of this species is the large sail-like dorsal fin and almost matching anal fin; both are patterned. Coloration of both fins and body may be variable in shades of brown overlaid with several vertical bands. The female fish is larger than the male.

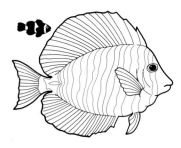

Zebrasoma xanthurum
Purple Sailfin Tang; Emperor Tang
● **Distribution:** Indo-Pacific, Red Sea.
● **Length:** 200mm/8in (wild).
● **Diet and feeding:** Protein foods and greenstuff. Bold grazer.
● **Aquarium behaviour:** Normally peaceful.

The body colour may vary from purplish blue to brown, depending on the fish's natural habitat. A number of dark spots cover the head and front part of the body. The caudal fin is bright yellow.

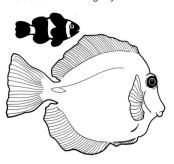

Right: **Zebrasoma xanthurum**
The specific name, xanthurum, *refers to the yellow caudal fin.*

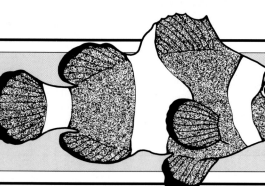

Common Clown (*Amphiprion ocellaris*)
Mature at 80mm (3.2in) and shown as a guide
to the maximum wild size of each species.

Family: APOGONIDAE
Cardinalfishes

Family characteristics
Cardinal fishes are generally slow-moving, often nocturnal fishes that hide among coral heads during the day. However, at the approach of a net, they can move very fast! They are usually found on coral reefs, but some frequent tidal pools and one species enters fresh water.

Unusually for a marine fish, the two separate dorsal fins are carried erect. This feature, together with the large head, mouth and eyes, is a characteristic of the Family.

Reproduction is by mouthbrooding. The male generally incubates the eggs, although in some species this task is undertaken by the female. In other species within the Family, both sexes share the responsibility.

Diet and feeding
Once acclimatized to aquarium conditions, Cardinalfishes will eat most live and dried foods (but never flake food). Do not keep them with fast-swimming boisterous fishes or they will lose out in the competition for food. It is a good idea to feed Cardinalfishes late in the evening, since this will suit their nocturnal lifestyle and may result in a greater willingness to accept new foods.

Aquarium behaviour
Hardy fishes that should be acclimatized gradually to the bright lights of the main aquarium. During the quarantine period, slowly increase the lighting level from dim to full strength.

Above:
Sphaeramia nematopterus
The body shape of this fish might be reminiscent of the freshwater tetras, although it boasts an extra dorsal fin and much larger eyes.

Right: **Apogon maculatus**
Much slimmer than the more common Pyjama Cardinalfish, the Flamefish is also a nocturnal species by nature, and prefers to share its aquarium with less boisterous fishes.

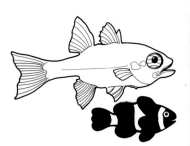

Apogon maculatus
Flamefish
● **Distribution:** Western Atlantic.
● **Length:** 150mm/6in (wild), 750mm/3in (aquarium).
● **Diet and feeding:** All foods. Shy.
● **Aquarium behaviour:** Prefers a quiet aquarium with fishes of a similar disposition.

This bright red fish with two white horizontal lines through the eye is very easy to identify. It has two dark spots on the body, one below the second dorsal fin and the other on the caudal peduncle (although faint at times). It is a nocturnal feeder and, although shy, usually settles down well in captivity.

Sphaeramia (Apogon) nematopterus
Pyjama Cardinalfish; Spotted Cardinalfish
● **Distribution:** Indo-Pacific.
● **Length:** 100mm/4in (wild), rarely seen above 75mm/3in in the aquarium.
● **Diet and feeding:** All foods. Keen.
● **Aquarium behaviour:** Do not keep with larger boisterous species.

This fish has three distinct colour sections to its striking body, each dissimilar to the next, almost as if it had been assembled like an 'identikit'. The large head section, back to the first of the two dorsal fins, is yellow-brown in colour. A dark brown vertical band joins the first dorsal fin to the pelvic fins. A spotted paler area covers the rear of the fish. The large eyes indicate a naturally nocturnal behaviour. It may be necessary to acclimatize this species with live foods, but once settled in the aquarium it will eat well. However, do not offer flake food. This fish was formerly known as *Apogon orbicularis*.

A practical reminder
If you intend 'upgrading' your system at a later date, be sure to allow enough room in your tank to house new equipment. Protein skimmers and similar systems need extra height.

Family: BALISTIDAE
Triggerfishes

Family characteristics
Members of this Family have acquired their common name from the characteristic locking and unlocking mechanism of the first dorsal fin. This fin is normally carried flat in a groove, but it can be locked into position by a third ray and prevents the fish from being eaten or withdrawn from a crevice in which it has taken refuge.

Triggerfishes are relatively poor swimmers. They achieve propulsion by undulating wave motions of the dorsal and anal fins, the caudal fin being saved for emergency accelerations when required. The pelvic, or ventral, fins are absent in most species, or are restricted to a single spine or knoblike protruberances.

Body coloration can range from the dull to the psychedelic. The patterning around the mouth is typically exaggerated, probably to deter rivals or predators. The teeth are very strong and often protrusive – ideal for eating shelled invertebrates and sea urchins. Needless to say, you should not keep Triggerfishes with invertebrates in the home aquarium. Also take care that they do not nip your fingers!

Reproduction takes place in pits dug in the sand within the territory of one of the female fish. These terrritories, in turn, are all enclosed within the dominant male's greater territory. The eggs, presumed to be demersal (i.e. heavier than water), are released either in an ascending swimming action or over a preselected site.

Some species guard the eggs, but others do not.

In the sea, Triggerfishes live alone and are intolerant of similar species in the aquarium. They may adopt peculiar resting positions, headstanding or even lying on their sides.

Diet and feeding
Triggerfishes are greedy feeders, accepting anything that is offered. Natural foods taken by the bottom-feeding species of the Family include echinoderms such as starfishes and sea urchins, which they devour complete with the spines. Triggerfishes consume the Crown of Thorns Starfish in a specific manner – they first blow the starfish over so that its spines are out of the way and then eat the soft unprotected underbelly. Species that occupy the middle and upper waters of the tank take plankton and green foods. Suitable aquarium foods include dried foods, chopped earthworms and small fishes (Guppies, *Gambusia* and other livebearing fry).

Aquarium behaviour
The behaviour of Triggerfishes in the aquarium varies from peaceful to unaccommodatingly aggressive, depending on the species. Fishes rest at night in crevices or caves, and so it is avisable to aquascape the aquarium to allow for this. Do not be surprised, however, if the fish take advantage of your thoughtfully provided refuges when you try to net them! In nature, they favour underwater cliff faces, especially the Caribbean species.

Balistapus undulatus
Undulate Triggerfish; Orange-green Trigger; Red-lined Triggerfish
● **Distribution:** Indo-Pacific.
● **Length:** 300mm/12in (wild), 200mm/8in (aquarium).
● **Diet and feeding:** Corals, crustaceans, molluscs, sea urchins. Bold grazer.
● **Aquarium behaviour:** The most aggressive Trigger of all. Keep out of aquariums that contain invertebrates and most fish. Using its powerful jaws, *B.undulatus* is in the habit of picking up lumps of coral and distributing them elsewhere in the aquarium. Despite its aggressive behaviour and potential size – in a large tank it will grow to about 300mm/12in – it is a rewarding fish to keep, becoming quite tame and enjoying a lot of fuss from its owner.

This species was first discovered in 1797 by the Scottish explorer Mungo Park. In the wild, it is found over a wide area of the Indo-Pacific, although not around Hawaii. The body coloration can vary quite markedly, as its common names suggest. Indian Ocean variants have orange tails,

while Pacific specimens have orange-rayed green caudal fins. Males are larger, with no orange banding on the head. Several large spines are arranged in two rows on the caudal peduncle.

Above: **Balistapus undulatus**
It is more than 190 years since this fish was first discovered and described for science and it is not difficult to understand why it might be regarded as an asset to the marine aquarium. However, its striking coloration, and the fact that it can become hand-tame must be taken into consideration along with another of its traits – it's a very aggressive fish.

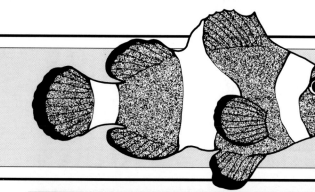

Common Clown (*Amphiprion ocellaris*)
Mature at 80mm (3.2in) and shown as a guide
to the maximum wild size of each species.

Above: **Balistes bursa**
The coloration around the mouth, together with the lighter body colours, accentuates and apparently enlarges the actual size of the mouth, a good deterrent against would-be predators. Like all Triggerfishes, the head appears disproportionately large compared to the rest of the body. Note the almost non-existent pelvic fins.

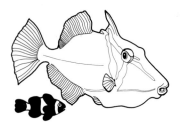

Balistes (Hemibalistes) bursa

White-lined Triggerfish; Bursa Trigger
● **Distribution:** Indo-Pacific.
● **Length:** 250mm/10in (wild), 150mm/6in (aquarium).
● **Diet and feeding:** All foods. Bold.
● **Aquarium behaviour:** Unsociable towards other Triggerfishes. Aggressive in general to other fishes.

The red and yellow lines on the head joining the eye to the pectoral fin and the snout to the pectoral fin are the principal clues to the identification of this fish. An area of light blue runs below the horizontal line from snout to vent. The fins are practically colourless. Males are larger and more colourful than females. This fish is also known as *Sufflamen bursa*.

Balistes vetula

Queen Triggerfish; Conchino; Peja Puerco
● **Distribution:** Tropical western Atlantic.
● **Length:** 500mm/20in (wild), 250mm/10in (aquarium).
● **Diet and feeding:** Crustaceans, molluscs, small fishes, usual frozen foods, etc. Bold; will take good-sized pieces.
● **Aquarium behaviour:** Do not keep with small fishes. Although peaceful with other species, it will quarrel with its own kind.

Dark lines radiate from around the eyes and there are striking blue facial markings. The tips of the dorsal fin and caudal fins become filamentous with age, especially in the male, which is larger and more colourful than the female. This beautifully marked species may become hand-tame in captivity.

Right: **Balistes vetula**
A characteristic of Triggerfishes is that many will become hand-tame in time. You should exercise care when hand-feeding, however, for their slightly protrusive teeth are very sharp. Impaling pieces of food on a cocktail stick before offering to the fish will be a safer method of hand-feeding, and the fish will not know the difference anyway.

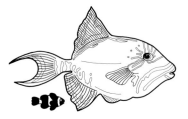

A practical reminder
Choose the correct size heater; allow about 2 watts per litre of water. Large tanks need two heaters. Do not test heaters out of water and always switch off power before adjusting thermostats.

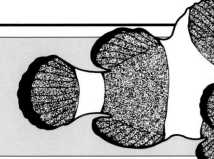

Common Clown (*Amphiprion ocellaris*)
Mature at 80mm (3.2in) and shown as a guide
to the maximum wild size of each species.

Balistoides conspicillum
Clown Trigger; Big-spotted Triggerfish
● **Distribution:** Indo-Pacific.
● **Length:** 500mm/20in (wild);
250mm/10in (aquarium).
● **Diet and feeding:** Crustaceans,
molluscs. Bold.
● **Aquarium behaviour:**
Aggressive. Do not keep with small
fishes.

An easily recognizable species,
with its large white-spotted lower
body. The 'brightly painted' yellow
mouth may deter enemies, while
the disruptive camouflage assists
species recognition. Both the
dorsal and anal fin are basically
pale yellow and the caudal fin is
dark edged. This fish is also known
as *Balistoides niger*.

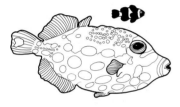

Right: **Balistoides conspicillum**
*With its spectacular coloration, the
Clown Trigger is an unmistakable
fish. An aggressive species.*

Below: **Melichthys ringens**
*A peaceful Indo-Pacific species
that is very similarly marked to
M.niger from the Caribbean.*

Melichthys ringens
Black-finned Triggerfish
● **Distribution:** Indo-Pacific.
● **Length:** 500mm/20in (wild),
250mm/10in (aquarium).
● **Diet and feeding:** All foods.
Bold grazer.
● **Aquarium behaviour:** Peaceful.
A very gentle Triggerfish.

The body is brownish and the fins
are black, but it is the white lines at
the base of the dorsal and anal fins
and the white-edged caudal fin
that distinguish this species.

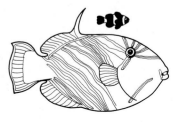

Odonus niger
Black Triggerfish
● **Distribution:** Indo-Pacific and Red Sea.
● **Length:** 500mm/20in (wild), 250mm/10in (aquarium).
● **Diet and feeding:** All foods. Bold.
● **Aquarium compatibility:** Fairly sociable and peaceful.

The body coloration of *O. niger* can vary from blue to green from day to day. The red teeth are often quite conspicuous. Propulsion is achieved by undulations of the dorsal, anal and caudal fins rather than by body movements. Red Sea specimens require a higher specific gravity than those from the Indo-Pacific Ocean.

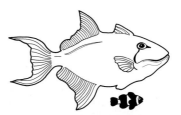

Below: **Odonus niger**
Maybe the photographer frightened the fish into erecting its first dorsal fin, in anticipation of perhaps capture or worse! Whilst Triggerfishes have apparently less means of manouevrability, by lacking pelvic fins, they manage very well by using dorsal and anal fins to equally good effect.

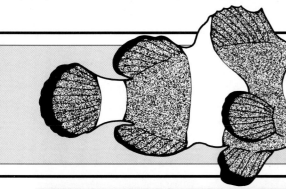

Common Clown (*Amphiprion ocellaris*)
Mature at 80mm (3.2in) and shown as a guide
to the maximum wild size of each species.

Rhinecanthus aculeatus
Picasso Trigger
● **Distribution:** Indo-Pacific, Red Sea.
● **Length:** 300mm/12in (wild), 230mm/9in (aquarium).
● **Diet and feeding:** Crustaceans, molluscs, sea meat foods. Bold.
● **Aquarium behaviour:** Aggressive towards members of the same species and towards other fish of the same size.

The 'avant garde' colours of this fish make it a popular species. A number of diagonal white bars slant upwards and forwards from the anal fin. The mouth and jawline are accentuated with colour and a blue and yellow-brown stripe across the head connects the eye with the pectoral fin base. This fish may emit a distinctive whirring sound when startled.

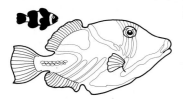

Family: BLENNIIDAE
Blennies

Family characteristics
Bluntheaded, elongate and constantly active, Blennies make a cheerful addition to the aquarium, although they should be kept in a species tank rather than in a community collection. They naturally frequent inshore waters, hiding in any handy cave or crevice, not always bothering to follow the tide out to sea. Provide suitable living quarters in the aquarium using short lengths of plastic piping, either laid on the aquarium floor or stacked up in small piles to form 'apartments'.
   The dorsal fin is long and there are cirri (hairy, bristle-like growths) above the high-set eyes. The skin is slimy, hence the alternative name of Slimefishes.
   Male Blennies tend to be larger and more colourful than females. During breeding, the male may undergo changes in colour during both the pre- and post-spawning periods. One member of the Family, the False Cleanerfish, lays its eggs in any handy shelter – empty shells are particularly acceptable – and the eggs are guarded by the male.

Diet and feeding
Blennies are completely omnivorous, eating everything from algae to small fishes and bits of large ones! They will even take dried foods with apparent relish.

Aquarium behaviour
Some Blennies are very aggressive to any other fishes; *Ophioblennius* is a typical case that should not be kept with any fish less than twice its size.

Above: **Rhinecanthus aculeatus**
Whether used for camouflage, species recognition or as a deterrent, the exaggerated patterns make the Picasso Trigger instantly distinguishable from other members of the Family. Here, the front dorsal fin is being carried flat.

Aspidontus taeniatus
False Cleanerfish; Sabre-toothed Blenny; Cleaner Mimic
● **Distribution:** Indo-Pacific.
● **Length:** 100mm/4in (wild).
● **Diet and feeding:** Skin, scales and flesh – preferably from living, unsuspecting victims! Sly and devious.
● **Aquarium behaviour:** Do not keep with other fishes.

Using its similarity in size, shape and colour to the true Cleanerfish, *Labroides dimidiatus*, this fish approaches its victims who expect the usual 'cleaning services'; instead they end up with a very nasty wound and a little bit wiser. Easily distinguished by its underslung mouth, which gives it a shark-like appearance. Because of its predatory nature, this species is

A practical reminder
Three things help maintain the correct
light levels in the aquarium: well-filtered
water, a spotlessly clean cover glass
and the regular renewal of lamps,
especially fluorescent tubes.

Above: **Ecsenius bicolor**
*The rearmost body colour of this
fish is often hidden from view,
since it spends much of the time in
the many hiding places carefully
provided by the hobbyist. It is
ironical – make a fish comfortable
and it promptly hides from view!*

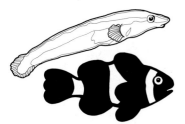

not recommended for inclusion in
the home marine aquarium under
any circumstances. It is featured
here primarily as a warning, so that
you can avoid it.

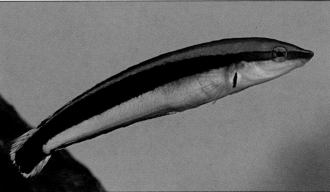

Above: **Aspidontus taeniatus**
*Familiarize yourself thoroughly with
this fish, for it is one you should
avoid at all costs. It uses its
coloration to mimic the true
Cleanerfish, Labroides dimidiatus,
and denude its unsuspecting
victims of large lumps of flesh!*

Ecsenius (Blennius) bicolor
Bicolor Blenny
● **Distribution:** Indo-Pacific.
● **Length:** 100mm/4in (wild).
● **Diet and feeding:** Meat foods
and algae. Bottom-feeding grazer.

● **Aquarium behaviour:** Shy with
larger fishes; provide plenty of
hiding places.

The front half of this fish is brown,
but the rear half is orange-red.
During spawning, the male turns
red with white bars. The female's
breeding colours are light brown
and yellow-orange. After
spawning, the male changes
colour again, becoming dark blue
with light patches on each side of
the body.

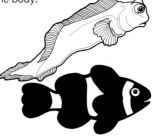

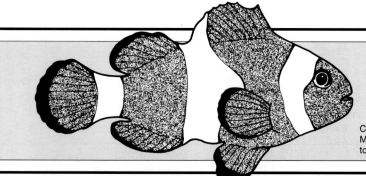

Common Clown (*Amphiprion ocellaris*)
Mature at 80mm (3.2in) and shown as a guide
to the maximum wild size of each species.

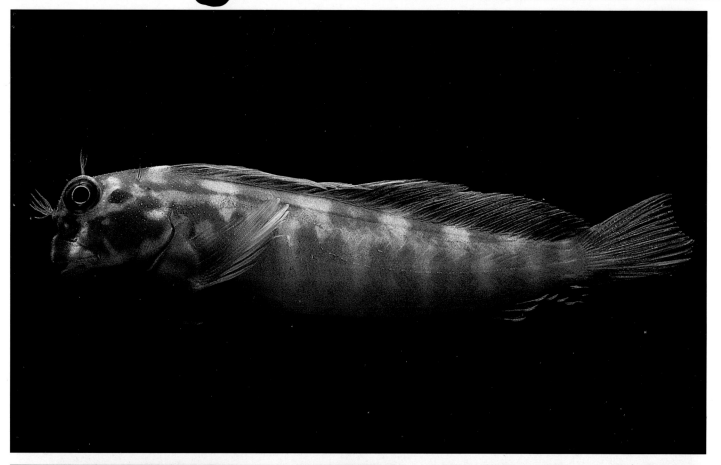

Above: **Salaria fasciatus**
It is a pity that Blennies are so keen on hiding away in caves and under rocks, for it is only when they emerge into more open areas that you can see their body colour patterns, long finnage and cirri – crestlike growths above the eyes.

Above left:
Ophioblennius atlanticus
A member of the combtooth Blennies group, the Redlip Blenny varies in colour from very dark to almost white. It is a very territorial fish and often perches on coral outcrops apparently on 'sentry duty' on the lookout for potential intruders.

Left: **Petroscirtes temmincki**
Striped Slimefish is hardly an attractive name, but Blennies in the aquarium often reveal endearing characteristics as they scurry around their territories. This highly camouflaged species lacks the usual cirri on the head.

Ophioblennius atlanticus
Redlip Blenny
● **Distribution:** Tropical western Atlantic.
● **Length:** 120mm/4.7in (wild).
● **Diet and feeding:** Meat foods and algae. Bottom-feeding grazer.
● **Aquarium behaviour:** Territorial, and it chases everything.

Keep this rare species in a community of small fishes and provide plenty of hiding places; lengths of plastic pipe are particularly suitable.

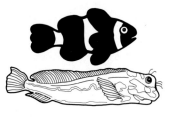

Petroscirtes temmincki
Striped Slimefish
● **Distribution:** Indo-Pacific.
● **Length:** 100mm/4in (wild).
● **Diet and feeding:** Algae, small animals. Bottom grazer.
● **Aquarium behaviour:** Can be kept in small groups of the same species.

The body shape is that of a typical Blenny, with the eyes set up high on the head. There are no cirri. The coloration is black with white blotches, plus bright blue spots on the head region.

Salaria fasciatus
Banded Blenny
● **Distribution:** Indo-Pacific.
● **Length:** 100mm/4in (wild).
● **Diet and feeding:** Small animal foods and algae. Bottom grazer.
● **Aquarium behaviour:** Requires plenty of hiding places.

The elongate body is covered with mottled light and dark brown vertical bands, extending into the long-based dorsal fin. The eye patterning – radiating stripes around the rim – is a particular feature.

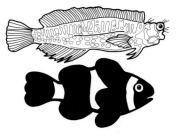

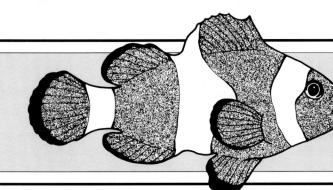

Common Clown (*Amphiprion ocellaris*)
Mature at 80mm (3.2in) and shown as a guide
to the maximum wild size of each species.

Family: CALLIONYMIDAE
Mandarinfishes

Family characteristics
Mandarinfishes and the related Dragonets are small, mainly
bottom-dwelling species that often bury themselves in the sand
during the day. Sometimes they will perch on a firm surface not too
far away from the aquarium floor.

Sexing these fish is fairly straightforward, males having longer
dorsal and anal fin extensions and brighter colours than females.
Reproduction is by internal fertilization, often following a ritualistic
courtship display and a clasping together of the two fishes. The
eggs are scattered in open water, and are normally described as
pelagic. (In contrast to so-called demersal eggs, which are
deposited on a surface). Although this behaviour has been
observed in aquariums, no fry have yet been raised in captivity.

Diet and feeding
Members of this Family feed predominantly on small marine
animals, such as crustaceans, that live among the debris on the
seabed. Provide the commercially available shrimps in the aquarium.

Aquarium behaviour
Mandarinfishes should be kept singly or in matched pairs. They are
ideally suited to a quiet aquarium containing fishes of a similar
disposition. Seahorses make suitable companions.

Synchiropus picturatus
Psychedelic Fish
● **Distribution:** Pacific.
● **Length:** 100mm/4in (wild).
● **Diet and feeding:** Small
crustaceans and algae. Shy
bottom-feeding grazer.
● **Aquarium behaviour:** Likely to
be intolerant of their own kind.
May be better able to cope with
livelier tankmates than
Synchiropus splendidus.

The basically green body is
adorned with lemon-edged, darker
green red-ringed patches. This
species is found in the Philippines
and Melanesia. It is less common
than *S. splendidus*.

Synchiropus splendidus
Mandarinfish
● **Distribution:** Pacific.
● **Length:** 100mm/4in (wild).
● **Diet and feeding:** Small
crustaceans and algae. Shy
bottom-feeding grazer.
● **Aquarium behaviour:** It is best
kept in a quiet aquarium away from
larger, more lively fishes.

This fish has much more red in its
coloration, in random streaks
around the body and fins. Males
usually develop a longer dorsal
spine. It is said that the skin mucus
of this and the previous species is
poisonous, a fact often signalled in
gaudily patterned fishes.

Below: **Synchiropus picturatus**
*Not quite so gaudily coloured as
the following species, the bottom-
dwelling, less common*

*Psychedelic Fish has bold patterns
clearly outlined against the
subdued green of its body. An
attractive subject for a quiet tank.*

A practical reminder
When checking the specific gravity or the pH value of the water, ensure that it is at the correct temperature; otherwise you will obtain false readings. Make adjustments gradually.

Below:
Synchiropus splendidus
The long extension to the dorsal fin of the male fish is well illustrated here. The fish may be showing off its vivid colours to a nearby female before joining her in a vertical courtship ascent in the water, prior to the release and fertilization of eggs during spawning.

Family: CENTRISCIDAE
Razorfishes/Shrimpfishes

Family characteristics
The Shrimpfish, the principal member of this Family, has a completely straight top to its body. This is because the first ray of the dorsal fin projects horizontally past the rear end of the body like a protective cover. This forces the dorsal and caudal fin to be bent downwards, below the horizontal line. The word 'horizontal' becomes meaningless, however, because these fishes typically swim in a head-down position. The mouth is very small and tubular.

Diet and feeding
Razorfishes need a diet of small live foods, such as brineshrimp and finely chopped shrimps, and dried food.

Aquarium behaviour
These are delicate fishes to transport, and can be difficult to keep, but they often make rewarding aquarium subjects because of their distinctive appearance and curious behaviour. They are ideal fishes for an invertebrate aquarium.

Aeoliscus strigatus
Razorfish; Shrimpfish
● **Distribution:** Indo-Pacific.
● **Length:** 125mm/5in (wild).
● **Diet and feeding:** Very small animal foods. Bottom grazer.
● **Aquarium behaviour:** Usually thrive best in a species aquarium of their own, but will live peacefully with Seahorses.

Their habit of feeding and resting in a head-down position makes these interesting fishes to observe. The longitudinal (turned vertical) black stripe provides perfect camouflage, especially when they hide among long-spined sea urchins. They are susceptible to the effects of copper, so accurate dosage when treating disease is vital. (See page 57 for guidance on using copper-based remedies in the marine aquarium.)

Above: **Aeoliscus strigatus**
No, the picture isn't printed the wrong way round, this is the normal swimming attitude of these fishes. Spot them among the long spines of sea urchins if you can!

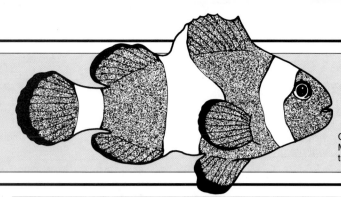

Common Clown (*Amphiprion ocellaris*)
Mature at 80mm (3.2in) and shown as a guide
to the maximum wild size of each species.

Family: CHAETODONTIDAE (including POMACANTHIDAE)
Angelfishes and Butterflyfishes

Family characteristics
This Family contains two very important groups of aquarium fishes: the Angelfishes and the Butterflyfishes, both favourites with the fishkeeper. The two groups are now classified separately as Chaetodontidae (Butterflyfishes) and Pomacanthidae (Angelfishes), but such is their similarity in appearance and aquarium requirements that it is more practical to treat them as one for the purposes of this book.

The body form is oval and laterally compressed. These features, together with the terminal mouth, provide a strong clue as to the their natural habitat: coral heads, where their thin-sectioned bodies can pass easily between the branches. Their amazing colour patterns camouflage and protect vulnerable parts of their bodies, and assist species identification. Juvenile Angelfishes have a different coloration pattern to the adults and it is not always possible to identify a young Angelfish with certainty; many species are similar at this stage – blue with white markings.

Of the two groups, Angelfishes are the most numerous. The surest way of distinguishing between the two groups is to look for the spine found on the gill cover of Angelfishes but not on Butterflyfishes.

There appear to be no external differences between the sexes, although at breeding times the females may become noticeably swollen with eggs. Both groups of fishes spawn in a similar manner, ascending in the water to release eggs and sperm. Once fertilized, the eggs float briefly until they hatch. The larvae then feed on plankton for some time before sinking to the bottom. One or two reports of aquarium spawnings indicate that demersal (i.e. non-floating) eggs were laid on a site, but these occurrences are presumed to be isolated incidents brought on by confinement and not typical of the Family as a whole.

Diet and feeding
Most members of the Chaetodontidae are grazing fishes that feed on algae, sponges and corals; some are omnivorous, however, and include small and planktonic animals in their diet. You will need to feed young fishes several times a day with live brineshrimp. Larger fish should be offered cultured worm foods (whiteworm, grindalworm, chopped earthworms, etc.) as well as dried foods. It is a good idea to get a new Angelfish feeding readily while in the quarantine tank, before introducing it into the main aquarium. Living corals, sea anemones and invertebrates will not last long in the same aquarium with Butterflyfishes, although Angels are less likely to prey on them. One or two species have evolved long snouts for reaching even further into crevices for food.

Aquarium behaviour
Although very attractive, these fishes are not really suitable for inexperienced fishkeepers. They can be difficult to maintain in captivity, particularly the algae- and sponge-eating species, while the polyp-eating species are practically impossible to sustain. These species are easily upset by changes in water conditions, usually showing any dissatisfaction with aquarium life by going on hunger strike; one day they are quite content with the diet you provide and the next day they will simply not touch it.

They are fairly territorial and Angels may be intolerant of their own kind, although most of the Butterflyfishes are compatible. Angelfishes are generally relatively tolerant of dissimilarly-sized fishes; smaller fishes do not alarm them, and they do not feel especially threatened by larger ones. However, when faced with a fish of the same proportions, quarrelling may occur. In a large aquarium with a good number of retreats, you can expect better results. Both Butterflyfishes and Angelfishes need refuges in which to shelter at night. Bear this in mind when decorating the tank; use rockwork and suitable pieces of coral – glue fragments together with sealant if necessary – to create hiding places.

ANGELFISHES

Apolemichthys arcuatus
Bandit Angelfish; Banded Angelfish
● **Distribution:** Pacific.
● **Length:** 180mm/7in (wild).
● **Diet and feeding:** Mainly sponges and algae, but freeze-dried foods can be offered. Grazer.
● **Aquarium behaviour:** Little information.

The diagonal white-edged dark stripe that runs from the eye to the rear of the dorsal fin gives this fish its apt common name. The anal and caudal fins are similarly dark with white edging and the dorsal fin is yellow-gold.

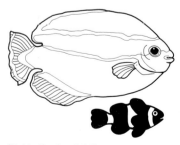

Right: **Apolemichthys arcuatus**
Whether the two common names are merely corruptions of one another or not, they both seem to suit this fish most aptly.

A practical reminder
Keep a close check on the nitrite content of the water, especially during the early weeks. It is safest to wait until it has fallen to a stable minimum before you introduce livestock.

Apolemichthys trimaculatus

Three-spot Angelfish
● **Habitat:** Indo-Pacific.
● **Length:** 250mm/10in (wild).
● **Diet and feeding:** Mainly algae, but offer freeze-dried foods and greenstuff. Grazer.
● **Aquarium behaviour:** Territorial, keep individual species only. This is not the easiest Angel to maintain in captivity.

The three 'spots' that give the fish its common name are around its head – one on top and one on each side of the body behind the gill covers. The lips are bright blue, and the anal fin is black with a broad white area immediately next to the body.

This species is fussy about water conditions and may also be difficult to acclimatize to aquarium life. Provide a variety of foods.

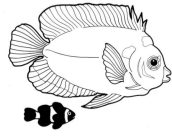

Above:
Apolemichthys trimaculatus
The specific name of this fish refers to the three prominent spots on the body, immediately behind the gill covers and on the top of the head. Note the contrasting band of black on the edge of the anal fin and the pale area close to the body. Needs care in captivity.

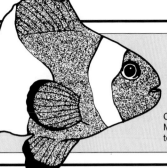

Common Clown (*Amphiprion ocellaris*)
Mature at 80mm (3.2in) and shown as a guide
to the maximum wild size of each species.

Arusetta asfur
Purple Moon Angel
● **Distribution:** Indian Ocean,
Persian Gulf and Red Sea.
● **Length:** 150mm/6in (wild).
● **Diet and feeding:** Meat foods
and plenty of greenstuff. Grazer.
● **Aquarium behaviour:** Territorial.

This species has a yellow vertical
bar across the blue body in front of
the anal fin. In this respect it differs
from a similar-looking species,
Pomacanthus maculosus, whose
yellow bar begins well into the anal
fin. The dorsal and anal fins are
elongated and the yellow colour is
repeated on the caudal fin.

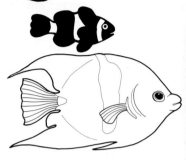

Right: **Arusetta asfur**
*Compare the extended dorsal and
anal fin outlines of this Indo-Pacific
Angelfish with those of the smaller
'dwarf' Centropyge species shown
below and on following pages.*

A practical reminder
To help mature the biological filter, add some sand from an established marine aquarium, use a maturing agent or introduce a pair of hardy nitrite-tolerant fishes, such as Damselfishes.

Genus Centropyge – DWARF ANGELFISHES
Species in the genus *Centropyge* deserve a special introduction, although we have maintained their position in the A-Z sequence of the Angelfish section.

These are ideal aquarium fishes, principally because they are miniature versions of the larger Angelfishes. An obvious bonus is that you can keep a greater number of fishes in the same relative space, and they may be less expensive too! In the wild, they are found more commonly at the base of the reef rather than among the coral polyps, although they are never far away from a safe retreat. Unlike some other Angelfishes, *Centropyge* species more often than not associate in pairs, with several pairs sharing the same area. Their main diet appears to be algae, which they graze from the reef surfaces. Should treatment be required, these fishes will accept lower doses of a copper-based remedy for a longer time than normal, but may not tolerate the higher doses given to larger related species.

Centropyge argi
Pygmy Angelfish; Cherubfish; Purple Fireball
- **Distribution:** Western Atlantic.
- **Length:** 75mm/3in (wild).
- **Diet and feeding:** Meat foods and plenty of greenstuff. Grazer.
- **Aquarium behaviour:** Often happier if kept in pairs.

A deeper water fish, which lives around the base of the reef rather than at the top. The colour patterns around the head may vary in detail from one species to another and there is no difference in the juvenile colour form, as in other Angelfishes. It is possible to keep compatible pairs in the aquarium, since natural territories are not particularly large.

Above: **Centropyge bicolor**
Literally, a two colour Angelfish. Juveniles are found in shallower waters than the adults. Despite its wide distribution in the Pacific, C.bicolor is not found in Hawaii.

Left: **Centropyge argi**
If two fishes of this attractive species appear to keep each other's company consistently, the result may be a spontaneous spawning in the aquarium.

Centropyge bicolor
Bicolor Cherub; Oriole Angel
- **Distribution:** Pacific.
- **Length:** 125mm/5in (wild).
- **Diet and feeding:** Meat foods and plenty of greenstuff. Grazer.
- **Aquarium behaviour:** Peaceful, providing plenty of hiding places are available.

The rear part of the body, from behind the head as far as the caudal fin, is bright purple-blue.

The small bar across the head over the eye is the same bright shade, while the head and caudal fin are yellow. In groups, a solitary male will dominate a 'harem' of females. If the male is removed from the group or – as in nature – dies, then one of the females will change sex to replace him. This procedure occurs every time the group becomes 'male-less'. This species is susceptible to disease. Use copper remedies with care.

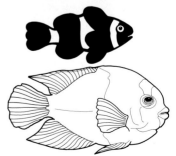

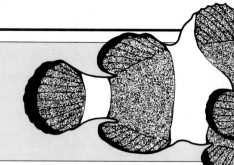

Common Clown (*Amphiprion ocellaris*)
Mature at 80mm (3.2in) and shown as a guide
to the maximum wild size of each species.

Centropyge bispinosus
Coral Beauty
● **Distribution:** Indo-Pacific.
● **Length:** 120mm/4.7in (wild).
● **Diet and feeding:** Meat foods
and plenty of greenstuff. Grazer.
● **Aquarium behaviour:** Will settle
down if retreats are close at hand.

In young specimens, the head and
body are outlined in deep purple;
red flanks are vertically crossed by
many thin purple lines. The adult
fish has much larger areas of gold/
yellow on the flanks, again crossed
by dark vertical stripes. The
pattern is very variable, however;
specimens from the Philippines,
for example, have more purple and
red coloration than those from
Australasian waters.

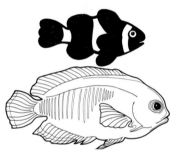

Below: **Centropyge bispinosus**
*The colour patterns of this species
vary according to its native home.*

A practical reminder
Biological filtration is vital in the marine aquarium; along with regular partial water changes, it is the most convenient and efficient way of reducing nitrogenous toxic wastes.

Centropyge eibli
Eibl's Angelfish
● **Distribution:** Indo-Pacific.
● **Length:** 150mm/6in (wild), 100mm/4in (aquarium)
● **Diet and feeding:** Most foods. Grazer.
● **Aquarium behaviour:** Peaceful.

The pale grey-gold body is crossed with gold and black lines, and some gold patterning appears in the anal fin. The rear part of the dorsal fin, the caudal peduncle and caudal fin are black, edged in pale blue. The eye is ringed with gold.

Centropyge acanthops
African Pygmy Angelfish
● **Distribution:** Indian Ocean, along the eastern seaboard of Africa.
● **Length:** 75mm/3in (wild).
● **Diet and feeding:** Meat foods and plenty of greenstuff. Grazer.
● **Aquarium behaviour:** Peaceful.

A blue fish with a yellow head and dorsal area, plus a pale yellow caudal fin. An ideal, peaceful aquarium subject. It is similar to *C. aurantonotus* (Flame-backed Angelfish) from the West Indies.

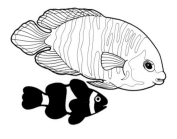

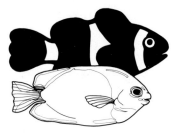

Left: **Centropyge eibli**
The combination of subtle colours of this fish come as a surprise – and very nearly a disappointment – when compared to the more vivid, even gaudy, hues of its relatives.

Below: **Centropyge acanthops**
The telltale spine on the gill cover distinguishes this species as an Angelfish, despite having a body shape more like a Damselfish. It is also often confused with C.fisheri.

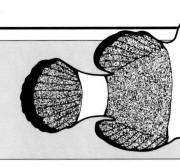

Common Clown (*Amphiprion ocellaris*)
Mature at 80mm (3.2in) and shown as a guide
to the maximum wild size of each species.

Centropyge flavissimus
Lemonpeel Angelfish
- **Distribution:** Indo-Pacific.
- **Length:** 100mm/4in (wild).
- **Diet and feeding:**
Predominantly greenstuff, but
might be persuaded to take meaty
foods. Grazer.
- **Aquarium behaviour:** Peaceful.

A plain yellow fish except for the
blue outlines around the eye,
bottom lip and gill cover edge.

A practical reminder
Water flow through biological filters, using the sand bed as the nitrifying bacterial colony, can be either downward or upward. Reverse-flow systems keep the sand cleaner.

Above left:
Centropyge flavissimus
A yellow fish with blue-ringed eyes.

Left: **Centropyge heraldi**
Unlike C.flavissimus, *this fish must be content with being plain yellow.*

Centropyge heraldi
Herald's Angelfish
● **Distribution:** Indo-Pacific.
● **Length:** 100mm/4in (wild).
● **Diet and feeding:** Mainly greenstuff, but also takes meaty foods. Grazer.
● **Aquarium behaviour:** Peaceful.

C.heraldi is also plain yellow, lacking even the blue details of *C.flavissimus.* Specimens collected from around Fiji have a black edge to the dorsal fin.

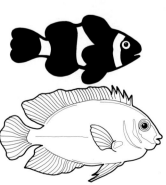

Centropyge loriculus
Flame Angelfish
● **Distribution:** Pacific.
● **Length:** 100mm/4in (wild).
● **Diet and feeding:** Meat foods and plenty of greenstuff. Grazer.
● **Aquarium behaviour:** Peaceful.

The fiery red-orange body has a central yellow area crossed by vertical dark bars. The dorsal and anal fins are similarly dark-tipped. The Flame Angelfish (often erroneously referred to as *C.flammeus*) is a hardy species and usually settles down quite well. Because of its peaceful disposition it may be kept in fairly small aquariums.

Above: **Centropyge loriculus**
There is no doubt at all about the identification of this species. Its vivid coloration distinguishes it from any other dwarf Angelfish.

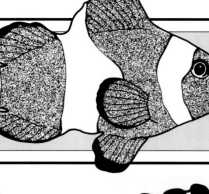

Common Clown (*Amphiprion ocellaris*)
Mature at 80mm (3.2in) and shown as a guide
to the maximum wild size of each species.

Centropyge multifasciatus

Multibarred Angelfish
● **Distribution:** Pacific.
● **Length:** 120mm/4.7in (wild).
● **Diet and feeding:** Mainly greenstuff. Grazer.
● **Aquarium behaviour:** Not known, but probably peaceful.

A rare fish, deeper bodied than the usual shape for the Family. The pale body is crossed by several vertical black bars that extend into the dorsal and anal fins, those on the anal fin turning yellow. The caudal fin is also black barred. The mouth and pelvic fins are yellow.

Centropyge vroliki

Pearl-scaled Angelfish
● **Habitat:** Pacific.
● **Length:** 120mm/4.7in (wild).
● **Diet and feeding:** Meat foods and plenty of greenstuff. Grazer.
● **Aquarium behaviour:** Territorial.

At first glance this species could be confused with *C.eibli*, but it lacks the vertical lines. The pale body is edged with dusky black dorsal, anal and caudal fins. The eye is ringed in gold, and the rear edge of the gill cover and the base of the pectoral fin are also gold. This species has hybridized with *C.flavissimus*.

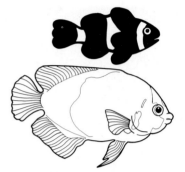

Although widely available, this species may be less popular with fishkeepers simply because of its muted colours.

Far left:
Centropyge multifasciatus
Another rare fish from the Pacific. Its patterning of vertical stripes should make it a popular variety.

Above: **Centropyge vroliki**
Like its relative, C.eibli, the Pearl-scaled Angelfish is not endowed with striking colours, but it deserves to be more popular.

Left:
Chaetodonplus conspicillatus
If you see one of these fishes, and are experienced enough to keep it successfully, be sure to snap it up.

Chaetodonplus conspicillatus

Conspicuous Angelfish
● **Distribution:** Pacific.
● **Length:** 250mm/10in (wild).
● **Diet and feeding:** Crustaceans, coral polyps, algae. Grazer.
● **Aquarium behaviour:** Little is known about how well this species adapts to life in the aquarium.

The brown body is ringed by blue-edged dorsal and anal fins. The clearly defined eyes are a 'conspicuous' feature of the vivid yellow face; the mouth is a contrasting blue. Further areas of bright yellow appear at the base of the pectoral and caudal fins; the pelvic fins are blue.

This rare species – considered by many marine fishkeepers to be the 'Jewel of the Angelfishes' – is found mainly around Lord Howe Island, about 640km(400 miles) off the east coast of Australia.

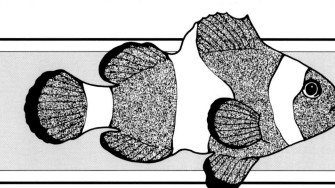

Common Clown (*Amphiprion ocellaris*)
Mature at 80mm (3.2in) and shown as a guide
to the maximum wild size of each species.

Chaetodonplus duboulayi

Scribbled Angelfish
● **Distribution:** Pacific.
● **Length:** 220mm/8.5in (wild).
● **Diet and feeding:** Crustaceans, coral polyps, algae. Grazer.
● **Aquarium behaviour:** Not known.

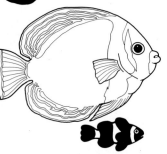

The rear portion of the body from the gills, together with the anal and dorsal fins, is dark blue with scribbled markings. A vertical yellow bar immediately behind the white gill cover is connected to the yellow caudal fin by a narrow yellow stripe along the top of the body. A dark bar covers the eye, and the mouth is yellow. A nitrate-free, but algae covered tank is ideal. Imported specimens are rarely available.

Chaetodonplus septentrionalis

Blue Striped Angelfish
● **Distribution:** Western Pacific.
● **Length:** 210mm/8.25in (wild).
● **Diet and feeding:** Crustaceans, coral polyps, algae. Grazer.
● **Aquarium behaviour:** Not known.

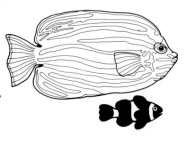

The brown body, dorsal and anal fins are covered with horizontal wavy blue lines. All the other fins are yellow. Juveniles are differently marked, being black with a yellow black-based caudal, and yellow margins to the dorsal and anal fins.

Below: **Chaetodonplus duboulayi**
Not a great deal is known about this recently introduced Angelfish. Provide it with the best of conditions and in time hobbyists will be able to find out more.

A practical reminder
Be careful when using ultraviolet lamps in sterilizers. Never remove the lamp from its casing when lit; it is dangerous to look directly at the lamp unless you have adequate eye protection.

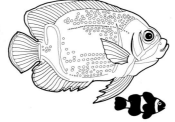

Euxiphipops navarchus
Blue-girdled Angelfish; Majestic Angelfish
● **Distribution:** Pacific.
● **Length:** 250mm/10in (wild).
● **Diet and feeding:** Meat foods and greenstuff. Grazer.
● **Aquarium behaviour:** Young specimens adapt better to aquarium life.

Left:
Chaetodonplus septentrionalis
The brown body of this Angelfish makes a contrasting background for the wavy blue stripes.

Below: **Euxiphipops navarchus**
When seen underwater, the dark blue areas, yellow saddle-back patch and yellow caudal fin help to confuse the 'fish shape' outline.

Blue-edged dark areas on the head and caudal peduncle of this fish are connected by a dark ventral surface. The rest of the body is rich orange flecked with fine blue iridescent spots. The plain orange anal and blue dorsal fins are both edged in pale blue, as are the dark pelvic fins. Like other large Angelfishes, the juvenile form is dark blue with vertical white stripes. (See pages 100 and 102.)

Common Clown (*Amphiprion ocellaris*)
Mature at 80mm (3.2in) and shown as a guide
to the maximum wild size of each species.

Euxiphipops xanthometapon

Blue-faced Angelfish; Yellow-faced Angelfish; Blue-masked Angelfish
● **Distribution:** Indo-Pacific.
● **Length:** 380mm/15in (wild), 300mm/12in (aquarium)
● **Diet and feeding:** Meat foods and greenstuff. Grazer.
● **Aquarium behaviour:** Young specimens adapt better to aquarium life.

Despite the inclusion of 'xantho' (the Greek word for yellow) in the specific name, this fish is usually known as the Blue-faced Angelfish. Obviously, some people feel that a greater part of the face is coloured blue, rather than yellow. Do not allow the attractive colouring and majestic appearance of this fish to tempt you unless you are an experienced fishkeeper; it needs special care. Juveniles are dark blue with white markings.

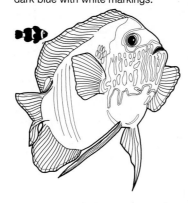

Holacanthus bermudensis (H.isabelita)

Blue Angelfish
● **Distribution:** Western Atlantic.
● **Length:** 450mm/18in (wild).
● **Diet and feeding:** Meat foods and greenstuff. Grazer.
● **Aquarium behaviour:** Aggressive when young; grows large.

When adult, these fish are blue-grey in colour with yellow tips to the dorsal and anal fins. The juveniles of this striking species can be distinguished from those of *H.ciliaris* by the straight blue vertical lines on dark blue bodies.

Above:
Euxiphipops xanthometapon
If any marine fish is capable of exhibiting sheer arrogance, then this spectacular species must be a front-running candidate. The eye is highlighted in yellow but a false eye on the dorsal fin makes an alternative, albeit false target.

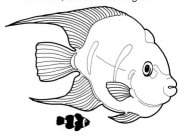

96

A practical reminder
Switch off power filters for a short time when feeding invertebrates; this will prevent their food (made by liquidizing usual aquarium foods) being extracted by the filtration system.

Above: **Holacanthus ciliaris**
When faced with this fish, who could deny its claim to be the Queen Angelfish? Young fish have royal blue vertical markings on a dark blue, gold-finned body. The body hues also appear to change under varying lighting conditions.

Left: **Holocanthus bermudensis**
This Blue Angelfish is nearly reaching full adulthood; the body stripe has yet to fade completely and in maturity the overall colour will become a delicate blue.

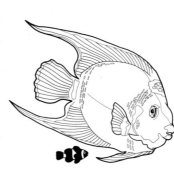

Holacanthus ciliaris
Queen Angelfish
● **Distribution:** Western Atlantic.
● **Length:** 450mm/18in (wild).
● **Diet and feeding:** Meat foods and greenstuff. Grazer.
● **Aquarium behaviour:**
Aggressive when young; grows large.

A very beautiful fish in the aquarium. Variations in colour pattern occur, but generally this species has more yellow than *H.bermudensis*. Hybrids between this species and *H.bermudensis* are classified as 'H.townsendi' but this is a non-valid name. Young specimens of *H.ciliaris* have more curving blue vertical lines on the dark blue body than the young of *H.bermudensis*.

Queen Angelfish are reported to be prone to outbreaks of white spot disease, but can be successfully treated with copper-based remedies. They are quite resistant to such treatment and may even withstand some degree of overdosing without ill effects.

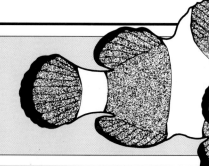

Common Clown (*Amphiprion ocellaris*)
Mature at 80mm (3.2in) and shown as a guide
to the maximum wild size of each species.

Holacanthus passer
King Angelfish
● **Distribution:** Pacific.
● **Length:** 450mm/18in (wild).
● **Diet and feeding:** Mainly greenstuff. Grazer.
● **Aquarium behaviour:** Aggressive; grows large.

The body is a dark brownish gold colour with a single vertical white stripe. The caudal fin is yellow. The dorsal and anal fins show gold patterning and edging. Young specimens have extra blue stripes on the rear of the body.

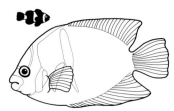

Below: **Holacanthus passer**
Only the yellow caudal fin and white stripe remain from the gold juvenile coloration. Blue stripes, previously separated, now merge.

Holacanthus (Apolemichthys) tricolor
Rock Beauty
● **Distribution:** Western Atlantic.
● **Length:** 600mm/24in (wild), 300mm/12in (aquarium).
● **Diet and feeding:** In nature, sponges. Will eat meat foods and algae but may not thrive. Grazer.
● **Aquarium behaviour:** Aggressive.

Juvenile forms of this fish are yellow with perhaps just a blue-edged dark spot on the body, but this enlarges to cover two-thirds of the body as the fish matures.

This good looking but very aggressive species will offer a challenge to the experienced fishkeeper with a spacious aquarium. Feeding can be a problem, requiring patience and care; even when they appear to be feeding well, these fishes miss their normal diet of marine sponges. If the aquarium conditions are good, however, and you feed good-quality frozen foods, then you may well achieve success with this fish.

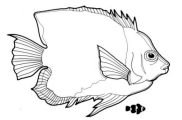

Pomacanthus (Pomacanthodes) annularis
Blue Ring Angelfish
● **Distribution:** Indo-Pacific.
● **Length:** 400mm/16in (wild), 250mm/10in (aquarium).
● **Diet and feeding:** Meat foods and greenstuff. Grazer.
● **Aquarium behaviour:** Territorial.

Blue lines run from either side of the eye diagonally across the brown body. The lines rejoin at the top of the rear portion of the body. A dominant blue ring lies behind the gill cover. Juveniles are blue with a distinctive pattern of almost straight transverse white lines.

Right: **Holacanthus tricolor**
The Rock Beauty is an extremely attractive fish. Before buying one, however, you should make sure it is eating readily; these fish feed naturally on sponges and can be hard to acclimatize to aquarium diets. Tends to be aggressive.

Below right:
Pomacanthus annularis
This head shot shows clearly how the common name of 'Blue Ring Angelfish' was inspired. Again, juveniles are blue with horizontal white markings, which turn blue and slant up more diagonally with approaching maturity.

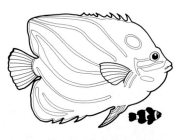

A practical reminder
Make regular use of a 'gravel-washer' to
clean the substrate. Use it when making
regular partial water changes; it will
remove substrate dirt along with a
portion of the aquarium water.

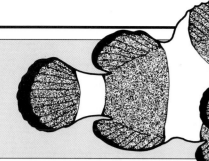

Common Clown (*Amphiprion ocellaris*)
Mature at 80mm (3.2in) and shown as a guide
to the maximum wild size of each species.

Pomacanthus imperator
Emperor Angelfish
● **Distribution:** Indo-Pacific.
● **Length:** 400mm/16in (wild),
300mm/12in (aquarium).
● **Diet and feeding:** Animal foods
and greenstuff. Grazer.
● **Aquarium behaviour:** Very
inquisitive towards new additions
to the aquarium.

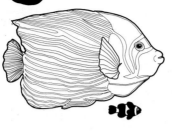

The yellow body is crossed with
diagonal blue lines. The dark blue
of the anal fin extends into a
vertical wedge behind the gill
cover. The eye is hidden in a blue-
edged dark band. The caudal fin is
yellow. Juveniles are dark blue
with white semicircular or oval
markings. Like all Angels, this
species requires the very best
water conditions possible. Many
fishkeepers have grown this
species on from juvenile to adult.

Right: **Pomacanthus imperator**
*Clearly a juvenile, with the
distinctive white markings on a
blue background. Such patterns
provide excellent disruptive
camouflage for the young fishes in
the dappled light of the coral reefs.*

Below: **Pomacanthus imperator**
*Despite the colour changes
apparent in this adult, the eye
remains hidden beneath a dark bar,
giving protection against attack.*

A practical reminder
Avoid building up coral structures too elaborately; you will find it difficult to reposition them without breaking and makes netting fish a frustrating task. Clean corals thoroughly before use.

Pomacanthus paru
French Angelfish
● **Distribution:** Western Atlantic.
● **Length:** 300mm/12in (wild).
● **Diet and feeding:** Meat foods and greenstuff. Grazer.
● **Aquarium behaviour:** Young specimens may be 'nippy', since they act as cleaner fishes.

The young fish is black with bright yellow vertical bands. The adult fish is predominantly grey with bright speckles. Juvenile members of the Atlantic Pomacanthids exhibit cleaning tendencies towards other fishes, and each Angel's territory is recognized as a cleaning station.

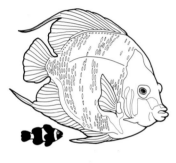

Right: **Pomacanthus paru**
This is the juvenile stage, with a pattern of yellow stripes on a black background. As the fish develops into a sub-adult (below) the stripes begin to fade and the adult coloration appears (seen fully developed at below right).

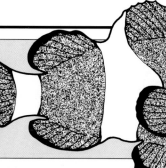

Common Clown (*Amphiprion ocellaris*)
Mature at 80mm (3.2in) and shown as a guide
to the maximum wild size of each species.

Pomacanthus semicirculatus

Koran Angelfish
● **Distribution:** Indo-Pacific, Red Sea.
● **Length:** 400mm/16in (wild), 380mm/15in (aquarium).
● **Diet and feeding:** Meat foods and greenstuff. Grazer.
● **Aquarium behaviour:** Territorial.

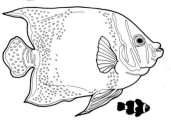

The body is golden brown with blue speckles and the fins are outlined in blue. There are vertical blue lines on the head. The white markings on the juvenile are in the shape of semicircles rather than straight lines. During the colour change to adulthood, the markings on the caudal fin often resemble Arabic characters in the Koran – hence the common name.

Right and below:
Pomacanthus semicirculatus
Like most Angelfishes, the juvenile form (right) is differently coloured to the adult. Again, the usual dark blue background is apparent and only the way in which the white markings are curved gives a clue to the species' indentity. The near-adult form (below) has almost lost the juvenile white markings.

A practical reminder
Marine algae, especially of the genus *Caulerpa*, bring welcome greenery to the marine tank and make fine substitutes for freshwater plants. Be sure to provide bright lighting.

Pygoplites diacanthus
Regal Angelfish; Royal Empress Angelfish
● **Distribution:** Indo-Pacific and Red Sea.
● **Length:** 250mm/10in (wild), 180mm/7in (aquarium).
● **Diet and feeding:** Sponges and algae in nature. In the tank, they will take frozen bloodworm, frozen *Mysis* shrimp, mussel meat, etc; even flake sometimes. Grazer.
● **Aquarium behaviour:** Shy, requires plenty of hiding places.

Dark-edged, bright orange slanting bands cross the body and extend into the dorsal and anal fins. The caudal fin is plain yellow. Feeding can be a problem, and may make it difficult to acclimatize this species to aquarium life. It requires a low nitrate level in the tank.

Specimens from the Philippines are relatively pale in colour, and consequently less desirable, and are virtually impossible to feed. Those from Sri Lanka, the Maldives and the Red Sea will eat in good water conditions and are brighter in colour. As some encouragement, one specimen of this species has grown 125mm (5in) during seven years in captivity.

Below: **Pygoplites diacanthus**
If you can keep this Regal Angelfish in the very best of conditions and provide it with just the right diet, then over a period of years it will repay you by displaying amazing colours and, indeed, a truly regal manner.

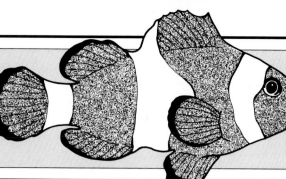

Common Clown (*Amphiprion ocellaris*)
Mature at 80mm (3.2in) and shown as a guide
to the maximum wild size of each species.

BUTTERFLYFISHES

Family characteristics
Butterflyfishes are colourful and attractive, but if they are not confident in the aquarium they will hide away from suspected dangers and provide you with little opportunity to appreciate them. Like many freshwater fishes, Butterflyfishes may undergo colour changes at night; the usual transformation is the appearance of darker splodges over parts of the body.

Diet and feeding
Feeding is of paramount importance to these mostly timid fishes, which may lose out in the rush for food. The result is that many Butterflyfishes may starve to death in a short space of time. Offer cultured worm foods (whiteworm, grindalworm, small earthworms etc.), dried foods and algae. A good alternative to worm foods – or any other terrestrial and/or freshwater aquatic live foods, which tend to stop wriggling very rapidly in sea water – are the many good-quality frozen foods available from your dealer. Live foods such as *Mysis* shrimp and brineshrimp will also be much appreciated by these elegant, if difficult, fishes.

Aquarium behaviour
Ensure that the aquarium has sufficient retreats and hideaways to give the fishes some form of security. Unfortunately, the most exotically coloured (and hence most desirable) Butterflyfishes often prove to be the most difficult to acclimatize to aquarium life. Although we feature some of these especially beautiful fishes in this section, they may prove to be expensive, shortlived disappointments in the aquarium. In this respect, many should simply be left in the sea. The tragedy is that in order to learn how to keep them successfully, so many die in the attempt.

Chaetodon (Anisochaetodon) auriga
Threadfin Butterflyfish
● **Distribution:** Indo-Pacific, Red Sea.
● **Length:** 200mm/8in (wild), 150mm/6in (aquarium).
● **Diet and feeding:** Crustaceans, coral polyps and algae in the wild. Offer suitable live and frozen foods in the aquarium. Grazer.
● **Aquarium behaviour:** Peaceful, but shy.

A black bar crosses the eye, and the mainly white flanks are decorated with a 'herring-bone' pattern of grey lines. The anal, dorsal and front part of the caudal fin are yellow, and there is a dark 'eye-spot' in the rear part of the dorsal fin. The common name refers to a threadlike extension to the dorsal fin. *C.auriga* is a hardy species that can be weaned on to food of your choice by gradual substitution.

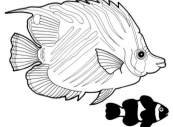

A practical reminder
Of the artificial decorations available,
moulded logs look the most natural, but
be sure that they are suitable for the
marine aquarium. Plastic plants may
have toxic supporting wires or fixings.

Left, below left: **Chaetodon auriga**
Juvenile Threadfin Butterflyfishes
do not have the long filament from
the rear of the dorsal. The eye-spot
on the dorsal fin does not fade
with adulthood in Indo-Pacific
specimens, but adults of the
subspecies C.a.auriga *from the*
Red Sea may lose it.

Below: **Chaetodon capistratus**
Colourful Butterflyfishes also
inhabit areas other than the usual
Indo-Pacific regions. This species
comes from the Caribbean.

Chaetodon capistratus
Four-eyed Butterflyfish
● **Distribution:** Western Atlantic
and Caribbean.
● **Length:** 150mm/6in (wild),
100mm/4in (aquarium).
● **Diet and feeding:** Crustaceans,
coral polyps, algae. Grazer.
● **Aquarium behaviour:** Once
settled in the aquarium it should
thrive, but it may be difficult to
acclimatize at first.

The white body has a series of
dark 'V' stripes and a false eye-
spot on each side of the caudal
peduncle. This extra pair of 'eyes'
on the rear of the body is an
excellent target for any predator;
imagine its annoyance when the
target swims rapidly away in the
opposite direction to that indicated
by the false decorations. (These,
together with the real pair of eyes,
give the fish its common name.) It
may be very difficult to accustom
this species to aquarium foods and
it may starve to death. Although
attractive, therefore, this is not
really a beginner's fish.

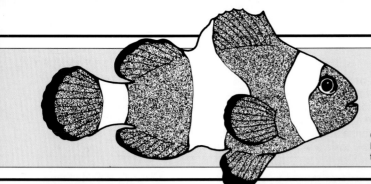

Common Clown (*Amphiprion ocellaris*)
Mature at 80mm (3.2in) and shown as a guide
to the maximum wild size of each species.

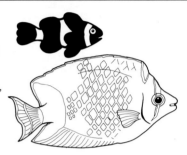

Chaetodon chrysurus
Pearlscale Butterflyfish
● **Distribution:** Indo-Pacific, Red Sea.
● **Length:** 150mm/6in (wild).
● **Diet and feeding:** Crustaceans, vegetable matter. Grazer.
● **Aquarium behaviour:** A shy species.

The scales on this species are partially dark-edged, giving the fish a lattice-covered, or checkered, pattern. The main feature is the bright orange arc connecting the rear of the dorsal and anal fins; a repeated orange band appears in the caudal fin. The fish's habitat is thought to be nearer to Africa, Mauritius and the Seychelles rather than spread widely over the Indo-Pacific area. It is rarely imported. The Red Sea variant C.chrysurus paucifasciatus has a faint spot in the dorsal fin and a slightly different shape to the orange area. *C.mertensii* and C.xanthurus are also very similar in appearance to C.chrysurus.

Left and below:
Chaetodon xanthurus
Despite having slightly different colorations, these two fishes are the same species. C.xanthurus is often confused with two other similarly marked species, but the almost identical C.chrysurus is imported less frequently; it can be distinguished by its smaller and less clearly defined scales.

Right: **Chaetodon ephippium**
The threadlike extension to the dorsal fin – typical of these fishes – can be clearly seen here, indicating a mature specimen.

Chaetodon ephippium
Saddleback Butterflyfish
● **Distribution:** Indo-Pacific.
● **Length:** 230mm/9in (wild).
● **Diet and feeding:**Crustaceans.
Grazer.
● **Aquarium behaviour:** May be
intolerant of other members of its
own, or other, species.

Easily recognizable by the white-
edged dark 'saddle' that covers
the rear upper portion of the body
and dorsal fin. The females
become plumper at breeding time.
It may be difficult to accustom
these fish to a successful aquarium
feeding pattern.

Chaetodon collare
Pakistani Butterflyfish
● **Distribution:** Indian Ocean.
● **Length:** 150mm/6in (wild),
100mm/4in (aquarium).
● **Diet and feeding:** Meat foods
and greenstuff. Grazer.
● **Aquarium behaviour:** May be
intolerant of other members of its
own, or other, species.

The brown coloration of *C. collare*
is unusual for a Butterflyfish. It is
reputed to be difficult to keep,
although not all authorities agree
on this. Species from different
locations may have different
feeding requirements, the species
from rocky outcrops being easier
to satisfy in captivity than those
from coral reefs. Not a suitable fish
for the beginner.

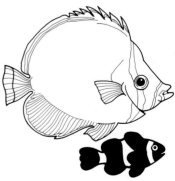

Left: **Chaetodon collare**
*From the coast of East Africa, right
across the Indian Ocean to
Melanesia, this fish is a common
sight around the coral reefs.*

107

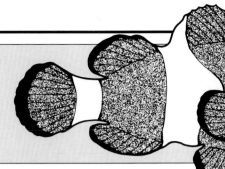

Common Clown (*Amphiprion ocellaris*)
Mature at 80mm (3.2in) and shown as a guide
to the maximum wild size of each species.

Chaetodon (Anisochaetodon) falcula

Double-saddled Butterflyfish; Pig-faced Butterflyfish

● **Distribution:** Indian Ocean.
● **Length:** 150mm/6in (wild), 100-125mm/4-5in (aquarium)
● **Diet and feeding:** Crustaceans, coral polyps, algae. Grazer.
● **Aquarium behaviour:** Aggressive towards similar species.

Two dark saddle markings cross the top of the body. The dorsal, anal and caudal fins are yellow, and there is a black spot or bar on the caudal peduncle. The body and head are white. A vertical black bar runs down the side of the head and there are many vertical thin lines on the body. This species is often confused with *C.ulietensis*, which is found across a wider area of the Pacific Ocean, and has slightly lower reaching 'saddles' and less yellow on top of the body and dorsal fin.

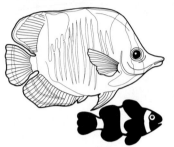

Right: **Chaetodon falcula**
The distribution of this Butterflyfish is confined to the Indian Ocean. C.ulietensis has similar markings, but is fairly easy to distinguish and is found in the wider-ranging Indo-Pacific waters.

A practical reminder
Find out the specific gravity of the water in your dealer's tanks before buying fishes so that you can adjust the initial conditions in your aquarium to suit your first introductions.

Left: **Chaetodon frembli**
The clearly visible dark spot just in front of the dorsal fin probably serves as an alternative 'eye-target' for any would-be predator. This species does not share the characteristic Butterflyfish pattern, in which the real eye is hidden in a vertical dark band.

Chaetodon frembli
Blue-striped Butterflyfish
● **Distribution:** Indo-Pacific, Red Sea.
● **Length:** 200mm/8in (wild).
● **Diet and feeding:** Crustaceans, coral polyps, algae. Grazer.
● **Aquarium behaviour:** Calm community fish.

The yellow body is marked with upward slanting diagonal blue lines. A black mark appears immediately in front of the dorsal fin, and the black of the caudal peduncle extends into the rear of the dorsal and anal fins. The caudal fin has white, black and yellow vertical bars. This Butterflyfish lacks the usual black bar through the eye. Not an easy species to keep.

Chaetodon (Anisochaetodon) kleini
Klein's Butterflyfish; Sunburst Butterflyfish
● **Distribution:** Indo-Pacific.
● **Length:** 125mm/5in (wild), 100mm/4in (aquarium).
● **Diet and feeding:** Crustaceans, coral polyps, algae. Grazer.
● **Aquarium behaviour:** Peaceful.

This is a more subtly coloured fish; its black eye bar is followed by a grey bar and the white forebody changes to a golden yellow. The dorsal and anal fins, plus the front part of the caudal fin, are a matching gold-yellow. The mouth is black. *C.kleini* is considered to be the easiest of all Butterflyfishes to keep, being hardy once it has settled into the aquarium.

Above: **Chaetodon kleini**
The obvious wide bands on this juvenile fish will fade with adulthood. Only the black bar will remain as a contrast to the sunburst colour of the body.

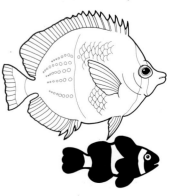

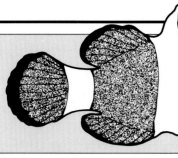

Common Clown (*Amphiprion ocellaris*)
Mature at 80mm (3.2in) and shown as a guide
to the maximum wild size of each species.

Chaetodon (Gonochaetodon) larvatus

Red-headed Butterflyfish
● **Distribution:** Red Sea.
● **Length:** 120mm/4.7in (wild).
● **Diet and feeding:** Crustaceans, coral polyps, algae. Grazer.
● **Aquarium behaviour:** Peaceful.

C.larvatus is reputed to be difficult to keep and a temperamental feeder. It has a dark brown-red head and the rear portion of body is black. The caudal fin is divided by a grey area crossed with white and yellow chevron markings.

Chaetodon lunula

Racoon Butterflyfish
● **Distribution:** Indo-Pacific.
● **Length:** 200mm/8in (wild)
● **Diet and feeding:** Crustaceans, coral polyps, algae. Grazer. Feeds well.
● **Aquarium behaviour:** Peaceful.

A white-edged black bar runs down over the eye and immediately sweeps up again into the mid-dorsal area. A white bar crosses this bar immediately behind the eye. A black blotch appears on the caudal peduncle, a feature missing in the otherwise similar species, *C.fasciatus*. *C.lunula* is fairly long-lived in the aquarium and will readily accept most foods.

Above: **Chaetodon lunula**
Juvenile forms of the Racoon Butterflyfish have an 'eye-spot' in the rear part of the dorsal fin, but this fades with age. Another difference between young and adult fishes is that the adult fish has more yellow on the snout.

Below: **Chaetodon larvatus**
If you feel that the colour of the head is not quite the shade of red you expected from the fish's popular name, but more of an orange-brown colour, then perhaps the alternative name of Hooded Butterflyfish is more apt.

A practical reminder
Always use plastic clips to fix heater-thermostats and other equipment in place. Avoid introducing any form of metal into the marine aquarium as it is likely to poison the fishes.

Chaetodon melannotus
Black-backed Butterflyfish
● **Distribution:** Indo-Pacific.
● **Length:** 150mm/6in (wild).
● **Diet and feeding:** Crustaceans, coral polyps, algae. Grazer.
● **Aquarium behaviour:** Peaceful.

The white body is crossed by diagonal thin black stripes and bordered by yellow dorsal, anal and caudal fins. A black eye bar divides the yellow head.

Chaetodon meyeri
Meyer's Butterflyfish
● **Distribution:** Indo-Pacific.
● **Length:** 150mm/6in (wild).
● **Diet and feeding:** Coral polyps. Grazer.
● **Aquarium behaviour:** May be intolerant of other members of its own, or other, species.

The striking vertical and diagonal black stripes are enclosed by the yellow border to the dorsal, anal and caudal fins. This species is extremely difficult to keep in the aquarium as it feeds mainly on polyps.

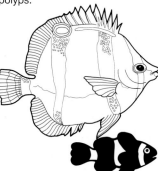

Above: **Chaetodon melannotus**
For hobbyists requiring absolute accuracy in fish descriptions, this species might be renamed the Black-sided Butterflyfish.

Below: **Chaetodon meyeri**
When young, diagonal stripes cover the whole body area behind the two vertical bars. The pattern becomes interrupted with age.

111

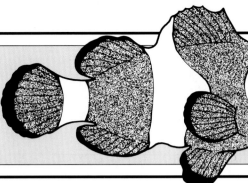

Common Clown (*Amphiprion ocellaris*)
Mature at 80mm (3.2in) and shown as a guide
to the maximum wild size of each species.

Chaetodon octofasciatus
Eight-banded Butterflyfish
● **Distribution:** Indo-Pacific.
● **Length:** 100mm/4in (wild).
● **Diet and feeding:** Coral polyps. Grazer.
● **Aquarium behaviour:** May be intolerant of other members of its own, or other, species.

The striking vertical black stripes are the main feature of this species. It is a difficult species to keep in the aquarium as its diet consists mainly of coral polyps. It may be worth trying brineshrimp.

Chaetodon ornatissimus
Ornate Coralfish
● **Distribution:** Pacific.
● **Length:** 180mm/7in (wild).
● **Diet and feeding:** Coral polyps. Grazer.
● **Aquarium behaviour:** May be intolerant of other members of its own, or other, species.

This fish is a swimming companion of *C.meyeri*. They share similar facial markings but in *C.ornatissimus* the diagonal lines are yellow. Like its companion, it can be difficult to keep because of feeding problems.

Below: **Chaetodon octofasciatus**
Try tempting this stunning, but difficult, fish with brineshrimp.

A practical reminder
Always increase the aeration rate in the treatment tank because many medications reduce the level of oxygen in the water. Vigorous aeration also helps to drive out carbon dioxide.

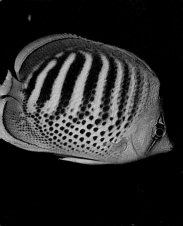

Above: **Chaetodon ornatissimus**
As in C. meyeri, *the diagonal stripes in the juvenile fish change to a more oval pattern as the fish reaches adulthood. This fish from the outer reefs ranges from the western Pacific to Hawaii, and needs plenty of swimming space.*

Left: **Chaetodon punctofasciatus**
This species' natural habitat ranges from the China Sea in the north, out to the Philippines and south as far as Australia's Great Barrier Reef. If you see it in your store, do buy it, since it is not difficult to keep, and may even obligingly take flaked foods.

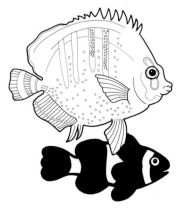

Chaetodon punctofasciatus
Spot-banded Butterflyfish
● **Distribution:** Pacific.
● **Length:** 100mm/4in (wild).
● **Diet and feeding:** Coral polyps. May accept flake foods in the aquarium. Grazer.
● **Aquarium behaviour:** May be intolerant of other members of its own, or other, species.

The vertical black stripes end halfway down the body, and turn into many spots. A black spot appears immediately in front of the dorsal fin. The eye bar is yellow with a black edge.

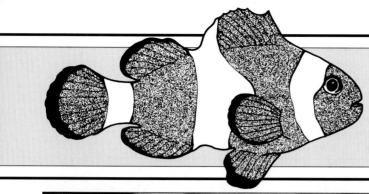

Common Clown (*Amphiprion ocellaris*)
Mature at 80mm (3.2in) and shown as a guide
to the maximum wild size of each species.

Chaetodon semilarvatus
Addis Butterflyfish
● **Distribution:** Indian Ocean, Red Sea.
● **Length:** 200mm/8in (wild).
● **Diet and feeding:** Crustaceans, coral polyps, algae. Grazer.
● **Aquarium behaviour:** May be intolerant of other members of its own, or other, species.

The yellow body is crossed by thin orange vertical lines. A blue-black inverted teardrop patch covers the eye. This species settles down readily in captivity. Specimens from the Red Sea are difficult to obtain and therefore very expensive.

Chaetodon striatus
Banded Butterflyfish
● **Distribution:** Tropical Atlantic Ocean.
● **Length:** 150mm/6in (wild).
● **Diet and feeding:** Crustaceans, coral polyps, algae. Grazer.
● **Aquarium behaviour:** May be intolerant of other members of its own, or other, species.

An easily recognizable species with four dark bands across its body. A continuous dark band passes through the outer edges of the dorsal, caudal and anal fins to connect with the ends of the third vertical band. The juvenile form has a white-ringed black spot on the soft dorsal fin. A good community fish.

Take care not to shock or otherwise stress this easily frightened fish during transportation and introduction into the aquarium.

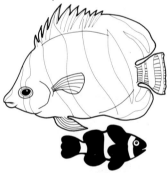

Left: **Chaetodon semilarvatus**
The bright colour and distinctive markings of this species make it a perfect photographic subject.

Above: **Chaetodon striatus**
Do the black and white stripes of the Banded Butterflyfish remind you of the freshwater Angelfish?

Below: **Chaetodon trifascialis**
This fish has a wide horizontal black band with white blotches as a fright, or night-time pattern.

Chaetodon trifascialis
Chevron Butterflyfish
● **Distribution:** Indo-Pacific, Red Sea.
● **Length:** 180mm/7in (wild).
● **Diet and feeding:** Coral polyps. Grazer.
● **Aquarium behaviour:** Aggressive.

In juveniles, the chevron-marked area of the white body is bordered by the black eye bar and a black area at the rear of the body, dorsal and anal fins. In adult fishes, the black rear area extends to cover the previously yellow caudal fin completely. These fish are almost impossible to keep due to the problem of providing a suitable diet; think twice before trying it.

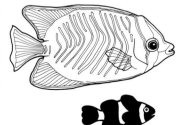

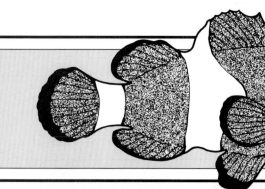

Common Clown (*Amphiprion ocellaris*)
Mature at 80mm (3.2in) and shown as a guide
to the maximum wild size of each species.

Chaetodon trifasciatus

Rainbow Butterflyfish, Redfin Butterflyfish
● **Distribution:** Indo-Pacific.
● **Length:** 150mm/6in (wild).
● **Diet and feeding:** Live coral polyps in nature. Grazer.
● **Aquarium behaviour:** Unknown.

In this species the blue-violet body is crossed with fine horizontal lines. Three crescent-shaped black bars cross the head. Variations in the colour of the front part of anal fin are said to indicate sexual differences: pink in the female, red in the male. Another difficult species to keep due to feeding problems, although juveniles seen feeding in dealers' tanks might be acclimatized with live brineshrimp, *Mysis* shrimp and/or *Tubifex*. *C.austriacus* from the Red Sea is similarly marked, but has less patterning in the anal fin.

Above: **Chaetodon trifasciatus**
Buying reasonably sized specimens of this stunningly beautiful fish is no guarantee that they will thrive in captivity; they may not adapt to aquarium foods.

Right: **Chaetodon austriacus**
The above species has a number of colour variants but this similar-looking fish is a different species altogether, being found in the Indian Ocean and the Red Sea.

A practical reminder
Avoid disturbing the substrate and tank decorations when filling the tank. To disperse the flow, direct the water carefully into a wide-mouthed jug or deep saucer standing on the substrate.

Chaetodon (Rhabdophorus) xanthocephalus

Yellowhead Butterflyfish; Goldrim Butterflyfish

● **Distribution:** Indian Ocean.
● **Length:** 200mm/8in (wild).
● **Diet and feeding:** Crustaceans, coral polyps, algae. Grazer.
● **Aquarium behaviour:** Hardy and peaceful; a good community fish. Once acclimatized, it will eat and thrive. Do not keep it with overly boisterous fishes.

This rare fish is much deeper-bodied than the other members of its Family, and it has a pronounced snout. The mouth and throat, and the dorsal and anal fins are yellow, and the thin eye bar is black. The lines on the body are bent and slightly chevron-shaped. Juveniles have more black in the dorsal and anal fins.

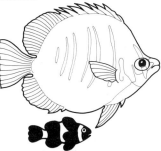

Below: **Chaetodon vagabundus**
The Vagabond Butterflyfish is a long-standing aquarium favourite, a good introduction to the Family.

Above:
Chaetodon xanthocephalus
Keep an eye open for this hardy species with a deeper body shape.

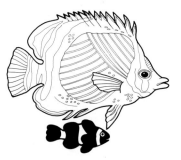

Chaetodon (Anisochaetodon) vagabundus

Vagabond Butterflyfish; Criss-cross Butterflyfish

● **Distribution:** Indo-Pacific.
● **Length:** 200mm/8in (wild).
● **Diet and feeding:** Crustaceans, coral polyps, algae. Grazer.
● **Aquarium behaviour:** Peaceful.

Diagonal lines cross the white body in two directions. Black bars cross the eye and fringe the rear part of the body. The rear part of the dorsal and anal fins are gold-yellow edged with black; the yellow caudal fin has two black vertical bars. A similar species is *C.pictus*, often classified as a subspecies or a colour variant. *C.vagabundus*, like all marines, appreciates good water conditions and regular partial water changes.

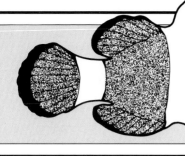

Common Clown (*Amphiprion ocellaris*)
Mature at 80mm (3.2in) and shown as a guide
to the maximum wild size of each species.

Chelmon rostratus
Copper-band Butterflyfish
● **Distribution:** Indo-Pacific, Red Sea.
● **Length:** 170mm/6.7in (wild).
● **Diet and feeding:** Frozen foods, small animal foods, algae. Picks in between coral heads.
● **Aquarium behaviour:** Aggressive towards members of its own species.

The yellow-orange vertical bands on the body have blue-black edging. These distinctive colours, coupled with the false 'eye-spot' at the rear of the upper body, make this fish difficult to confuse with any other. It may take time to acclimatize to aquarium foods but should adapt if taught by other, bolder tankmates. It is very sensitive to deteriorating water conditions in the aquarium.

Forcipiger flavissimus
Long-nosed Butterflyfish
● **Distribution:** Indo-Pacific, Red Sea.
● **Length:** 200mm/8in (wild), 100-150mm/4-6in (aquarium).
● **Diet and feeding:** Small animal foods, algae. Picks in between coral heads.
● **Aquarium behaviour:** Not as aggressive as the previous species.

The body, dorsal, anal, and pelvic fins are bright yellow, but a black triangle disrupts the contours of the head. The lower jaw is white, and the caudal fin is clear. A false 'eye spot' on the anal fin confuses predators. It is similar in its aquarium requirements and treatment to *C.rostratus*. The Big Long-nosed Butterflyfish (*F.longirostris*) is a similar species with a proportionately longer snout, although overall it is shorter than *F.flavissimus*. It is less frequently imported.

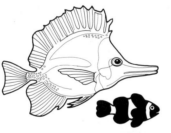

Above: **Chelmon rostratus**
The outstanding colours and attractive and slightly unusual shape of the Copper-band Butterflyfish should be all the inducement you need to keep it in the best aquarium conditions.

Below: **Forcipiger flavissimus**
If the Copper-band Butterflyfish needed a rival in picking out food from among the crevices in the coral, then this fish would be a good candidate. Note how the black triangle camouflages the eye.

A practical reminder
Reduce the pressure of water returning
from power filters by using a spray bar
to disperse the water across the surface
of the aquarium. Make sure that all hose
connections are securely fixed in place.

Above: **Heniochus acuminatus**
*The Wimplefish, with its long
trailing extension to the dorsal fin,
is often confused with the Moorish
Idol* (Zanclus sp.). *However, it
lacks the extraordinary facial
markings of that species. The plain
yellow dorsal and caudal fins are
other very useful features that help
to distinguish this fish.*

Left: **Forcipiger longirostris**
This species of Forcipiger *is at a
natural advantage over similar
long-snouted fishes when it comes
to searching for food; with its
much longer snout it is able to
probe into parts of the coral
inaccessible to other fishes.*

Heniochus acuminatus

*Wimplefish, Pennant Coralfish,
Poor Man's Moorish Idol*
● **Distribution:** Indo-Pacific,
Red Sea.
● **Length:** 180mm/7in (wild).
● **Diet and feeding:** Meat foods
and greenstuff. Grazer.
● **Aquarium behaviour:**
Companionable.

Two wide, forward-sloping black
bands cross the white body. The
rear parts of the dorsal, pectoral
and anal fins are yellow while the
pelvic fins are black. The front few
rays of the dorsal fin are much
extended. Young specimens act as
cleanerfishes and all these fish
appreciate plenty of swimming
room. Other species, such as the
Horned Coralfish (*H.chrysostomus*
or *H.permutatus*) are rarely
imported. While *H. acuminatus*
varies little in juvenile and adult
coloration, other species in the
genus do differ; some adults
develop protuberances on the
forehead.
  Heniochus is easier to keep than
the lookalike *Zanclus*. It is a
shoaling fish, but the natural leader
in a group in captivity may well
develop into a bully.

Common Clown (*Amphiprion ocellaris*)
Mature at 80mm (3.2in) and shown as a guide
to the maximum wild size of each species.

Family. CIRRHITIDAE
Hawkfishes

Family chacteristics
Despite their attractive appearance and friendliness, Hawkfishes are predators – albeit of small prey. They rest or 'perch' on a piece of coral and wait for food to pass by, at which point they dash out and seize it. Reproduction in these fishes is by demersal eggs, i.e. the eggs are laid and fertilized on a firm surface, where they subsequently hatch.

Diet and feeding
In the wild, these fishes will take small invertebrates – shrimps, etc. – and smaller fishes. In the aquarium, provide live foods and suitable meaty frozen foods.

Aquarium behaviour
Hawkfishes will appreciate plenty of 'perching places' in the aquarium. Despite their predatory nature, they appear not to harm sedentary invertebrates such as tubeworms, soft corals, etc.

Oxycirrhites typus
Longnosed Hawkfish
● **Distribution:** Indian Ocean mainly.
● **Length:** 100mm/4in (wild).
● **Diet and feeding:** Meat foods. Sits on a rock or coral, then dashes out to grab food.
● **Aquarium behaviour:** Peaceful. Does well in small groups.

The elongate body of this hardy fish is covered with a squared pattern of bright red lines. The snout is very long and suited to probing the coral crevices for food. There are small cirri, or crestlike growths, at the end of each dorsal fin ray and on the nostrils. The female is larger than the male and the male has darker red lower jaws. There are black edges to both the pelvic and caudal fins.

In nature, spawnings occur from dusk onwards. Reports of aquarium 'spawnings' suggest that the female lays patches of adhesive eggs after courtship activity.

Below: **Oxycirrhites typus**
The Longnosed Hawkfish cannot depend on its natural colouring for camouflage, as it perches on coral outcrops waiting to pounce on its next unsuspecting meal.

A practical reminder
Remove uneaten food once the fishes lose interest in it, otherwise it will begin to pollute the water. You should, in any case, feed most fishes only a little at a time, but at regular intervals.

Family: DIODONTIDAE

Porcupinefishes

Family characteristics
Porcupinefishes are very similar to the other 'inflatable' fishes, the Puffers. They can be distinguished from the Pufferfishes, however, by the spines on their scales and by their front teeth, which are fused together. Hard crustacean foods present little problem to them. The pelvic fins are absent. Normally the spines are held flat, but in times of danger they stand out from the body as the fish inflates itself. Their appearance and inflatability make them interesting subjects for the aquarium.

Diet and feeding
Earthworms, shrimps, crab meat and other meaty foods can be given, but cut food into pieces for smaller specimens. Young fish, such as livebearing fry, are also accepted.

Aquarium behaviour
Although they grow very large in the wild, Porcupinefishes rarely grow as big in captivity. Nevertheless, be sure to keep them alone in a large aquarium. You may find that specimens measuring 125-180mm/5-7in appear to recognize the fishkeeper.

Chilomycterus schoepfi
Spiny Boxfish; Striped Burrfish; Burrfish
● **Distribution:** Tropical Atlantic, Caribbean.
● **Length:** 300mm/12in (wild).
● **Diet and feeding:** Crustaceans, molluscs, meat foods. Bold.
● **Aquarium behaviour:** Aggressive among themselves. Do not keep them with small fishes.

The undulating dark lines on its yellow body provide *C.schoepfi* with excellent camouflage, and a first line of defence; then the short spines – fixed and usually held erect – may be called upon to play their part. Not as liable to inflate itself as other species. Importations of this fish are rare.

Diodon hystrix
Common Porcupinefish; Porcupine Puffer
● **Distribution:** All warm seas.
● **Length:** 900mm/36in (wild), considerably smaller in the aquarium.
● **Diet and feeding:** Crustaceans, molluscs, meat foods. Bold.
● **Aquarium behaviour:** Generally peaceful with other fishes.

This species has longer spines held more flatly against the body. They are not constantly active, remaining at rest for long periods until hunger or some other action-provoking event stirs them. Keep the tank efficiently filtered to cope with these fishes that can sometimes prove 'messy eaters'.

Top: **Chilomycterus schoepfi**
The short spines of this species are kept erect, a constant defence against predation or capture.

Above: **Diodon hystrix**
Despite its formidable adult size, the Common Porcupinefish poses little threat to smaller fishes.

Diodon holacanthus
Long-spined Porcupinefish
● **Distribution:** All warm seas.
● **Length:** 500mm/20in (wild), 150mm/6in (aquarium).
● **Diet and feeding:** Crustaceans, molluscs, meat foods. Bold.
● **Aquarium behaviour:** Do not keep with small fishes.

The colour patterning on this species is blotched rather than lined, but it serves the same excellent purpose – to disguise the fish as part of the surrounding underwater scenery.

Right: **Diodon holacanthus**
The Long-spined Porcupinefish is one of the most commonly found species, being native worldwide. It feeds on crustaceans, using its powerful front teeth, so do not include it in a tank containing invertebrates.

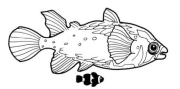

Common Clown (*Amphiprion ocellaris*)
Mature at 80mm (3.2in) and shown as a guide
to the maximum wild size of each species.

Family: GOBIIDAE
Gobies

Family characteristics

Comparatively little is known about this very large Family, which – paradoxically – contains one of the smallest vertebrates (*Pandaka* sp). In the wild, Gobies are found in several different locations: tidal shallow beaches; on the coral reef itself; and on the muddy seabed. Some species are found in fresh water. All rely on having a secure bolthole in which to hide when danger threatens. Such 'boltholes' may be located within sponges, caves, crevices or simply burrows in the seabed.

The Gobies are endearing little characters for the aquarium. Unlike the Blennies, the colours of the Gobies can be quite brilliant. Their bodies are elongate, the head blunt with high-set eyes. Gobies can be further distinguished from Blennies, with whom they share a similar habitat, by the presence of a 'suction-disc' formed by the fusion of the pelvic fins.

Sexing Gobies is difficult, although females may become distended with eggs at breeding time and there are the typical differences in the size and shape of the genital papillae – if you can see them! (The genital papillae are breeding tubes that extend from the vent of each fish; usually longer in females than in males.) In some species, the male may change colour or develop longer fins during the breeding period. Spawning occurs in burrows or in sheltered areas, with the eggs being guarded by the male. Several Gobies have been spawned in captivity. *Gobiosoma oceanops* and *Lythrypnus dalli*, for example, will breed willingly in the aquarium, but rearing the young fry is not easy. The young of *G.oceanops* have been reared with more success than the smaller fry of *L.dalli*.

Diet and feeding

Gobies are carnivorous bottom-dwelling fishes that will eat brineshrimp, finely chopped meat foods, dried foods and *Daphnia* in the aquarium.

Aquarium behaviour

Many reef-dwelling species provide cleaning services for larger fishes, the cleaning sequence following the pattern described for the Cleaner Wrasse (see page 130).

Gobiosoma oceanops
Neon Goby
● **Distribution:** Western Atlantic, especially Florida, and the Gulf of Mexico.
● **Length:** 60mm/2.4in (wild), 25mm/1in (aquarium)
● **Diet and feeding:** Parasites, small crustaceans and plankton. Bold nibbler; bottom feeder.
● **Aquarium behaviour:** Peaceful and uninhibited.

Two characteristics distinguish this most familiar Goby: the electric blue coloration of the longitudinal line on the body and the cleaning services it offers to other fishes. The species can be positively identified by the gap visible between the two blue lines on the snout when the fish is seen from above; other species have connected lines or other markings between the ends of the lines.

G.oceanops has been bred in the aquarium. Pairing occurs spontaneously, and if you intend breeding the fishes try to buy any 'pairs' of fishes seen to be keeping close company with each other. Before spawning, the male's colour darkens and he courts the female with exaggerated swimming motions, assuming a position on the aquarium floor until the female takes notice of him. Spawning activity occurs in a cave or other similar sheltered area – an upright plastic tube stuck in the aquarium floor is often more than acceptable. The fertilized eggs hatch after 7-12 days. In the wild, the fry feed on planktonic foods for the first few weeks. In the aquarium, start the fry off with liquid fry foods, cultured rotifers and newly hatched brineshrimp. After three to four months, the young fish will pair off themselves, even though they will not spawn for another few months.

Unfortunately, these eminently suitable (and practicable) aquarium subjects are relatively shortlived – perhaps only a year, but their breeding possibilities should enable you to continue the species without too much trouble.

Lythrypnus dalli
Blue-banded Goby; Catalina Goby
● **Distribution:** Californian Pacific coast.
● **Length:** 60mm/2.4in (wild), 25mm/1in (aquarium).
● **Diet and feeding:** Small crustaceans and other small marine organisms. Bottom feeder.
● **Aquarium behaviour:** Peaceful with small fishes.

The red body is crossed by brilliant blue vertical lines and the first dorsal fin has an elongated ray. The male has longer dorsal fin spines than the female. Several fish will share even a reasonably small aquarium quite happily, but they are not naturally a longlived species. This species does not require the same high water temperatures as other marine fish; do not exceed a maximum of 22°C(72°F). This fish has been bred successfully in the aquarium; the fry are much smaller than those of the Neon Goby.

Left: **Gobiosoma oceanops**
The brilliantly coloured Neon Goby has much in its favour as a subject for the marine aquarium. Its tank need not be too large, and the fish will spawn quite readily.

A practical reminder
Remember that many marine fishes are herbivorous and welcome green matter in their diet. This is another reason for the bright lighting; it encourages lush growths of algae for fishes to feed on.

Above: **Lythrypnus dalli**
A number of Blue-banded Gobies could share a reasonably sized tank without too much quarrelling.

Left: **Nemateleotris splendida**
Also known as a 'hovering' Goby, the Firefish never ventures too far from the safety of its bolthole.

Nemateleotris splendida
Firefish
● **Distribution:** Indo-Pacific.
● **Length:** 60mm/2.4in (wild).
● **Diet and feeding:** Small crustaceans, plankton and other small live foods. Bottom feeder.
● **Aquarium behaviour:** Peaceful once established.

This beautifully coloured fish makes a burrow in the substrate and only when it has organized this bolthole will it settle down in the aquarium. The blue, green and yellow on the body gradually give way to a magnificent fiery red on the rear of the body and on the dorsal, anal and caudal fins. The first dorsal fin is much elongated.

123

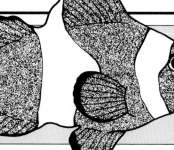

Common Clown (*Amphiprion ocellaris*)
Mature at 80mm (3.2in) and shown as a guide
to the maximum wild size of each species.

Family: HOLOCENTRIDAE
Squirrelfishes

Family characteristics
Squirrelfishes are large-eyed nocturnal fishes that hide by day
among crevices in the coral reefs of the Indo-Pacific and Atlantic
Oceans. They usually have red patterning on their elongate bodies,
spines on the gill covers and sharp rays on the fins. The dorsal fin
looks as if it has two separate parts: a long-based spiny part at the
front and a high triangular softer rayed section at the back.

Diet and feeding
In the aquarium, they rapidly adjust to a daytime eating routine and
a diet consisting of chopped worm foods and small fish.

Aquarium behaviour
Squirrelfishes are very active and need a sufficiently large
aquarium to accommodate their energetic way of life. Remember
that small fishes may not welcome such boisterous companions.

Holocentrus (Adioryx) diadema
Common Squirrelfish
● **Distribution:** Indo-Pacific.
● **Length:** 300m/12in (wild).
● **Diet and feeding:** All foods.
Bold.
● **Aquarium behaviour:** Do not
keep with small fishes.

Horizontal red lines and a red
dorsal fin make this common fish a
very colourful addition to any
sufficiently large aquarium. In
nature, it is a nocturnal species
and therefore needs some hiding
places in which to rest during the
day. It does adapt to aquarium life,
however, and will swim around in
daylight hours.

Below: **Holocentrus diadema**
*In the wild, these strikingly
attractive fishes swim in large
shoals among the coral reefs. Their
relatively large size and constant
activity render them less suited to
an aquarium of modest
proportions. However, if you can
provide adequate swimming space
and plenty of companions, the
Common Squirrelfish will prove a
worthwhile addition to the tank.*

A practical reminder
Always use non-metallic (non-toxic)
containers when making up synthetic
sea water. Similarly, you should use
plastic containers to store sea water for
future partial water changes.

Holocentrus rufus
White-tip Squirrelfish
● **Distribution:** Western Atlantic.
● **Length:** 200mm/8in (wild).
● **Diet and feeding:** Crustaceans
and meaty foods. Bold.
● **Aquarium behaviour:** Shoaling
fish for a large aquarium.

Holocentrus rufus is a similar
colour to other Squirrelfishes, but it
has a white triangular mark on
each dorsal fin ray.

Right: **Holocentrus rufus**
*A feature of this species is the long
rear part of the dorsal fin; the
upper part of the caudal fin is
larger than the lower. Reasonably
fearless, predatory Squirrelfishes
can hold their own with Grunts and
even Moray Eels; they will meet
any attempts to threaten their
territorial safety with grunting
noises and quivering actions.*

Left: **Myripristis murdjan**
*The Big-eye Squirrelfish clearly
lives up to its popular name! The
organs in question are used to
good advantage at night, when the
fish is active. It lacks the spine on
the rear of the gill cover that is
carried by members of the genus
Holocentrus. Although peaceful,
do not be tempted to include
smaller fishes in their tank.*

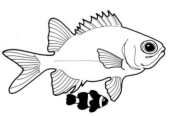

Myripristis murdjan
Big-eye Squirrelfish; Blotcheye
● **Distribution:** Indo-Pacific.
● **Length:** 300mm/12in (wild).
● **Diet and feeding:** Crustaceans
and meaty foods. Bold.
● **Aquarium behaviour:** Peaceful.

The red edge on each scale gives
this fish a reticulated appearance.
There is a dark red vertical area
immediately behind the gill cover.

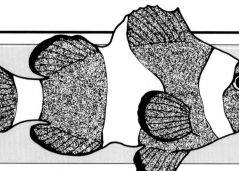

Common Clown (*Amphiprion ocellaris*)
Mature at 80mm (3.2in) and shown as a guide
to the maximum wild size of each species.

Family: LABRIDAE
Wrasses and Rainbowfishes

Family characteristics
The Labridae is a very large Family, encompassing about 400 species. It is not surprising, therefore, that the body shape varies; some Wrasses are cylindrical, while others are much deeper bodied. Like many other marine fishes, Wrasses swim without making much use of the caudal fin, which is mainly used for steering or held in reserve for emergencies. The main propulsion comes from the pectoral fins.

Sex reversal is quite common in Wrasses, the necessary change occurring in single-sexed groups as required. Reproductive activity can occur between pairs or collectively in groups. In both cases, the fishes spiral upwards towards the surface to spawn. Occasionally, this activity is based around a preselected territory. Coastal species take advantage of the outgoing tide to sweep the fertilized eggs away from the reef to safety. Species from temperate zones in Europe and the Mediterranean build spawning nests of algae or sand.

Diet and feeding
Feeding habits vary from species to species, but most relish molluscs and crustaceans. They will take brineshrimps, shrimps, earthworms and also green foods.

Aquarium behaviour
Juvenile forms are quite suitable for the aquarium. Wrasses and Rainbowfishes are interesting for several reasons: the juvenile coloration patterns are different from those of adult fishes; many bury themselves at night, or spin mucus cocoons in which to rest; and a number of fishes perform 'cleaning services' on other species, removing parasites in the process. Fishes in this group are usually quite active and therefore may disturb more sedate fishes in the aquarium.

Bodianus pulchellus
Cuban Hogfish
- **Distribution:** Western Atlantic.
- **Length:** 250mm/10in (wild), 150mm/6in (aquarium)
- **Diet and feeding:** Crustaceans, shellfish meat. Bold bottom feeder.
- **Aquarium behaviour:** Generally peaceful although small fishes in the aquarium may not be entirely safe.

The front of the body is red, divided by a white horizontal band; the upper part of the back is bright yellow. There is a black spot at the end of the pectoral fins. Juveniles are yellow with a dark spot on the front of the dorsal fin, a colour scheme similar to that of the juvenile form of *Thalassoma bifasciatum* (see page 132). It is likely that both these species have evolved similar markings to signal their cleaning services. Usually it is quite easy to acclimatize these fishes to aquarium foods.

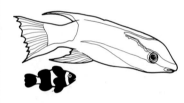

Bodianus rufus
Spanish Hogfish
- **Distribution:** Western Atlantic.
- **Length:** 600mm/24in (wild), 200mm/8in (aquarium)
- **Diet and feeding:** Crustaceans, shellfish meat. Bold bottom feeder.
- **Aquarium behaviour:** Peaceful.

Juvenile specimens are yellow with an area of blue along the upper body. Adult fishes show the standard red and yellow coloration, although the proportions may vary according to the habitat and depth of water. Like other members of the genus, juveniles perform cleaning actions on other fishes.

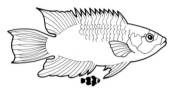

Coris angulata
Twin-spot Wrasse
- **Distribution:** Indo-Pacific, Red Sea.
- **Length:** 1200mm/48in (wild), 200-300mm/8-12in (aquarium).
- **Diet and feeding:** Small marine animals, live foods. Bottom feeder.
- **Aquarium behaviour:** Peaceful but grows very quickly.

A spectacularly coloured species, both as a juvenile and as an adult. When young, this fish is white with two prominent orange spots on the dorsal surface (hence the above common name). The front of the body, together with the fins, is covered with dark spots and there are two white-edged black blotches on the dorsal fin. The adult fish is green with yellow-edged purple fins.

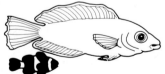

Left: **Bodianus pulchellus**
This smart Cuban Hogfish from the western Atlantic is easy to acclimatize to aquarium life.

Above right: **Bodianus rufus**
A brightly coloured juvenile specimen of this wrasse from the Caribbean. A peaceful fish.

Right: **Coris angulata**
The adult Twin-spot Wrasse not only loses the two spots seen in this juvenile, but also outgrows the domestically sized aquarium.

A practical reminder
You can lessen the risk of disease in the
aquarium by using only the highest
quality foods from reliable sources.
Gamma-irradiated foods are safe, fish
from the local fishmongers may not be.

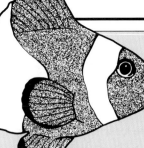

Common Clown (*Amphiprion ocellaris*)
Mature at 80mm (3.2in) and shown as a guide
to the maximum wild size of each species.

Coris formosa
African Clown Wrasse
● **Distribution:** Indian Ocean.
● **Length:** 300mm/12in (wild),
200mm/8in (aquarium).
● **Diet and feeding:** Small marine
animals, live foods. Bottom feeder.
● **Aquarium behaviour:** Peaceful
but grows large.

The juvenile fish is dark brown with
a thick vertical white band crossing
the body and dorsal fin just behind
the gill cover. Two shorter bands
cross the head and two more
appear on the rear of the dorsal fin
and caudal peduncle. The caudal
fin is white. In the adult, the head
and body are green-brown and
two green-blue stripes run in front
of and behind the gill cover. The
dorsal fin is red with an elongated
first ray, the anal fin is green and
purple, and the caudal fin is red,
bordered with white.

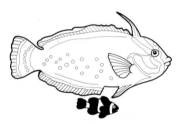

Above right: **Coris formosa**
*The African Clown Wrasse
eventually loses the juvenile white
markings shown here. The adult's
dorsal fin has an extended first ray.*

Below: **Coris gaimardi**
*The first colour stage of the Clown
Wrasse is orange, with similar, but
less extensive, white markings on
the body than the above species.*

Above opposite: *As the Clown
Wrasse matures, the orange body
of the juvenile fades, accompanied
by darkening of the fins, head, and
edges of the white markings.*

Below opposite: *Here, the final
adult colours are established. The
blue facial markings and spotted
body bear little resemblance to the
appearance of the young fish.*

A practical reminder
Marine fishes are very susceptible to shock. Equalize temperatures in the transportation bag and tank and release the fishes into the aquarium under dim lighting conditions, if possible.

Coris gaimardi
Clown Wrasse; Red Labrid
● **Distribution:** Indo-Pacific.
● **Length:** 300mm/12in (wild), 150mm/6in (aquarium).
● **Diet and feeding:** Crustaceans, shellfish meat. Bold bottom feeder.
● **Aquarium behaviour:** May quarrel among themselves.

Juveniles are similar to *C.formosa* but are orange rather than brown; the middle white band does not extend right down the body and the dorsal fin lacks a spot. Adults are brown-violet with many blue spots. The dorsal and anal fins are red, the caudal fin is yellow. There are blue markings on the face. These can be nervous fishes that dash about when first introduced into the aquarium, so try not to shock them.

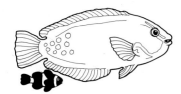

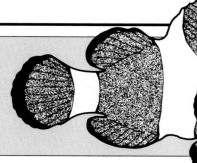

Common Clown (*Amphiprion ocellaris*)
Mature at 80mm (3.2in) and shown as a guide
to the maximum wild size of each species.

Gomphosus coeruleus
Birdmouth Wrasse
- **Distribution:** Indo-Pacific.
- **Length:** 250mm/10in (wild).
- **Diet and feeding:** Small animal life gathered from coral crevices. In the aquarium, they will take brineshrimp, *Mysis* shrimp, krill and chopped fish meats, plus some green foods. Grazer.
- **Aquarium behaviour:** Peaceful.

The body in adult males is blue-green; younger males, and females, are brown. The snout is elongated. A very active fish that is constantly on the move around the aquarium. This species looks and swims like a dolphin. Young fishes act as cleaners.

Labroides dimidiatus
Cleaner Wrasse
- **Distribution:** Indo-Pacific.
- **Length:** 100mm/4in (wild).
- **Diet and feeding:** Skin parasites of other fishes in the wild; in captivity, finely chopped meat foods make an excellent substitute. Bold.
- **Aquarium behaviour:** Peaceful.

This is the most familiar of the Wrasses because of its cleaning activities. This cleaning process, also practised by some Gobies and Cleaner Shrimps, is almost ritualistic. When approached by a Cleaner Wrasse, the subject fish – or host – often remains stationary with fins spread, in a head-up or head-down attitude. Sometimes the colours of the host fish fade, maybe so that the Cleaner Wrasse can see any parasites more clearly. The elongate blue body of the Cleaner Wrasse has a horizontal dark stripe from snout to caudal fin. The mouth is terminal, and it is this feature that distinguishes *L.dimidiatus* from the predatory lookalike *Aspidontus taeniatus*, the so-called False Cleanerfish.

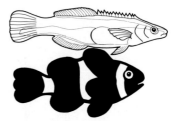

Below: **Gomphosus coeruleus**
The Birdmouth Wrasse is a very active species, always on the move around the aquarium. Generally, it is very peaceful, and minds its own business, but its constant movement may annoy more leisurely or smaller species.

Right: **Labroides dimidiatus**
One of the true assets to the marine aquarium, the Cleanerfish provides a service much appreciated by the other inmates of the tank. Be sure that the fish you introduce is the true Cleanerfish; look for the mouth at the extreme tip of the snout: an underslung mouth indicates the False Cleanerfish, (Aspidontus taeniatus), which will bite instead of clean its host.

Below opposite: *Here, a beautiful Butterflyfish (Chaetodon trifasciatus) is taking advantage of the Cleanerfish's services. Many fishes make a point of visiting the territory of the Cleanerfish, literally a 'cleaning station'. They wait their turn to have parasites removed from their skin, gills or even mouth, advertising their willingness to be cleaned by adopting a motionless head-up or head-down attitude.*

A practical reminder
Reject any fishes which are too thin,
have obvious physical faults or will not
feed. Not all marine fishes swim with
erect fins and so clamped fins are not
necessarily a sign of ill health.

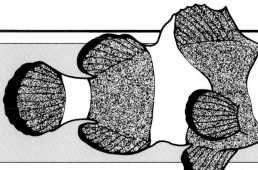

Common Clown (*Amphiprion ocellaris*)
Mature at 80mm (3.2in) and shown as a guide
to the maximum wild size of each species.

Novaculichthys taeniurus

Reindeer Wrasse
- **Distribution:** Indo-Pacific.
- **Length:** 30mm/1.2in (wild).
- **Diet and feeding:** Crustaceans, meaty foods. Bottom feeder.
- **Aquarium behaviour:** Peaceful.

The blotchy green coloration and elongated first rays of the dorsal fin are features of the juvenile; adult fishes are brown with marks radiating from the eye; these fade as the fish grows older. Because this fish is so small, be sure to keep it with similarly sized or non-predatory tankmates.

Right: **Novaculichthys taeniurus**
Keep this Wrasse in a species tank or with equal-sized tankmates.

Below: **Thalassoma bifasciatum**
Only dominant males of the species have the blue head.

Thalassoma bifasciatum

Bluehead (Juveniles are known as Banana Wrasse)
- **Distribution:** Caribbean.
- **Length:** 140mm/5.5in (wild).
- **Diet and feeding:** Crustaceans, meaty foods. Bottom feeder. Most specimens have a very healthy appetite but may need weaning off live brineshrimp on to other, more convenient, meaty foods.
- **Aquarium behaviour:** Peaceful.

This fish undergoes remarkable colour changes: juveniles are yellow (the shallow water types are white) with a dark spot on the front of the dorsal fin and/or a dark horizontal stripe along the body. Dominant males then develop the characteristic blue head and green body separated by contrasting black and white bands.

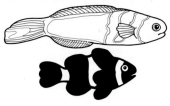

Thalassoma lunare

Moon Wrasse; Lyretail Wrasse;
Green Parrot Wrasse

● **Distribution:** Indo-Pacific,
Red Sea.
● **Length:** 330mm/13in (wild).
● **Diet and feeding:** All meaty
foods. Greedy bottom feeder.
● **Aquarium behaviour:** Active all
day, then sleeps deeply at night.
Its constant daytime movement
may disturb smaller fishes and it
may attack new additions to the
tank, regardless of their size.
Needs plenty of room.

Adult specimens lose the dark
blotches of the juvenile and are
bright green with red and blue
patterns on the head. The centre of
the caudal fin is bright yellow.

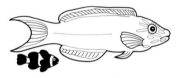

Right: **Thalassoma lunare**
The radiating facial patterns
around the eye of this adult Moon
Wrasse are a feature of its adult
coloration; many species share
this striking characteristic.

Below: **Thalassoma lunare**
A Moon Wrasse in adult colours. A
distinguishing feature of this
species is the bright yellow central
section to the caudal fin.

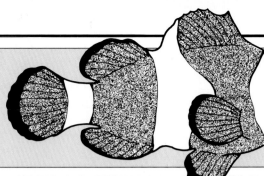

Common Clown (*Amphiprion ocellaris*)
Mature at 80mm (3.2in) and shown as a guide
to the maximum wild size of each species.

Filefishes

Family characteristics
Filefishes, like the Triggerfishes to whom they are related (and with whom they are classified by some authorites), have two dorsal fins, the first being a rudimentary spine which can be locked into position. The ventral fins are reduced to a single spine. The skin is rough in texture, which has given rise to the fishes' alternative common name of Leatherjackets.

Diet and feeding
In the wild, these fishes use their tiny mouths to feed mainly on polyps and algae. This may cause initial problems in the aquarium until they can be persuaded to accept alternative foods.

Aquarium behaviour
Despite their scientific similarity to Triggerfishes, Filefishes are generally smaller, less active and – once acclimatized and feeding well – make good additions to the aquarium community.

Oxymonocanthus longirostris
Long-nosed Filefish; Orange-green Filefish; Beaked Leatherjacket
● **Distribution:** Indo-Pacific.
● **Length:** 100mm/4in (wild).
● **Diet and feeding:** Polyps and algae in the wild; animal foods such as crustaceans and shellfish meat in captivity. Grazer.
● **Aquarium behaviour:** Shy; best kept in groups of two or more with non-boisterous fishes, or in a species aquarium.

The body is bright green with orange spots, and this pattern continues into the caudal fin. The dorsal and anal fins are yellow. The orange eyes have radial patterning and the snout is also orange. The green and orange first dorsal fin is held erect. The male has orange in the fins, and a black-edged red ventral flap of skin that joins the body to the rudimentary ventral fins. Females have colourless fins and a black-edged grey ventral flap.

Below:
Oxymonocanthus longirostris
The head-standing attitude of this fish is quite normal behaviour.

A practical reminder
Some fishes are difficult to acclimatize to aquarium diets. Be guided by your dealer and don't be tempted by very exotic species – they may be a bad investment if they simply won't feed.

Family: MONOCENTRIDAE

Pine-cone Fishes

Family characteristics

This small Family contains some interesting fishes known to have existed millions of years ago. Their bodies are enclosed in the rigid covering of a few large scales fused together. They are deepwater fishes and it is thought that they use their light-generating organs to attract prey. These fishes are only occasionally available through dealers and therefore command a high price.

Diet and feeding

Because of their deepwater origins, little is known of their natural diet. It probably consists mainly of small marine animals attracted to them by their light-generating organs. In the aquarium, offer live foods and then try to wean them on to other suitable foods.

Aquarium behaviour

You may find it advisable to keep these fishes in a species tank so that you can study them more closely.

Monocentrus japonicus

Pine-cone Fish
● **Distribution:** Indo-Pacific.
● **Length:** 160mm/6.3in (wild), 100-150mm/4-6in (aquarium).
● **Diet and feeding:** Provide chopped white fish meat or shellfish meat, such as boiled mussel. Also supply frozen meaty foods.
● **Aquarium behaviour:** Keep in a dimly lit species aquarium.

The head forms about one third of the body size. The large brass-coloured scales have dark edges and spiny centres. Spiny dorsal rays alternate from left to right. The pelvic fins are restricted to strong spines. Does not thrive if kept at temperatures above 23°C(74°F) for long periods.

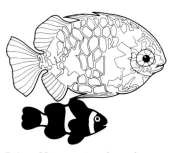

Below: **Monocentrus japonicus**
The Pine-cone Fish, one of the more unusual fishes for the aquarium, can boast an ancestry going back some millions of years. Although not commonly encountered in retail outlets, it is worth considering if you are looking for something different for the marine aquarium.

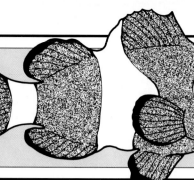

Common Clown (*Amphiprion ocellaris*)
Mature at 80mm (3.2in) and shown as a guide
to the maximum wild size of each species.

Family: MONODACTYLIDAE
Fingerfishes

Family characteristics
These silver rhomboidal fishes are reminiscent of the freshwater
Angelfishes. They are found in coastal waters, particularly
estuaries, often entering brackish or even fresh water. Although
young specimens will thrive in slightly brackish water, they do even
better in full strength salt water. Along with *Scatophagus* spp, they
are scavengers, frequently found in dirty waters, where they
appear to thrive in the conditions!

Diet and feeding
These fishes will eat any foods, including *Tubifex* worms.

Aquarium behaviour
Fast-moving shoaling fishes that may reach up to 150mm(6in) long
in captivity.

Below: **Monodactylus argenteus**
*Although young specimens may be
kept successfully in freshwater or
brackish water tanks, as it grows,
the Fingerfish really thrives in full-
strength sea water. In common
with its relative, the similar but less
widely seen Striped Fingerfish
(M.sebae), this is an active
shoaling species that needs plenty
of swimming space in the
aquarium to really feel at home.*

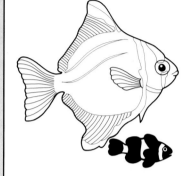

Monodactylus argenteus
*Fingerfish; Malayan Angel;
Silver Batfish*
● **Distribution:** Indo-Pacific.
● **Length:** 230mm/9in (wild).
● **Diet and feeding:** Will eat
anything. Bold scavenger.
● **Aquarium behaviour:** Peaceful
but constantly active.

One or two black bars cross the
front part of the silver body and the
fins are yellow. The pelvic fins are
rudimentary. These fishes are very
fast swimmers when disturbed,
and can be difficult to catch in the
aquarium.

Monodactylus sebae
Striped Fingerfish
● **Distribution:** Eastern Atlantic,
West African coast.
● **Length:** 200mm/8in (wild).
● **Diet and feeding:** Will eat
anything. Bold scavenger
● **Aquarium behaviour:** Peaceful,
but restless.

Monodactylus sebae is slightly
darker than the previous species
and the body is much taller. Two
additional dark vertical stripes
cross the body, one connecting
the tips of the dorsal and anal fins,
the other crossing the extreme end
of the caudal peduncle. The pelvic
fins are rudimentary. They appear
to be less hardy than the more
commonly kept species.

A practical reminder
Marine fishes will often accept aquatic
livefoods as used in the freshwater
aquarium, but remember that such food
may not live as long in sea water.
Livebearer fry may survive longer.

Family: MURAENIDAE
Moray Eels

The tropical eels are often splendidly marked and all grow very
long. Many are nocturnal and are hardly seen during the day, since
they hide among caves and crevices. They detect their food by
smell and are usually quite undemanding in captivity, providing
that they have sufficient room, refuges and food. Keeping them in
the company of small 'bite-sized' fishes is tempting providence a
little too much. Needless to say, the aquarium should be tightly
covered – and beware your fingers when feeding them.

Breeding Moray Eels in captivity is unlikely because sexual
maturity is reached only when the eels attain a large size. This
stage is not normally reached in the confines of a domestic
aquarium, and so successful breeding is doubtful even if a
sufficient number of specimens are kept together to allow natural
pairings to take place. A further complication is that many eels
need to undertake migratory journeys before spawning occurs.

Gymnothorax tesselatus
Reticulated Moray; Leopard Moray
● **Distribution:** Indo-Pacific.
● **Length:** 1500mm/60in (wild).
● **Diet and feeding:** Will eat
anything they can swallow.
Predatory ambushers.
● **Aquarium behaviour:** Do not
keep with anything small.

The dark body is covered with a
reticulated pattern of pale
markings, producing an effect very
similar to a giraffe's markings. The
nostrils are tubular. This species is
sometimes called *Lycodontis
tesselata*.

Below: **Gymnothorax tesselatus**
*Concentrating on the 'business
end' of this species is very wise.
The bite can be very painful, even
leading to infection (and that's only
for humans). Just imagine
encountering this predator if you
were a fish! Only for the 'big tank'
hobbyist or public aquariums.*

Above:
Rhinomuraenia amboinensis
*Asking anyone to estimate the
length of this fish in your tank
could lead to you winning a few
bets. Putting two in your tank
could really confuse people. It
does attract a lot of attention, with
its fine colours, length and coils.*

Rhinomuraenia amboinensis
Blue Ribbon Eel
● **Distribution:** Pacific.
● **Length:** 750mm/30in (wild).
● **Diet and feeding:** Meat eater
that needs live foods. Often
difficult to feed. Nocturnal.
● **Aquarium behaviour:** Usually
peaceful, but boisterous inquisitive
fishes, such as Damsels, may
annoy it.

The body is dark blue-black and
the dorsal fin is bright yellow. The
long nostrils, positioned at the very
tip of the pointed snout, are
constantly erect.

Evidence has shown that a
certain amount of hermaphroditism
exists within this species, and this
has led to some confusion with
species identification.
R.amboinensis is black, but
appears to transform with age, first
into the blue form known as
R.quaesita and then into a yellow
female form. (It may be that
R.quaesita is the only valid
species, merely passing through
several colour phases during its
development.)

These are favourite show fishes.
Be sure to fit a secure lid on their
tank; these snakelike fishes can
escape very easily.

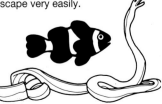

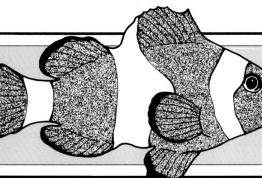

Common Clown (*Amphiprion ocellaris*)
Mature at 80mm (3.2in) and shown as a guide
to the maximum wild size of each species.

Family: OPISTHOGNATHIDAE
Jawfishes

Family characteristics
Behind the large mouth and eyes of these fish is a tapering cylindrical body. The main appeal of Jawfishes is their habit of constructing tunnels or burrows in the substrate into which they retreat when threatened. At night they use a small pebble or shell to cover the entrance.

While the commonly kept Yellow-headed Jawfish (*Opisthognathus aurifrons*) shows no sexual dimorphism, males of other less familiar species, such as the Atlantic Yellow Jawfish (*O.gilberti*) and the Pacific Blue-Spotted Jawfish do undergo colour changes at breeding times. Perhaps the best guide to the sexes is the fact that males take on the incubation of the eggs.

Diet and feeding
Hovering close to their burrowed tunnels, Jawfishes wait for their prey of crustaceans, small fishes and plankton. Some species are not so adventurous, preferring to remain in their holes waiting for small live foods to pass by.

Aquarium behaviour
Providing sufficient 'accommodation' is available, a number of these fishes can be kept together. They are very hardy but easily frightened, retreating into their holes like lightning. These tolerant fishes bother nobody, but may be harassed by other cave-dwelling species that may have designs on their living quarters. Jawfishes are excellent jumpers, so ensure that the aquarium has a closely fitting cover to prevent escapes.

Above: **Opisthognathus aurifrons**
The normal pose, at peace with the world. How the fish manages to retreat into its hole tail-first at such speed almost defies belief.

Below: **Opisthognathus aurifrons**
Once seen outside its usual safe retreat, the Yellow-headed Jawfish reveals that its slim body has the most delicate coloration.

Opisthognathus aurifrons
Yellow-headed Jawfish
- **Distribution:** Western Atlantic.
- **Length:** 125mm/5in (wild).
- **Diet and feeding:** Finely chopped shellfish meat. Makes rapid lunges from a vertical hovering position near its burrow to grab any passing food.
- **Aquarium behaviour:** Peaceful and rarely disturbed by other fishes, although the Royal Gramma (*Gramma loreto*) may try to steal its territory given the opportunity.

The delicately coloured yellow head is normally all you see of this fish, but the rest of the body is an equally beautiful pale blue. The eyes are large. It needs a reasonably soft substrate in which to excavate a burrow, entering the hole tail first at any sign of trouble. A good jumper.

Family: OSTRACIONTIDAE
Boxfishes and Trunkfishes

Family characteristics
These fishes have a rigid body made up of bony plates covered with a sensitive skin that may be damaged by Cleanerfishes. The only flexible part is the caudal peduncle, where the most obvious growth occurs rearwards. The pelvic fins are missing, although bony stumps may appear at the corners of the body box in some species. They are slow moving – some have been designated 'hovercraft fishes' by imaginative authors – and they do indeed have a similar form of locomotion, making rapid movements of the dorsal, anal and pectoral fins to good effect. When buying these fishes, avoid any with concave looking sides, as these never recover from this probable semi-starved state.

Most are poisonous, releasing a poison into the water when threatened. In the confines of the aquarium, or in the transportation container, this often proves fatal both to the Boxfish and to other fishes. Some authorities advocate introducing these fish into the aquarium in advance of other fishes to reduce the chances of fatal consequences should the Boxfishes become frightened.

Diet and feeding
These fishes will try anything, but appear to relish worm foods, especially *Tubifex* (obtained from a disease-free source).

Aquarium behaviour
Some reports suggest that these fish resent the attentions of Cleaner Gobies or any other inquisitive fishes perhaps attracted by their slow swimming action.

Lactoria cornuta
Long-horned Cowfish
● **Distribution:** Indo-Pacific.
● **Length:** 500mm/20in (wild), 400mm/16in (aquarium).
● **Diet and feeding:** Crustaceans and greenstuff. Shy bottom feeders.
● **Aquarium behaviour:** Intolerant of each other.

The two 'horns' on the head and two more projections at the bottom rear of the body make for easy identification. The body is brilliant yellow with bright blue spots in the centre of each segment of body 'armour plating'. Specimens in domestic aquariums do not reach very large sizes.

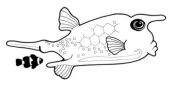

Above: **Lactoria cornuta**
The large horny projections serve a more specific purpose than merely providing the fish with its popular name of Long-horned Cowfish: they make the fish hard to swallow by predators, although its poisonous flesh would inflict justifiable retribution in any event.

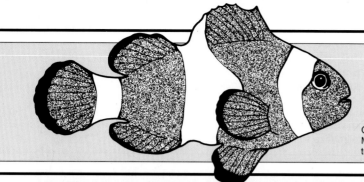

Common Clown (*Amphiprion ocellaris*)
Mature at 80mm (3.2in) and shown as a guide
to the maximum wild size of each species.

A practical reminder
Calculate copper-based medication doses accurately by using a copper test kit. Do not use activated carbon in filters used in treatment tanks as it will remove the medication from the water.

Left: **Ostracion lentiginosum**
Although named lentiginosum, *there are strong grounds for believing that this fish is the male form of O.meleagris. The confusion arises because of the obvious differences in colour patterning on the body, which make it hard to believe that the two are related.*

Below left: **Ostracion meleagris**
Although often confused with young specimens of Pufferfish, especially Arothron meleagris, *Boxfishes rely on poisonous secretions to ward off predators rather than inflating their bodies. According to recent information, the fish shown here is probably a female or juvenile form of the vividly coloured fish above.*

Below right:
Ostracion tuberculatum
This species really lives up to its popular name of Boxfish, especially when viewed from the angle captured here. However, a side view would soon reveal yellow fins, a pointed snout and longish caudal peduncle.

Ostracion lentiginosum
Blue-spotted Boxfish
● **Distribution:** Indo-Pacific.
● **Length:** 200mm/8in (wild), 100mm/4in (aquarium).
● **Diet and feeding:** Crustaceans. Bottom feeder.
● **Aquarium behaviour:** Peaceful, but do not keep in the same aquarium as inquisitive fishes.

This is a most colourful species. The top of the body is black with white spots and the lower flanks are violet with yellow spots. The two sections are separated by a yellow line. The eye is yellow-gold and the face is a similar colour. The body patterning dwindles away two-thirds of the way through the caudal fin. The male is much darker than the female.

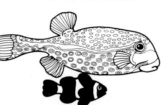

Ostracion meleagris
White-spotted Boxfish; Pacific Boxfish
● **Distribution:** Indo-Pacific.
● **Length:** 160mm/6.3in (wild).
● **Diet and feeding:** Crustaceans and greenstuff. Bottom feeder.
● **Aquarium behaviour:** Peaceful.

There is much confusion between this and the previous species since *O.meleagris* is also black with a covering of white spots. Some authorities believe that both are the same species, one being the male, the other the female. The problem is that they cannot agree which one is which! Start feeding with brineshrimp, *Daphnia* etc.

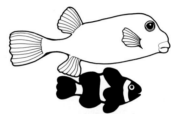

Ostracion tuberculatum
Blue-spotted Boxfish
● **Distribution:** Indo-Pacific.
● **Length:** 450mm/18in (wild).
● **Diet and feeding:** Crustaceans and greenstuff. Bottom feeder.
● **Aquarium behaviour:** Peaceful; best left undisturbed.

The almost cube-shaped body of juveniles is light cream or yellow with dark blue spots; it is easy to imagine that they are animated dice, slowly swimming around looking for food. Adult fishes develop a more elongate body and the colour changes to a yellowy green, while the armoured plates on the body become more clearly defined. The fins are tinted yellow.

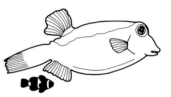

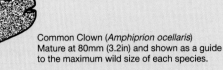

Common Clown (*Amphiprion ocellaris*)
Mature at 80mm (3.2in) and shown as a guide
to the maximum wild size of each species.

Family: PLATACIDAE
Batfishes

Family characteristics
The oval-bodied, high-finned Batfish is unmistakable. It is found in coastal and brackish waters and in mangrove swamps. It often lies on its side 'playing dead', floating like a leaf to avoid capture or detection. There is still unresolved speculation as to whether there is only one true species, with the variously coloured forms being regarded as subspecies. According to commercial sources, there may be three species of Batfishes available, with possibly a rarer fourth: *Platax orbicularis*, *P.tiera* (Longfinned Batfish), *P.pinnatus*, and a marbled type as yet un-named. In the light of such varied speculations, it is not surprising that positive species identification is difficult, but it is known that adult fishes have less coloration than juveniles.

Diet and feeding
These greedy fishes will usually accept all manner of foods.

Aquarium behaviour
The Batfish usually adapts to captivity well, not quarrelling with similarly sized tankmates. It does need a spacious tank, however, as it grows very quickly.

Platax orbicularis
Batfish; Orbiculate Batfish;
Round Batfish
● **Distribution:** Indo-Pacific.
● **Length:** 500mm/20in (wild), 380mm/15in (aquarium).
● **Diet and feeding:** Will eat anything. Scavenger.
● **Aquarium behaviour:** Peaceful, but grows fast. Keep away from boisterous fin-nipping species.

The body is round, with large rounded fins. There are one or two dark stripes on the head and front part of the body, but these fade with age. Young specimens have more elongated fins and also more red coloration.

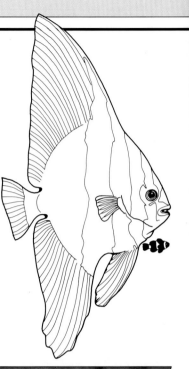

Below: **Platax orbicularis**
A young specimen, showing the typical dark red-brown stripes. Allow a generous depth of water for these tall-finned fishes.

A practical reminder
Do not leap to conclusions in
diagnosing fish diseases or treat fishes
with more than one remedy at a time.
Avoid treating a tank containing
invertebrates with copper-based cures.

Platax pinnatus
Red-faced Batfish
● **Distribution:** Indo-Pacific.
● **Length:** 500mm/20in (wild),
450mm/18in (aquarium).
● **Diet and feeding:** Will eat
anything. Scavenger.
● **Aquarium behaviour:** Peaceful,
but grows fast. Keep away from
boisterous fin-nipping species.

Platax pinnatus may be a separate
species of Batfish; the body shape
is much shorter and higher than in
P.orbicularis and the fins are very
elongate. The colour is much
darker, with a red outline to the
body and fins. It is a pity that it
should lose such magnificent
colours and gracefulness with
advancing age.

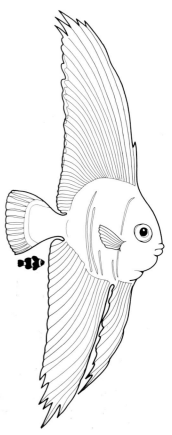

Left: **Platax pinnatus**
*This splendid fish makes a
majestic picture, the red edges of
the fins outlining the fish to
perfection. It is quite easy to see
how tempting the tall fins might be
to other fishes with a fin-nipping
disposition. Luckily (for the fish
although not for the hobbyist)
these attractive colours fade with
increasing age. Similar in body
shape to the freshwater Angelfish,
the fish's slender body enables it
to move with ease through dense
mangrove roots in coastal areas.*

143

Common Clown (*Amphiprion ocellaris*)
Mature at 80mm (3.2in) and shown as a guide
to the maximum wild size of each species.

Family: PLECTORHYNCHIDAE
Sweetlips

Family characteristics
Fishes in this Family are often classified in the Pomadasydae. They resemble Snappers, but differ from them in dentition details. The coloration of juveniles and adults differs quite dramatically. The Sweetlips are confined to the Indo-Pacific Ocean areas.

Diet and feeding
Crustaceans, live animal and meaty foods. Shy slow eaters.

Aquarium behaviour
Juveniles are excellent subjects for a large quiet aquarium.

Plectorhynchus albovittatus

Yellow Sweetlips; Yellow-lined Sweetlips
● **Distribution:** Indo-Pacific, Red Sea.
● **Length:** 200mm/8in (wild).
● **Diet and feeding:** Crustaceans, animal and meaty foods. Bottom feeder.
● **Aquarium behaviour:** Hardy, but keep with non-boisterous fishes.

In juveniles the body is yellow, with two white-bordered dark bands

running the length of the body. The lower band is level with the terminal mouth and centre line of the fish. The patterning of the body extends into the rear of the yellow dorsal fin and into the caudal fin. Adult fishes lose this interesting coloration and become brown.

Below:
Plectorhynchus albovittatus
When seen in dealer's tanks, the juveniles look very appealing, but they lose these colours with age.

Above and right:
Plectorhynchus chaetodonoides
Another striking difference in body colours, this time between young and adult Harlequin Sweetlips.

A practical reminder
Collect seashore specimens carefully. If you have to remove them from stones, replace these with substitutes to retain natural refuges. Don't transport fishes and invertebrates in the same container.

Plectorhynchus chaetodonoides
Harlequin Sweetlips; Clown Sweetlips; Polka-dot Grunt
● **Distribution:** Pacific.
● **Length:** 450mm/18in (wild).
● **Diet and feeding:** Crustaceans, animal and meaty foods. (Small live or frozen shrimps will often get them feeding in the aquarium.) Bottom feeder.
● **Aquarium behaviour:** Shy; keep with non-boisterous fishes.

Juveniles have a dark brown body covered with well-defined white blotches and this pattern is repeated on the fins. Adult fishes are a drab brown with dark dots. Feeding requires special attention; be sure to offer only small portions.

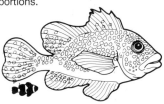

Plectorhynchus orientalis
Oriental Sweetlips
● **Distribution:** Indo-Pacific.
● **Length:** 400mm/16in (wild).
● **Diet and feeding:** Crustaceans, animal and meaty foods. Bottom feeder.
● **Aquarium behaviour:** Shy; keep with non-boisterous fishes.

Juvenile fishes have large cream-yellow patches on a dark background. Adults may sometimes be confused with young *P.albovittatus*, although there are more stripes on *P.orientalis* and the coloration is not quite so yellow.

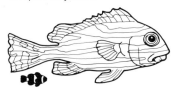

Left: **Plectorhynchus orientalis**
Members of the Sweetlips group are surprisingly shy; another even more unexpected feature is their habit of taking small morsels of food. Adult Oriental Sweetlips, similar in coloration to the juvenile Yellow Sweetlips shown opposite, reverse the usual colour sequence, ending up with stripes in contrast to the juvenile's creamy patches.

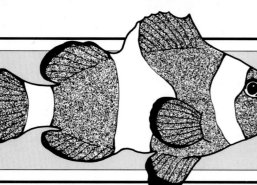

Common Clown (*Amphiprion ocellaris*)
Mature at 80mm (3.2in) and shown as a guide
to the maximum wild size of each species.

Family: PLOTOSIDAE
Catfishes

Family characteristics
Two features make it easy to identify the marine Catfishes: the second dorsal and anal fins merge with the caudal fin, and there are barbels around the mouth. The spines preceding the dorsal and pectoral fins are poisonous.

These fishes are very gregarious when young – species grouping together in a tight ball for safety – but this habit is lost (along with any colour pattern) when adult. In the wild, adult fishes may enter river systems.

Diet and feeding
Chopped shellfish meats form an ideal food in the aquarium.

Aquarium behaviour
Only juvenile specimens are suitable for the aquarium, as the adult fishes not only outgrow their juvenile coloration but also can become dangerous to inexperienced handlers.

Plotosus lineatus
Saltwater Catfish
- **Distribution:** Indo-Pacific.
- **Length:** 300mm/12in (wild).
- **Diet and feeding:** Chopped shellfish meats. Bottom feeder.
- **Aquarium behaviour:** Peaceful.

Two parallel white lines run along the length of the dark body. The second dorsal and anal fins are very long-based and merge with the caudal fin. In the wild, young specimens shoal together, forming a tight, ball-like clump when threatened. In the aquarium, they are best kept in small shoals, since solitary specimens seem to pine away. The spines are poisonous, so handle these fishes with care. (For action if stung, see page 168 – introduction to Scorpaenidae.)

This species presumably spawns in the same way as the freshwater Plotosid *Tandanus*, which constructs a nest of debris, sand or gravel. The male (usually identified simply because it does not lay the eggs) is said to guard the eggs after spawning has taken place. This fish is also known as *Plotosus anguillaris*.

Top right and right:
Plotosus lineatus
The horizontal stripes of the young Catfish make for a smart-looking fish, and the habit of young specimens congregating together suggests that it may be a good community subject. However, this fast-growing species soon loses its stripes and sociable nature as it matures in the aquarium.

A practical reminder
Never collect more native animals than you can accommodate in the tank. If the specimens outgrow their quarters, you can return them to the wild and capture smaller replacements at the same time.

Family: POMACENTRIDAE
Anemonefishes (Clownfishes) and Damselfishes

Family characteristics
Fishes within this Family are usually divided into two distinct groups: the Anemonefishes and the Damselfishes. They are very important to the marine aquarist, because they are brilliantly coloured, of modest size, and are also very hardy. These attributes make them ideal starter fishes, Damselfishes being especially suitable because they are nitrite tolerant. Here, we discuss the Anemonefishes. Damselfishes are described from page 154.

The curious 'waddling' swimming action of the Anemonefishes, together with their clearly defined markings, has given them their other collective common name of Clownfishes. As their principal common name suggests, the Anemonefishes live in close association with sea anemones, especially *Discosoma*, *Radianthus* and *Stoichactus* species. The Anemonefish was thought to be immune to the stinging cells of the sea anemone, but it now appears that the mucus on the fish prevents the stinging cells from being activated. This relationship is usually referred to as being symbiotic, but 'commensalism' might be a more accurate description. In this context, commensalism means that the fishes and sea anemones live in close proximity to one another, often to their mutual benefit. There may be some doubt about the benefit derived by the sea anemone in return for not stinging the fish. One belief is that the fish drops morsels of food for the sea anemone to eat, or entices would-be predators near enough to the sea anemone to be stung by its tentacles. Another theory is that the Anemonefishes, being territorial by nature, chase away fishes that might eat the sea anemone.

It could be that the Clownfish/sea anemone relationship is more like that of a patient and doctor. Some observers have noticed that the sea anemone appears to remove *Oodinium* parasites, not only from the Clownfish but also from any other similarly infected fish that cares to enter the sea anemone's tentacles. However, it is only the Clownfish that carries on with further visits to the sea anemone once the parasitic infection has cleared up. (It would appear that non-infected fishes cannot avoid the effects of the stings.)

Not all Anemonefishes are dependent upon sea anemones to the same degree. It seems that poor swimmers are the most reliant, whereas the more able swimmers venture further away with more confidence in their ability to survive without the immediate protection offered by the embracing tentacles.

Despite their close relationship in the wild, Anemonefishes will live quite happily in the aquarium without a sea anemone (and vice-versa), but then you will not see the fish behave as it does in nature. Large sea anemones can 'accommodate' several Anemonefishes. A single fish occupying a small sea anemone, on the other hand, will become territorial, defending its 'own' anemone from intruders. In the absence of a sea anemone, the fishes do not develop this territorial behaviour.

There may be some variation in the colour patterns of juvenile and adult forms and also between the same species from different localities. However, in most cases there are very few external physical differences between the sexes, although *Amphiprion perideraion* is reported to offer more positive clues in this respect (see page 150). Also, studies of some species in the wild have shown that, generally, mature females are longer than males. Like the Damselfishes, Anemonefishes exhibit hermaphrodite capabilities (i.e. fishes will change sex to 'even up' the numbers) to ensure the continuity of the species. Spawning has occurred in the aquarium and the eggs are laid on a selected site and guarded.

Diet and feeding
In the wild, small crustaceans, plankton and algae are the main diet. In the aquarium, these fishes will take live foods, algae, fish meat-based foods and flakes, etc.

Aquarium behaviour
Because of their territorial tendencies, Anemonefishes are eminently suitable for keeping in the aquarium, where they will naturally associate with suitable anemones. In this way, you can keep a few Anemonefishes in a relatively small tank.

ANEMONEFISHES

Amphiprion akallopisos
Yellow Skunk Clown
● **Distribution:** Indo-Pacific.
● **Length:** 75mm/3in (wild), 40-50mm/1.6-2in (aquarium).
● **Diet and feeding:** Small crustaceans, small live foods, algae, vegetable-based foods. Bold feeder.
● **Aquarium behaviour:** Peaceful.

A white line runs along the very top of the brown-topped golden body, from a point level with the eye to the caudal peduncle. Some Anemonefishes do not live up to the Family's reputation as sea anemone dwellers, but this species seems to need the association more than others.

Above: **Amphiprion akallopisos**
Here, the Yellow Skunk Clown is doing what comes naturally, resting among the tentacles of its home sea anemone which, providing it is large enough, can play host to several fishes. Radianthus ritteri *is a sea anemone often associated with this fish.*

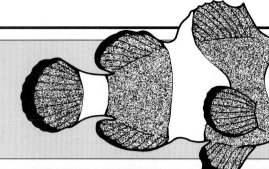

Common Clown (*Amphiprion ocellaris*)
Mature at 80mm (3.2in) and shown as a guide
to the maximum wild size of each species.

Amphiprion bicinctus
Two-banded Anemonefish;
Banded Clown
● **Distribution:** Red Sea, Indo-Pacific.
● **Length:** 120mm/4.7in (wild), 75mm/3in (aquarium).
● **Diet and feeding:** Small crustaceans, small live foods, algae, vegetable-based foods. Bold feeder.
● **Aquarium behaviour:** Peaceful.

The body is predominantly dark brown but for the ventral regions, which are yellow. All the fins, with the exception of the paler caudal fins, are bright yellow. Two tapering white vertical bars divide the body into thirds; in juvenile forms, there is a third white bar across the rear of the body.

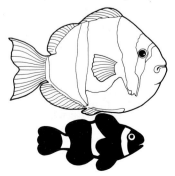

Amphiprion ephippium
Tomato Clown; Fire Clown; Red
Saddleback Clown
● **Distribution:** Indo-Pacific.
● **Length:** 120mm/4.7in (wild), 75mm/3in (aquarium).
● **Diet and feeding:** Small crustaceans, small live foods, algae, vegetable-based foods. Bold feeder.
● **Aquarium behaviour:** Can be aggressive.

This fish is often confused with *A.frenatus*, since both are a rich tomato-red with a black blurred blotch on the body rearwards of the gill cover. Occasionally, juveniles have a white vertical bar just behind the head, but some authorities maintain that this is never the case. According to some sources, imported species of *E.ephippium* are really *E.rubrocinctus*.

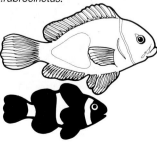

Amphiprion frenatus
Tomato Clown; Fire Clown; Bridled
Clownfish
● **Distribution:** Pacific.
● **Length:** 75mm/3in (wild).
● **Diet and feeding:** Small crustaceans, small live foods, algae, vegetable-based foods. Bold feeder.
● **Aquarium behaviour:** May be quarrelsome in confined spaces.

A.frenatus is very similar to *A.ephippium*, but it has the white stripe behind the head (sometimes two in juveniles) and the body blotch is often larger. The confusion between the two species is not helped by the fact that some authorities call this fish *A.ephippium* or *A.melanopus*. Another name for it is *A.polylepis*.

Above: **Amphiprion bicinctus**
An adult specimen. Juvenile forms are darker in body colour; there may also be dark patches in the caudal fin and rear of the dorsal fin, both disappearing with age. Two other species are similarly marked: the Indian Ocean A. allardi, the juveniles having saddle-like markings on the caudal peduncle, and A. chrysopterus, in which the adult is less orange.

Opposite top:
Amphiprion ephippium
This juvenile Tomato Clown is but one species of Amphiprion so named, many others having the similar rich red body coloration with a dark patch. The distinctions centre upon the presence or absence of the white vertical stripe; true adult A. ephippium do not have one, although it may persist from the juvenile for a time.

Right: **Amphiprion frenatus**
Unlike the previous species, adult specimens of this Tomato Clown retain the vertical white stripe into adulthood. As with all fishes with similar features that are gathered over very wide areas by collectors not aware of other's efforts or descriptions, there is bound to be confusion with classifications.

A practical reminder
A coldwater marine tank may overheat in the summer months. To compensate, increase aeration, add ice cubes in a plastic bag, or pass the filter's output tube through a bucket of cold water.

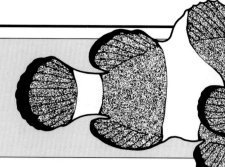

Common Clown (*Amphiprion ocellaris*)
Mature at 80mm (3.2in) and shown as a guide
to the maximum wild size of each species.

Amphiprion nigripes
Black-footed Clownfish
- **Distribution:** Indian Ocean.
- **Length:** 80mm/3.2in (wild), 50mm/2in (aquarium).
- **Diet and feeding:** Eats plankton and crustaceans in the wild, but finely chopped foods are ideal in captivity. Bold feeder.
- **Aquarium behaviour:** Best kept with other Anemonefishes.

Although it is similar to the two previous species, *A.nigripes* is much more subtly coloured. It is a soft golden brown with a white stripe just behind the head. The ventral fins are black, but the anal fin is not always so, hence the common name.

Amphiprion ocellaris
Common Clown; Percula Clown
- **Distribution:** Indo-Pacific.
- **Length:** 80mm/3.2in (wild), 50mm/2in (aquarium).
- **Diet and feeding:** Finely chopped foods. Bold feeder.
- **Aquarium behaviour:** Will sometimes exclude other Anemonefishes from its territory.

This is the Clownfish that everyone recognises, for the simple reason that it is the species most often imported. It is frequently confused with *A.percula*, which has slightly more black, especially in the dorsal fin, between the first two white bands, and on the pectoral and caudal fins.

Amphiprion perideraion
Salmon Clownfish; Pink Skunk Clownfish
- **Distribution:** Pacific Ocean.
- **Length:** 80mm/3.2in (wild), 38mm/1.5in (aquarium).
- **Diet and feeding:** Finely chopped foods. Not quite as bold as other species.
- **Aquarium behaviour:** Shy.

This species is very similar in colour to *A.akallopisos*, but can be easily distinguished from it by the vertical bar just behind the head. The body colour is perhaps a little more subdued and a white stripe reaches the snout. *A.perideraion* is rather more sensitive than other species and is best kept in a species tank with adequate space for sea anemones. Males have orange edging to the soft-rayed part of the dorsal fin and at the top and bottom of the caudal fin.

Below: **Amphiprion nigripes**
The Black-footed Clownfish is found off the Maldive Islands in the Indian Ocean. Its colours are not as rich as those of some other Clownfishes, and in this respect it is very similar to A.perideraion.

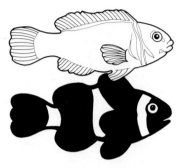

Right: **Amphiprion ocellaris**
The Common Clown can be found with some variations in its body colour. Based on scientific experimentation in similar species, this has been attributed to the relatively darker colours of their chosen sea anemones; it would seem that pale Anemonefishes become darker to blend in with their host anemone.

Below right:
Amphiprion perideraion
The Skunk Clownfish has a vertical bar, and a pink hue to the body, which helps distinguish it from similar white-backed species. It is also one of the few Clownfishes that show signs of sex differences.

A practical reminder
Keep a close-fitting lid on the tank, especially if it contains invertebrates, as many are great escape artists. Provide hermit crabs with variously sized shells to use as continuing 'homes'.

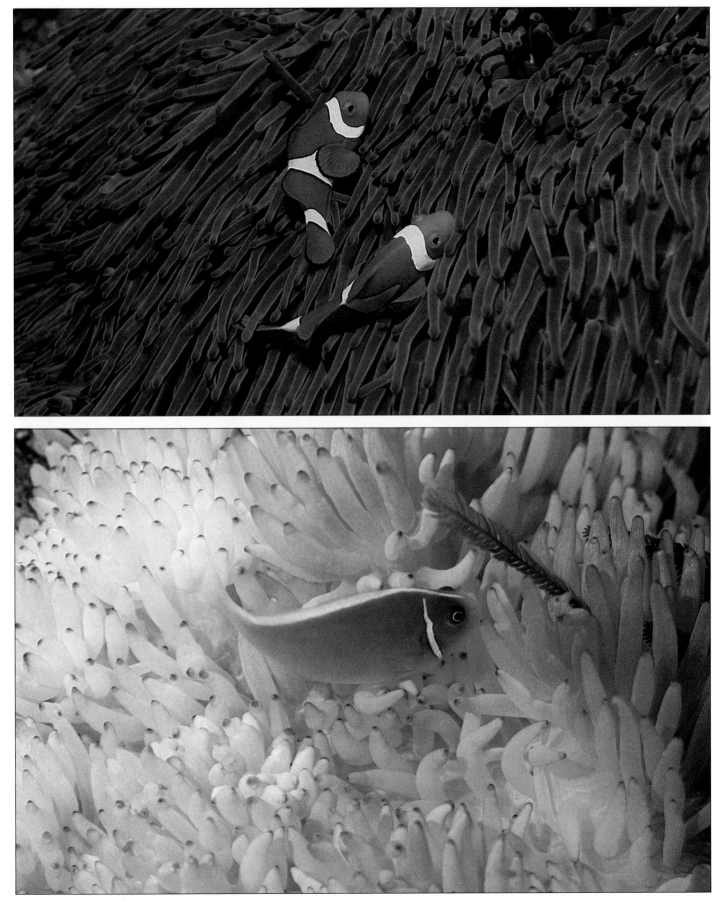

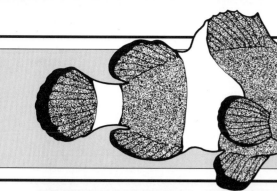

Common Clown (*Amphiprion ocellaris*)
Mature at 80mm (3.2in) and shown as a guide
to the maximum wild size of each species.

Above: **Amphiprion polymnus**
*The white markings on the dorsal
area make recognition quite
positive. An alternate scientific
name offered for the White-
saddled Clownfish is A.laticlavius.*

Amphiprion polymnus
White-saddled Clownfish
● **Distribution:** Pacific.
● **Length:** 120mm/4.7in (wild),
100mm/4in (aquarium).
● **Diet and feeding:** Small
crustaceans, small live foods,
algae, vegetable-based foods.
Bold feeder.
● **Aquarium behaviour:** Can be
territorial.

The dark red-brown body is
marked by two white bands; one
broad band lies just behind the
head, the other begins in the
middle of the body and curves
upwards into the rear part of the
dorsal fin. There is also a dash of
white along the top of the caudal
fin. Not an easy fish to maintain.

Premnas biaculeatus
Maroon Clownfish
● **Distribution:** Pacific Ocean.
● **Length:** 150mm/6in (wild),
100mm/4in (aquarium).
● **Diet and feeding:** Finely
chopped foods. Bold.
● **Aquarium behaviour:**
Aggressive towards other
Anemonefishes.

This larger species differs from
other Clownfishes by having two
spines beneath the eye, as well as
the usual small spines on the back
edge of the gill cover. The body is
a deep rich red colour with three
narrow white bands crossing it,
one behind the head, one midway
along the body and one just
behind the dorsal and anal fins.

Right: **Premnas biaculeatus**
*Recent scientific work has put
forward the suggestion that the
genus Premnas should be treated
as a subgenus of Amphiprion, but
aquarium hobbyists are sometimes
slow to readjust to such moves,
just in case the names change
again in a short space of time!*

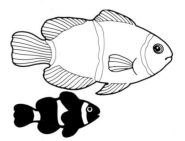

A practical reminder
You should take extra care when handling fishes that have venomous, or even merely sharp, spines. Even if fishes become hand-tame it may be prudent to offer food impaled on a stick.

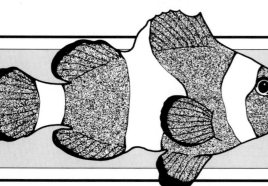

Common Clown (*Amphiprion ocellaris*)
Mature at 80mm (3.2in) and shown as a guide
to the maximum wild size of each species.

Family: POMACENTRIDAE
Damselfishes

Family characteristics

Damselfishes are small, busy fishes that bob constantly around the coral heads, using them as their territory and retreating into them when threatened. Consequently, they are among the most agile of fishes – particularly when you are trying to catch them!

There are a number of similar looking 'Electric-blue' or 'Blue Devil' fishes and also several blue-and-yellow coloured species. Because of these similarities, there is much confusion about the correct taxonomic classification. Sometimes Damsels lose their brilliant colours in captivity. Fading the colours may be a response that helps the fishes to blend in more effectively with the surroundings.

Normally, there are no clear distinctions between the sexes. An internal examination – usually beyond the scope or immediate interest of the hobbyist – will reveal differences more clearly. However, during courtship and breeding periods, colour changes do occur: *Abudefduf* males usually turn pale; the Atlantic *Eupomacentrus* species develop a mask over the eyes, head or other dorsal part of the body; and Pacific *Eupomacentrus* develop a contrasting colour around the pupil of the eye. There is one method of determining sex by external observation – a technique similar to that used for determining sex in freshwater Cichlids – and that is by looking at the genital papillae (often called the ovipositor). The male genital papilla is narrower and more pointed than the female's. Unfortunately, it takes a keen eye to make the necessary observations and these are best delayed until breeding activity is noticed, when the papillae are easier to see.

Spawning in Damselfishes entails the selection of a site and the laying and subsequent guarding of eggs.

Diet and feeding

Finely chopped meats, algae and greenstuff, but all species of Damselfishes will take dried foods readily.

Aquarium behaviour

When confident of a nearby safe refuge, they are delightful fishes, but they may transfer their nervous energy into quarrels among themselves. They can be aggressive. Provide a spacious aquarium if you wish to keep several fishes together.

Abudefduf cyaneus
(A. assimilis)

Blue Damsel
● **Distribution:** Indo-Pacific.
● **Length:** 60mm/2.4in (wild).
● **Diet and feeding:** Finely chopped meats, algae and greenstuff. Will take dried food. Bold feeder.
● **Aquarium behaviour:** May squabble with members of its own species. Keep singly or in shoals.

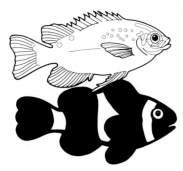

Although some specimens may have yellow markings on the caudal fin and ventral area, the predominant colour of this fish is a stunning royal blue. There is some confusion about the positive classification of this species, since some authorities refer to it as *Glyphidodontops*.

Above right: **Abudefduf cyaneus**
One of the many blue Damselfishes, this species probably has more synonyms than most. Doubts will always arise due to colour variations between fishes of different age, sex and location.

Right:
Glyphidodontops hemicyaneus
This is another name often applied to several bright blue species, all with varying amounts of yellow on fins and body. Such a coloration may be merely intermittent or a locality feature, rather than a positive identification factor.

A practical reminder
Make sure you can differentiate between species and their lookalikes, which may be predatory. The true Cleanerfish removes parasites from fishes; the False Cleaner takes skin!

Above: **Abudefduf oxyodon**
As with all marine fishes, it is vital that imported specimens are in the very best of health if they are to thrive in captivity. This handsome fish from the Pacific Ocean may not always adapt well if in less than tip-top condition.

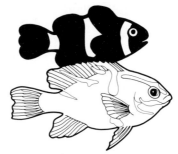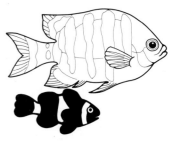

Abudefduf oxyodon
Blue-velvet Damselfish; Black Neon Damselfish
● **Distribution:** Pacific.
● **Length:** 110mm/4.3in (wild), 75mm/3in (aquarium).
● **Diet and feeding:** Finely chopped meats, algae and greenstuff. Bold.
● **Aquarium behaviour:** Aggressive.

A vertical yellow stripe crosses the deep blue-black body just behind the head. The electric blue wavy lines on the head and upper part of the body may fade with age.

Left: **Abudefduf saxatilis**
The Sergeant Major is widely distributed throughout the tropics. The male changes colour and an ovipositor appears from the vent during spawning, which occurs between territorial males and visiting females. Eggs are laid on rocks, shells or coral branches.

Abudefduf saxatilis
Sergeant Major
● **Distribution:** Indo-Pacific, tropical Atlantic.
● **Length:** 150mm/6in (wild), 50mm/2in (aquarium).
● **Diet and feeding:** Finely chopped meats, algae and greenstuff. Bold grazer.
● **Aquarium behaviour:** Juveniles are very active; adults can become aggressive.

Five vertical dark bars cross the yellow/silvery body. Depending on the geographic location of the individuals, the caudal fin may be a dusky colour. Juvenile forms in the Atlantic have bright yellow upper parts on an otherwise silver body. However, it may lose its colours when disturbed. This is a hardy fish, and a good choice for the beginner. A shoal in a large tank is impressive. *A.saxatilis* is a good teacher fish for 'educating' new fish to accept food and to help mature a newly set up aquarium.

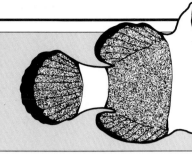

Common Clown (*Amphiprion ocellaris*)
Mature at 80mm (3.2in) and shown as a guide
to the maximum wild size of each species.

Chromis caerulea
Green Chromis
- **Distribution:** Indo-Pacific, Red Sea.
- **Length:** 100mm/4in (wild), 50mm/2in (aquarium).
- **Diet and feeding:** Chopped meats. Shy.
- **Aquarium behaviour:** Generally peaceful.

This hardy colourful shoaling species has a brilliant green-blue sheen to the scales. The caudal fin is more deeply forked than in some Damselfishes. Keep these fishes in shoals; individuals may go into decline in the aquarium.

Chromis cyanea
Blue Chromis
- **Distribution:** Tropical Atlantic.
- **Length:** 50mm/2in (wild).
- **Diet and feeding:** Chopped meats. Dried foods. Average.
- **Aquarium behaviour:** A peaceable shoaling fish that prefers to be with some of its own kind to feel at home.

This species thrives in vigorously aerated water. The body colour is brilliant blue with some black specks, topped with a black dorsal surface. There are black edges to the dorsal and caudal fins. The eye is also dark. In shape and size (but not colour) *C.cyanea* closely resembles *C.multilineata*, the Grey Chromis. The Blue Hamlet (*Hypoplectrus gemma*) is a colour mimic of *Chromis cyanea*, using its 'disguise' to prey upon unsuspecting fishes and crustaceans – which assume the 'Blue Chromis' to be harmless.

At breeding time, a brown ovipositor extends from just in front of the anal fin in a similar manner to that of freshwater Cichlids (see also page 154).

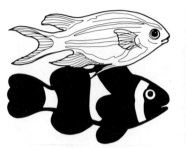

Right: **Chromis cyanea**
The normally narrow black area on the top of the male Blue Chromis spreads during spawning time and a brown ovipositor appears. The male usually guards the eggs.

Below right: **Chromis xanthurus**
Compare this species to the picture on p.154. There appears to be more yellow in the pelvic fins, a spot on the gill cover and at the bottom of the rear dorsal fin.

Below: **Chromis caerulea**
Like many Damselfishes, the peaceful Green Chromis has a gregarious nature and appreciates being kept in a small shoal. A lively and attractive species.

A practical reminder
Replenish water losses through evaporation by adding *fresh* water, as none of the sea salt is lost during evaporation. Adding sea water would alter the specific gravity of the water.

Chromis xanthurus
Yellow-tailed Damselfish
● **Distribution:** Indo-Pacific.
● **Length:** 100mm/4in (wild), 50mm/2in (aquarium).
● **Diet and feeding:** Chopped meats. Dried foods. Bold.
● **Aquarium behaviour:** A peaceable shoaling fish that prefers to be with some of its own kind to thrive.

The deep royal blue body contrasts sharply with the bright yellow caudal fin and caudal peduncle. Again, there is some confusion over the correct name of this species, both *Pomacentrus caeruleus* and *Abudefduf parasema* are given by other sources.

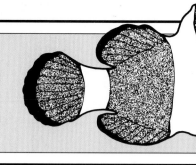

Common Clown (*Amphiprion ocellaris*)
Mature at 80mm (3.2in) and shown as a guide
to the maximum wild size of each species.

Dascyllus aruanus
Humbug
● **Distribution:** Indo-Pacific.
● **Length:** 80mm/3.2in (wild), 75mm/3in (aquarium).
● **Diet and feeding:** Chopped meats. Bold feeder.
● **Aquarium behaviour:** Aggressive towards its own kind and very territorial.

This white fish has three black bars across the body. The front bar covers the eye and follows the slope of the head up into the first rays of the dorsal fin. The rear two bars extend into the pelvic and anal fins and also into the dorsal fin, where they are linked by a horizontal bar along the top part of the fin. The caudal fin is unmarked. This is the hardiest of the Damsels.

Below: **Dascyllus aruanus**
Was the Humbug named by someone with a sweet tooth? It shares its popular name with a similarly coloured confection.

Dascyllus carneus
Cloudy Damsel
● **Distribution:** Indo-Pacific.
● **Length:** 80mm/3.2in (wild).
● **Diet and feeding:** Chopped foods. Dried foods. Bold.
● **Aquarium behaviour:** Aggressive towards its own kind.

All the fins, except the white caudal, are black and the body is greyish brown with a pattern of blue dots. There is a white patch on the top of the body, towards the front part of the dorsal fin and immediately behind a black bar, which covers the pectoral fin. A similar fish, *D.reticulatus*, is more an overall grey in colour, lacks the white patch and has a vertical black bar running from the rear dorsal to the rear of the anal fin.

Right: **Dascyllus carneus**
Of a similar size, but less starkly coloured than the previous species, the Cloudy Damsel has more grey-brown in its body.

A practical reminder
Keep a careful watch on algae growing in the tank. Although it should be thriving for the benefit of the fishes, thin it out if it becomes too lush; if it dies, it could cause pollution problems.

Left: **Dascyllus marginatus**
No doubt the dark margin to the dorsal fin inspired this fish's popular and scientific name.

Dascyllus marginatus
Marginate Damselfish; Marginate Puller
● **Distribution:** Red Sea.
● **Length:** 100mm/4in (wild).
● **Diet and feeding:** Chopped meats. Dried foods. Bold feeder.
● **Aquarium behaviour:** Aggressive and territorial.

A brown area slopes backwards from the front of the black-edged dorsal fin to the point of the anal fin. The rest of the body is cream in colour. Like all *Dascyllus* species, this fish occasionally makes quite audible purring or clicking sounds. This active fish will shelter among coral during the night.

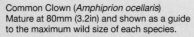
Common Clown (*Amphiprion ocellaris*)
Mature at 80mm (3.2in) and shown as a guide
to the maximum wild size of each species.

Dascyllus melanurus
Black-tailed Humbug
- **Distribution:** West Pacific.
- **Length:** 75mm/3in (wild).
- **Diet and feeding:** Chopped foods. Dried foods. Bold feeder.
- **Aquarium behaviour:** Aggressive and territorial.

This fish is very similar to *D.aruanus*, except that the black bars are more vertical and, as indicated by the common name, a black bar crosses the caudal fin.

Above: **Dascyllus melanurus**
This black and white Damsel is, like its almost lookalike relative the Humbug, a shoaling fish. It is found over a more limited area, however, being limited to the western Pacific Ocean around the Philippines and Melanesia.

Right: **Dascyllus trimaculatus**
This very common Damselfish, the Domino, is instantly recognizable by the three white spots on the body, and it would be very hard to imagine any other popular name for it. A similarly marked species from Hawaii, D.albisella, also carries three spots when young but these are more likely to fade.

A practical reminder
Even if you know how many fishes your tank can hold, always build up to this figure gradually so that the biological filter can cope with the increasing amounts of waste products.

Dascyllus trimaculatus
Domino Damsel; Three-spot Damselfish
● **Distribution:** Indo-Pacific, Red Sea.
● **Length:** 125mm/5in (wild), 75mm/3in (aquarium).
● **Diet and feeding:** Chopped meats and dried foods. Bold.
● **Aquarium behaviour:** Territorial.

This fish is velvety black overall, including the fins. The only markings are the three spots from which the comon name is derived. There is one white spot on each upper flank, midway along the length of the dorsal fin; the third spot is situated on the centre of the head, just behind the eye. The spots may fade with age.

Eupomacentrus leucostictus
Beau Gregory

● **Distribution:** Caribbean.
● **Length:** 150mm/6in (wild), 50mm/2in (aquarium).
● **Diet and feeding:** Animal and vegetable matter. Dried foods. Bold feeder.
● **Aquarium behaviour:** Aggressive.

The yellow body is topped by a golden brown area covered in bright blue dots. There is a dark blotch at the rear of the dorsal fin. All the other fins are yellow. This common Damsel is hardy enough for the beginner, but may bully fishes with similar feeding habits; kept alongside species with different feeding habits it is not so aggressive.

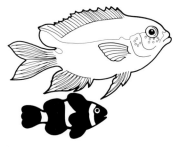

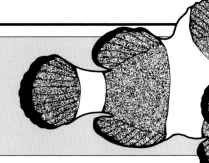

Common Clown (*Amphiprion ocellaris*)
Mature at 80mm (3.2in) and shown as a guide
to the maximum wild size of each species.

Paraglyphidodon (Abudefduf) melanopus
Yellow-backed Damselfish
- **Distribution:** Indo-Pacific.
- **Length:** 75mm/3in (wild).
- **Diet and feeding:** Chopped meats. Bold feeder.
- **Aquarium behaviour:** May be aggressive towards its own, and smaller, species.

An oblique bright yellow band runs from the snout to the tip of the dorsal fin above a pale violet body. The anal and pelvic fins are light blue, edged with black. The caudal fin is edged with yellow. A spacious tank with plenty of hiding places suits this brilliantly coloured fish very well.

Pomacentrus coeruleus
Blue Devil; Electric-blue Damsel
- **Distribution:** Indo-Pacific.
- **Length:** 100mm/4in (wild), 50mm/2in (aquarium).
- **Diet and feeding:** Chopped meats. Dried food. Bold feeder.
- **Aquarium behaviour:** Pugnacious.

The bright blue coloration of this fish really makes it stand out in the aquarium. There may be some black facial markings. It is a hardy species and, being smaller than most *Dascyllus* sp., poses less of a threat to other tank inmates. It lives peacefully in small groups when young but may turn aggressive when adult.

Pomacentrus melanochir
Blue-finned Damsel
- **Distribution:** Pacific.
- **Length:** 80mm/3.2in (wild).
- **Diet and feeding:** Chopped meats. Dried foods.
- **Aquarium behaviour:** Pugnacious. Less of a threat than *Dascyllus* sp.

At first sight, this looks like yet another yellow-tailed blue fish. However, closer inspection will reveal that each scale is dark-edged and that the blue patterning on the head is more obvious. The pelvic fins are yellowish.

Below:
Paraglyphidodon melanopus
The combination of black-edged pelvic fins and brilliant colours of this Damselfish has inspired several alternative common names: Bow-tie Damsel, Bluefin Damsel and Royal Damsel being just a few more to conjure with. This superbly attractive fish is found over a wide area of the Indo-Pacific Oceans.

Right: **Pomacentrus coeruleus**
The brilliant electric blue colour of the Blue Devil makes it an instant eye-catcher in the dealer's tanks, and it will certainly add an extra splash of colour to the home aquarium. Although generally peaceful, it may well alter its ways.

Below right:
Pomacentrus melanochir
Apparently, it takes one of two factors to make a positive identification of the many bright blue fishes with yellow markings: a reliable source of information or a large slice of luck. Such is the confusion over the many similar-looking species that the hobbyist often depends on the second.

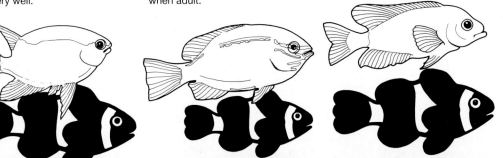

162

A practical reminder
Use light fittings with waterproofed connectors for the aquarium. Cover glasses reduce the risk of spray or condensation damage to lamps, and also prevent dust entering the tank.

Family: POMADASYIDAE
Grunts

Family characteristics
Grunts can be distinguished from the similar-looking Snappers by differences in their dentition. Many grind their pharyngeal teeth, the resulting sound being amplified by the swimbladder. Juveniles often perform cleaning services for other fishes.

Diet and feeding
Members of this Family of fishes eat well, enjoying a diet of small fishes, shrimps and dried foods.

Aquarium behaviour
Grunts may grow too quickly for the average aquarium.

Below: **Anisotremus virginicus**
This fine adult specimen displays the typical bright blue streaks and dark vertical bars. A similarly marked 'twin' species, A.taeniatus occurs in the Pacific Ocean.

Anisotremus virginicus
Porkfish
● **Distribution:** Caribbean.
● **Length:** 300mm/12in (wild), 150mm/6in (aquarium).
● **Diet and feeding:** In the wild, brittle starfish, crustaceans, etc. In the aquarium, worms, chopped meat foods, etc. Nocturnal feeder.
● **Aquarium behaviour:** Keep juvenile specimens only. A large tank will suit them well.

The body is triangular, the highest part being just behind the head. The steep forehead is fairly long and the eyes are large. The yellow body is streaked with bright blue lines and two black bars cross the head region, one through the eye and one just behind the gill cover.

The juvenile coloration is different: the cream body has black horizontal stripes and a black blotch on the caudal peduncle. The head is yellow and the larger fins have red marks on their edges.

The common collective name of Grunts comes from the noise these fishes make when they are taken from the water. They are very similar to the Majestic Snapper, *Symphorichthys spilurus.*

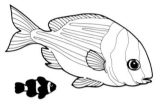

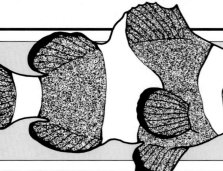

Common Clown (*Amphiprion ocellaris*)
Mature at 80mm (3.2in) and shown as a guide
to the maximum wild size of each species.

Family: SCATOPHAGIDAE
Butterfishes

Family characteristics
Like the Monodactylidae, the fishes in this Family are also estuarine and can be kept with some success in brackish water or even freshwater aquariums.

Diet and feeding
These fishes will eat anything, including greenfood, such as lettuce, spinach and green peas.

Aquarium behaviour
It is usual to keep Scats in the company of *Monodactylus* species.

Scatophagus argus
Scat; Argus Fish
● **Distribution:** Indo-Pacific.
● **Length:** 300mm/12in (wild).
● **Diet and feeding:** Will eat anything, including greenstuff. Scavenger.
● **Aquarium behaviour:** Peaceful.

Like *Monodactylus* sp., the Scat is almost equally at home in salt, brackish or even fresh water, but it thrives best in sea water. It frequents coastal and estuarine waters, where it is assured of a good supply of animal waste and other unsavoury material. (Its scientific name means 'excrement eater'). The oblong body is laterally compressed and reminiscent of Butterflyfishes and Angelfishes. It is green-brown with a number of large dark spots, which become less prominent on adult fishes. A deep notch divides the spiny first part and the soft-rayed rear section of the dorsal fin. Juveniles have more red coloration, especially on the fins.

Below: **Scatophagus argus**
The Scat is a familiar fish to hobbyists, as it can be kept with varying degrees of success in both brackish and fresh water. Adult specimens require full-strength sea water to develop fully. An active fish that will eat anything.

A practical reminder
Remember that the number of tropical marine fishes you can keep is much smaller than the number of coldwater or tropical freshwater species that you could accommodate in a similar tank.

Family: SCIAENIDAE
Croakers and Drums

Family characteristics
Most of the species likely to be suitable for the aquarium come from the western Atlantic, although a species from the opposite side of the American continent, in the eastern Pacific, is another possible contender.

The fishes in this Family are also capable of making sounds by resonating the swimbladder. Their strikingly marked bodies are usually elongated, often with a high first dorsal fin.

Diet and feeding
Most species may pose problems in their day to day care, being somewhat fussy eaters; success in the aquarium relies upon a constant supply of small live foods.

Aquarium behaviour
Fine with peacable tankmates. Will spawn in ideal conditions.

Equetus acuminatus
Cubbyu; High Hat
- **Distribution:** Caribbean.
- **Length:** 250mm/10in (wild), 150mm/6in (aquarium).
- **Diet and feeding:** Crustaceans, molluscs, soft-bodied invertebrates; live foods preferred in captivity. Slow bottom feeder.
- **Aquarium behaviour:** The long fins may be tempting to other fish, so be sure to keep them with non-agressive tankmates.

The main feature of this fish is the very tall first dorsal fin, which is carried erect. The pale body is covered with many horizontal black bands and the black fins have white leading rays. The chin barbels are used to detect food swimming below the fish, which then snaps downward to catch its prey. This species is probably the hardiest of the genus.

Left: **Equetus acuminatus**
The small barbels underneath the mouth are a good indication that the Cubbyu, or High Hat, is a bottom-feeding species.

Equetus lanceolatus
Jack-knife Fish; Ribbonfish
- **Distribution:** Caribbean.
- **Length:** 250mm/10in (wild).
- **Diet and feeding:** Crustaceans, molluscs, soft-bodied invertebrates. Slow bottom feeder.
- **Aquarium behaviour:** Its fins may be attacked by other fish. Can be aggressive towards its own kind when adult.

The high first dorsal fin of this very beautiful fish has a white-edged black line through it, that continues like a crescent through the body to the tip of the caudal fin. This gives the fish a forward sloping appearance. Further vertical black bars cross the eye and the body just behind the head. A delicate fish in captivity, which may be susceptible to skin infections for no apparent reason.

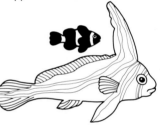

Below: **Equetus lanceolatus**
The strikingly attractive Jack-knife Fish is unfortunately rather delicate, and succumbs easily to shock and stress.

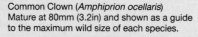

Common Clown (*Amphiprion ocellaris*)
Mature at 80mm (3.2in) and shown as a guide
to the maximum wild size of each species.

Family: SCORPAENIDAE

Dragonfishes, Lionfishes, Scorpionfishes and Turkeyfishes

Here are the exotic 'villains' of the aquarium. They are predatory carnivores that glide up to their prey and engulf it with their large mouths. The highly ornamental fins are not just there for decoration, since they have poisonous stinging cells and will inflict a very painful wound. HANDLE THESE FISHES WITH CARE. If you are stung, bathing the affected area in very hot water will alleviate the pain and help to 'coagulate' the poison.

During spawning, the pair of fishes rises to the upper levels of the water and a gelatinous ball of eggs is released. When they are 10-12mm (about 0.5in) long, the fry sink to the bottom.

Diet and feeding

As you might expect, these fishes require some form of live food – usually goldfishes – if they are to thrive in captivity. Feeding periods can be spaced apart, providing enough food has been taken; in practical terms this can be several goldfish at one 'sitting'. However, they can quite easily be weaned on to a diet of fish meats, suitable frozen foods and dead Lancefish.

Aquarium behaviour

Members of the Scorpaenidae are usually peaceful in captivity, but do not put temptation their way by keeping them with small fishes.

Dendrochirus (Brachirus) brachypterus

Turkeyfish

● **Distribution:** Indo-Pacific, Red Sea.
● **Length:** 170mm/6.7in (wild), 100mm/4in (aquarium).
● **Diet and feeding:** Small fishes, meat foods. Sedentary, engulfs passing prey.
● **Aquarium behaviour:** Keep in a species aquarium or together with larger fish.

A very ornate fish. The red-brown body has many white-edged vertical bars. The dorsal fin is multirayed and tissue spans the elongated rays. When spread, the fins have more obvious transverse patterning. The male has a longer pectoral fin and larger head than the female. At breeding time, the male darkens in colour; females become paler. This species does not grow as large as *Pterois* spp. It has attracted the alternative popular name of Dwarf Lionfish.

Below:
Dendrochirus brachypterus
It is well worth spending some time examining the very fine details of finnage, coloration and the overall appearance of this fish. Camouflage and species-recognition colour patterns, very poisonous defence mechanisms, together with a very healthy appetite, are all combined in this magnificent fish. A talking point for any visitor who sees one of these fishes in your aquarium.

A practical reminder
Fishes caught by means of drugs and explosives are often cheaper, but they are a lot less hardy and likely to have a shorter lifespan than fishes caught by more traditional, respectable methods.

Pterois antennata
Scorpionfish
● **Distribution:** Indo-Pacific, Red Sea.
● **Length:** 250mm/10in (wild), 100-150mm/4-6in (aquarium).
● **Diet and feeding:** Generally live foods such as small fishes, but all Lionfishes can be acclimatized to take frozen shrimps and similar items in the aquarium.
● **Aquarium behaviour:** Predatory.

The red bands on the body are wider and less numerous than on *P.volitans*. The white rays of the dorsal and pectoral fins are very elongated. It is possible to distinguish the sexes of all *Pterois* sp. at breeding time since the males darken and the females become paler and have noticeably larger abdomens. A slow-swimming fish that takes sudden gulps of food.

Above: **Pterois antennata**
Considering the bewildering array of fins slowly undulating in the water currents, it is not surprising that the stationary lurking Scorpionfish is often dismissed by its unsuspecting victims as a harmless piece of floating seaweed - until it is too late to escape that great gulping mouth. Perhaps this is its true fascination for some hobbyists who keep these fishes.

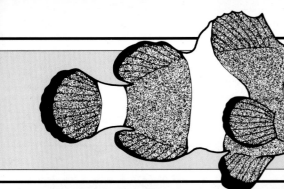

Common Clown (*Amphiprion ocellaris*)
Mature at 80mm (3.2in) and shown as a guide
to the maximum wild size of each species.

Above: **Pterois radiata**
*The dark bars across the head
(from the hornlike growths to the
bottom rear edge of the gill cover)
and body are accentuated by thin
white borders on each side.
Lionfishes often remain motionless
under ledges or in cave mouths
waiting for a potential meal to pass.*

Pterois radiata
White-fin Lionfish
● **Distribution:** Indo-Pacific,
Red Sea.
● **Length:** 250mm/10in (wild),
150mm/6in (aquarium).
● **Diet and feeding:** Smaller fishes
and meaty foods as described for
P. antennata. Slow-swimming
sudden gulper.
● **Aquarium behaviour:** Predatory.

Again, the red bands on the body
are wider and less numerous than
on *P.volitans.* The white rays of the
dorsal and pectoral fins are very
elongated and give this fish a very
graceful appearance. This species
is also known by the alternative
name of *Pteropterus radiatus.*

Pterois volitans
Lionfish; Scorpionfish
● **Distribution:** Indo-Pacific.
● **Length:** 350mm/14in (wild).
● **Diet and feeding:** Smaller fishes
and suitable meaty foods. Slow-
swimming sudden gulper.
● **Aquarium behaviour:**
Unsociable.

Pterois volitans is the most well-
known fish in this group. The
dorsal fin rays are quite separate
and the pectoral fins are only
partially filled with tissue. The
pelvic fins are red, and the anal
and caudal fins are comparatively
clear. Thick and thin red bands
alternate across the body and
there are tentacle-like growths
above the eyes.

Right: **Pterois volitans**
*This 'victim's eye view' of the
Lionfish illustrates another method
of capture; prey is manoeuvred
into a corner or area of no retreat,
the outspread fins preventing any
possibility of escape. Then the
usual quick gulp, and it's all over.*

A practical reminder
It is vitally important that you keep a
constant check on the water conditions
in your marine aquarium; the fishes are
less tolerant of changing conditions
than their freshwater counterparts.

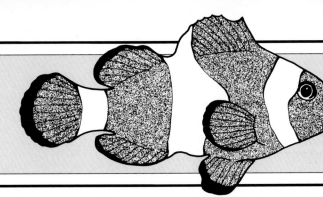

Common Clown (*Amphiprion ocellaris*)
Mature at 80mm (3.2in) and shown as a guide
to the maximum wild size of each species.

Family: SERRANIDAE
Sea Basses and Groupers

Family characteristics
Many juvenile forms of this large Family of predatory fishes have become aquarium favourites. Equally popular are the Basslets, whose brilliant colours ensure them a permanent place in the marine aquarium.

Most of the species within this group are hermaphrodite and therefore lack any clear sexual dimorphism. Even so, many species undergo colour changes during breeding, turning darker, paler, or taking on a bicolour pattern. Not surprisingly, 'females' become distended with eggs – another clue to their likely functional sex.

Diet and feeding
Include crustaceans and meaty foods in the diet of these fishes.

Aquarium behaviour
The majority of species need a large aquarium.

Anthias squamipinnis
*Wreckfish; Orange Sea Perch;
Lyre-tail Coralfish*
● **Distribution:** Indo-Pacific.
● **Length:** 125mm/5in (wild).
● **Diet and feeding:** Preferably live foods, or meat foods. Bold and prefers moving foods.
● **Aquarium behaviour:** Peaceful.

This very beautiful orange-red fish has elongated rays in the dorsal fin, a deeply forked caudal fin and long pelvic fins. It is a shoaling species that needs companions of the same species. Males have an elongated third dorsal spine are usually larger and more conspicuously coloured than females. Dominant males are quite happy for a harem to follow them.

Below: **Anthias squamipinnis**
The gorgeous colour and extended fins of the male Wreckfish are bound to attract the attention of a passing female, only too happy to join a growing band of admirers.

172

A practical reminder
Maintain the pH value of the water in the aquarium in the range 7.9-8.3. A falling pH value means that the water is losing its ability to remain in a stable condition; carry out a water change.

Calloplesiops altivelis
Marine Betta
● **Distribution:** Indo-Pacific.
● **Length:** 150mm/6in (wild).
● **Diet and feeding:** Small fishes, meaty foods. Predatory.
● **Aquarium behaviour:** Err on the side of caution, and do not keep with small fishes.

A very beautiful and deceptive fish: the trick is to decide which way it is facing, since the dorsal fin has a 'false-eye' marking near its rear edge. The dark brown body is covered with light blue spots and all the fins are very elongated. This species swims near the top of the aquarium.

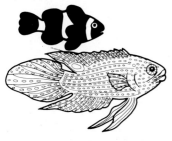

Right: **Calloplesiops altivelis**
The fins of this fish are very similar to those of the freshwater Siamese Fighting Fish, Betta splendens, *hence the popular name.*

Left: **Cephalopholis miniatus**
Ranging from the Red Sea to the mid-Pacific, the Coral Trout inhabits the coral reefs, looking for a meal of smaller fishes. It often hides away in caves or under ledges, denying the fishkeeper a view of its spectacular colouring. An alternative, and very apt, name for this species is Jewel Bass.

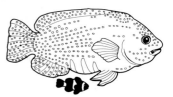

Cephalopholis miniatus
Coral Trout; Red Grouper
● **Distribution:** Indo-Pacific.
● **Length:** 450mm/18in (wild).
● **Diet and feeding:** Smaller fishes and meaty foods. Predatory.
● **Aquarium behaviour:** Do not keep with small fishes.

The body and the dorsal, anal and caudal fins of *C. miniatus* are bright red and covered with bright blue spots. However, the pectoral and pelvic fins are plain red. Other fishes bear a resemblance to this species, but they do not have the distinguishing rounded caudal fin.

173

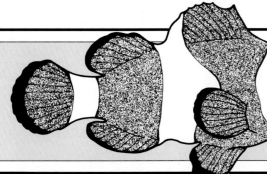

Common Clown (*Amphiprion ocellaris*)
Mature at 80mm (3.2in) and shown as a guide
to the maximum wild size of each species.

Chromileptis altivelis

Pantherfish; Polka-Dot Grouper
● **Distribution:** Indo-Pacific.
● **Length:** 500mm/20in (wild),
300mm/12in (aquarium).
● **Diet and feeding:** Live foods.
Bold feeder.
● **Aquarium behaviour:** It is better
not to keep this species with
smaller fishes. However, its

smallish mouth makes it the least
harmful of all the Grouper fishes.

Juveniles have black blotches on a
white body – effective disruptive
camouflage. As the fish matures,
these blotches increase in number
but decrease in size. The result is a
very graceful fish, and one that is
constantly on the move in the tank.

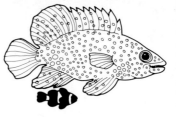

Above: **Chromileptis altivelis**
*A splendid juvenile in fine colour,
living up to its common name of
Polka-Dot Grouper. As is often the
case, the most beautiful of fishes
are quite likely to be the most
predatory. For this reason, do not
be tempted to keep this fish with
smaller species in the aquarium.*

A practical reminder
Cutting corners to reduce expenses is a false economy, especially in the delicately balanced world of the marine tank. Neglecting regular maintenance practices is another recipe for failure.

Gramma loreto
Royal Gramma
● **Distribution:** Western Atlantic.
● **Length:** 130mm/5in (wild), 75mm/3in (aquarium).
● **Diet and feeding:** Eats a wide variety of foods, including chopped shrimp, greenstuff and dried foods.
● **Aquarium behaviour:** This cave-dwelling fish should be acclimatized gradually to bright light. It may resent other cave-dwelling species, particularly the Yellow-headed Jawfish, *Opisthognathus aurifrons.* Aggressive towards its own kind.

The main feature of this species is its remarkable colouring. The front half of the body is magenta, the rear half bright golden-yellow. A thin black line slants backwards through the eye. These somewhat secretive cave dwellers should not be kept with boisterous species. An almost identical species, *Pseudochromis paccagnellae*, has a narrow white line dividing the two main body colours.

Spawning activity has been observed – paradoxically, not in nature but in captivity. Four fish grouped themselves into two 'pairs', each comprising one small and one large fish. The larger fish lined a cave with algal threads and then appeared to incubate a mouthful of eggs. The eggs were later rejected and proved to be infertile, but this does shed light on the possible reproductive methods practised by this species. The dissimilar sizes of the fishes making up the 'pairs' seems to bear out other reports that the male fish is usually larger than the female.

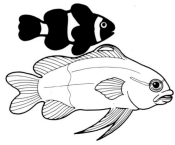

Left: **Gramma loreto**
As far as coloration goes, if big is beautiful then small can be simply stunning – as this Royal Gramma clearly demonstrates. A cave-dwelling fish, it is often very possessive, positively resenting any intrusion by other fishes into its chosen home. An aquarium stocked with many soft corals and hideaways suits this fish perfectly.

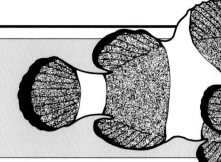

Common Clown (*Amphiprion ocellaris*)
Mature at 80mm (3.2in) and shown as a guide
to the maximum wild size of each species.

Grammistes sexlineatus

*Golden-striped Grouper; White/
Black-Striped Sea Bass*
● **Distribution:** Indo-Pacific.
● **Length:** 250mm/10in (wild).
● **Diet and feeding:** Animal and
meaty foods. Bold.
● **Aquarium behaviour:** Do not
keep with smaller fishes.

Alternate black and white
horizontal stripes cover the body.
Although a good aquarium subject,
it can give off toxic secretions
when frightened, annoyed or even
in the process of dying. It is
unlikely to reach its full size when
kept in captivity.

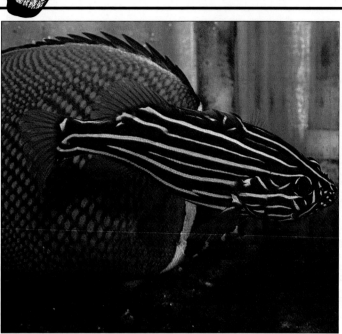

Above: **Grammistes sexlineatus**
*This fish secretes a toxin if
frightened or disturbed, a trait it
shares with the Boxfishes. A large*
aquarium containing this grouper
(introduced ahead of suitably sized
tankmates), may prove successful;
the grouper may become tame.

Mirolabrichthys tuka

Purple Queen; Butterfly Perch
● **Distribution:** Pacific.
● **Length:** 125mm/5in (wild).
● **Diet and feeding:** Chopped
meaty foods. Bold.
● **Aquarium behaviour:** Generally
peaceful.

The sides of the body are purple,
topped with yellow. The head is
also yellow, while the fins are light
blue. Its gorgeous colours and
pointed snout make this fish easy
to recognize. Unfortunately, this
species does not survive long in
captivity. In the similarly coloured
species, *M.evansi*, the yellow at
the top of the body extends into
the caudal fin.

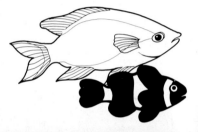

Lutjanus sebae

Emperor Snapper
● **Distribution:** Indo-Pacific.
● **Length:** 900mm/36in (wild).
● **Diet and feeding:** Animal and
meaty foods. Bold.
● **Aquarium behaviour:** Although
peaceful, do not keep this species
with smaller fishes. Despite its
attractive coloration, it will soon
outgrow the tank, and is therefore
not really suitable for anything but
the largest public aquarium.

The white body has three red-
brown transverse bands: the first
runs from the snout up the
forehead and the second is
'L-shaped' running vertically down
from the dorsal fin to the pelvic fins
and along the ventral surface into
the front half of the anal fin. The
third band is crescent shaped,
beginning in the rear of the dorsal
fin and crossing the caudal
peduncle into the lower half of the
caudal fin, which has a similarly
coloured bar on the top edge.

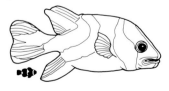

Right: **Lutjanus sebae**
*This Emperor Snapper is not only a
favourite with marine aquarists, it
also makes good eating! Sadly, the
bold coloration fades with age.*

A practical reminder
Cultivate a good relationship with your dealer. This will enable him to get to know your system and your fishes and thus be in a better position to offer advice in the event of any problems.

Left: **Mirolabrichthys tuka**
The delicate colours and 'snouty' appearance make this species both easy to identify and tempting to own, but it is a delicate species.

Above: **Mirolabrichthys evansi**
Another very attractive and related species, the yellow extending into the caudal fin; like M.tuka, it is difficult to keep in captivity.

Pseudochromis paccagnella
False Gramma; Dottyback; Royal Dottyback; Paccagnella's Dottyback
● **Distribution:** Pacific.
● **Length:** 50mm/2in (wild).
● **Diet and feeding:** Finely chopped meat foods, brineshrimp.
● **Aquarium behaviour:** Do not keep with lively fishes. May tend to nip at other fishes.

This species is almost identical to *Gramma loreto*, but a thin white line – often incomplete or hard to see – divides the two main body colours.

Left:
Pseudochromis paccagnella
The False Gramma – or Dottyback – requires similar aquarium conditions to its lookalike relative, the Royal Gramma. Provide a tank well stocked with soft corals and convenient retreats to ensure a sense of security.

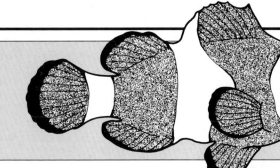

Common Clown (*Amphiprion ocellaris*)
Mature at 80mm (3.2in) and shown as a guide
to the maximum wild size of each species.

Symphorichthys spilurus
Majestic Snapper
● **Distribution:** Pacific.
● **Length:** 320mm/12.6in (wild).
● **Diet and feeding:** Meaty foods. Bold feeder.
● **Aquarium behaviour:** Do not keep with smaller fishes.

This fish is almost identical in colour to *Anisotremus virginicus*, the Atlantic Porkfish. The yellow body has horizontal blue lines and the fins are yellow. Two vertical black bars cross the head and there is a distinguishing white-ringed black blotch on the caudal peduncle. The dorsal fin develops extremely long filamentous extensions.

Above: **Symphorichthys spilurus**
Only the narrow band of land between the Pacific and Atlantic cuts off this species from the almost identical Atlantic Porkfish, Anisotremus virginicus *(described on page 165), which lacks the long extensions and caudal spot.*

Family: SIGANIDAE
Rabbitfishes

Family characteristics
The Rabbitfishes have deep oblong bodies and are fairly laterally compressed. The mouth is small and equipped for browsing on algae and other vegetation. The spines on the dorsal and anal fins are poisonous and so be sure to handle these fishes extremely carefully. Their alternative common name is 'Spinefoot', a reference to the fact that unsuspecting waders who disturb grazing fish risk a wound on the foot caused by the fishes' spines. Juveniles are often more brightly coloured than adults.

Only a dozen or so species belong to this Family, but they have an economic significance in the tropics, where they are caught for food. The one species that is especially familiar to hobbyists, *Lo (Siganus) vulpinus*, has a tubular mouth, which contrasts with the normal rabbit-shaped mouth of the Family.

Some reports of spawning in captivity – albeit of species not featured here – indicate that changing some of the water, or even decreasing its depth, may trigger off spawning activities.

Diet and feeding
Rabbitfishes must have vegetable matter in their diet, although they will adapt to established dried foods and live foods in the aquarium.

Aquarium behaviour
Active, fast-growing fishes that need plenty of swimming space.

Lo (Siganus) vulpinus
Foxface; Fox-fish; Badgerfish
● **Distribution:** Pacific.
● **Length:** 250mm/10in (wild).
● **Diet and feeding:** Most foods, but must have vegetable matter. Bold grazer that adopts a typical 'head-down' feeding attitude.
● **Aquarium behaviour:** Lively but peaceable, although it may be aggressive towards members of its own species.

The white head has two broad black bands: one runs obliquely back from the snout, through the eye and up the forehead; the second band is triangular, beginning below the throat and ending behind the gill cover. This coloration obviously gave rise to the common name of Badgerfish among European hobbyists, more familiar with the Badger than other hobbyists who, for some reason, feel the fish's face looks more like that of a fox. Although physically similar to the Surgeonfishes, it has no spine on the caudal peduncle, and the pelvic fins are not very well

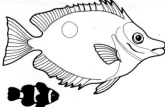

developed, having only a few rays.

Females are generally larger than males; at breeding time, the females are plumper, with larger genital openings.

Above: **Lo vulpinus**
The Foxface, or Badgerfish, has a tubular mouth, which is rather at variance with the more rabbitlike shape characteristic of other members of this Family.

Above right: **Siganus virgatus**
The Silver Badgerfish has a more typically shaped mouth, which is ideally suited to grazing and rasping algae from firm surfaces. Remember that the dorsal and anal spines are dangerous.

A practical reminder
If you can consistently patronize one dealer you will be able to locate the source of any problems. This will be frustrated if you have bought fishes or equipment from many different sources.

Family: SYNANCEIIDAE

Stonefishes

Family characteristics
Like sharks, these fishes hold a morbid fascination for many fishkeepers. The lifestyle of these fishes is quite simple; they lie almost completely concealed among rocks and seaweed, or semi-buried in the sand, waiting for food to come along. Their body colour and irregular shape provide the perfect disguise. These very dangerous fishes have erectile spines that can inject an extremely poisonous toxin. Although a wound may not be fatal, an affected limb may have to be amputated. Handle these species with extreme caution. If you should ever visit the natural habitat of these fish, always wear protective shoes and investigate rocks and corals with a stick, never with your hands.

Diet and feeding
Predators, but almost by default in that they wait for unsuspecting prey to venture too close to them.

Aquarium behaviour
Apart from their 'horror' value, these fishes are not likely to display a great deal of activity. They are usually kept as 'status symbols' in species tanks.

Above: **Synanceja horrida**
If you were a fish, this is about the only part of the Stonefish that you would recognize as it lies in wait for passing prey, the rest being perfectly camouflaged against the substrate. As a fishkeeper, be sure to handle this fish with extreme care, principally because of the very poisonous spines.

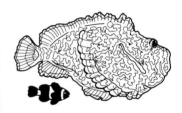

Synanceja horrida
Stonefish
- **Distribution:** Indo-Pacific.
- **Length:** 300mm/12in (wild).
- **Diet and feeding:** Will eat anything that it can swallow. Sedentary.
- **Aquarium behaviour:** Keep only with larger fish; in a species aquarium it will not require quite as much space as the more free-swimming species.

So effective is the natural camouflage of this species that it is almost impossible to describe! Generally, it is a mottled brown, with spots of more brown or red. The interior of the mouth is a paler colour. Beware of moving rocks or other similar decorations in the tank, just in case they aren't entirely what they seem!

Siganus virgatus
Silver Badgerfish
- **Distribution:** Pacific.
- **Length:** 260mm/10.2in (wild).
- **Diet and feeding:** Live foods, meat foods and plenty of greenstuff. Bold grazer.
- **Aquarium behaviour:** Lively but peaceable, although it may be aggressive towards fellow members of its own species.

The silvery yellow body is more oval and the head more rounded than in the previous species. Again, the head has two badger-like black bars, the second of which begins narrowly just below the pectoral fins and broadens as it runs up to the top of the body. The head and forepart of the body are covered with blue lines, producing an intricate pattern.

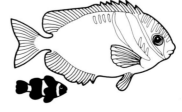

179

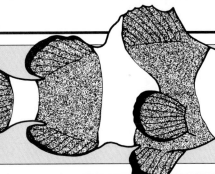

Common Clown (*Amphiprion ocellaris*)
Mature at 80mm (3.2in) and shown as a guide
to the maximum wild size of each species.

Family: SYNGNATHIDAE
Pipefishes and Seahorses

Family characteristics
Every fishkeeper loves the Seahorse, and the equally appealing Pipefish, which could be described as a 'straightened out' version of the Seahorse. Pipefishes are found among crevices on coral reefs, whereas Seahorses, being poor swimmers, anchor themselves to coral branches with their prehensile tails. Many Pipefishes are estuarine species, and are therefore able to tolerate varying salinities, even entering fresh water.

When Seahorses reproduce, the female uses her ovopositor tube to deposit the eggs into the male's abdominal pouch, where they are fertilized and subsequently incubated. Incubation periods range from two weeks to two months, depending on the species.

Diet and feeding
Seahorses and Pipefishes have small mouths and require quantities of small live foods to thrive; brineshrimp and rotifers are suitable, but some fishkeepers use Guppy fry.

Aquarium behaviour
Pipefishes and Seahorses do best in a quiet aquarium.

Dunkerocampus dactyliophorus
Banded Pipefish
● **Distribution:** Pacific.
● **Length:** 180mm/7in (wild).
● **Diet and feeding:** Very small live foods. Browser.
● **Aquarium behaviour:** Needs a quiet aquarium.

The entire length of the body is covered with alternate light and dark rings. The most distinctive feature of the fish is the disproportionately large caudal fin, which is white with a red central blotch. The other fins are small and hard to see, and there are no pelvic fins. The snout is very long. The eggs are carried by the male on the ventral surface of the body.

Right: **Hippocampus hudsonius**
A pinkish individual of this elegant species. Seahorses adopt a vertical position when at rest. When swimming, they lean forward, propulsion being provided by the fan-like dorsal fin.

Below:
Dunkerocampus dactyliophorus
The Banded (or Harlequin) Pipefish is a brightly coloured and fascinating addition to a quiet aquarium. Note the tiny pectoral fins and dorsal fin halfway along.

A practical reminder
As interest in marine fishkeeping grows around the world, the hobby magazines have increased their marine-orientated articles. These offer a good source of information on up-to-date practices.

Hippocampus hudsonius

Florida Seahorse
● **Distribution:** Western Atlantic.
● **Length:** 150mm/6in (wild).
● **Diet and feeding:** Small animal foods. Browser.
● **Aquarium behaviour:** Needs a quiet, non-boisterous aquarium.

The pelvic and caudal fins are absent, and the anal fin is very small. The tail is prehensile. The coloration of this species is variable; individuals may be grey, brown, yellow or red. The male incubates the young in the abdominal pouch.

Hippocampus kuda

Yellow Seahorse
● **Distribution:** Indo-Pacific.
● **Length:** 250mm/10in (wild) – measured vertically.
● **Diet and feeding:** Plenty of live foods, young freshwater livebearer fry, very small crustaceans, brineshrimp. *Daphnia* etc. Browser.
● **Aquarium behaviour:** Best kept in a species tank.

Newly imported specimens may be grey, but once they have settled into the aquarium, the body takes on the a yellow hue. An irresistible fish with a fascinating method of reproduction. The male incubates the fertilized eggs in his pouch for four to five weeks before they hatch. This species needs anchorage points in the aquarium, such as marine algae and other suitably branched decorations.

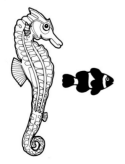

Above: **Hippocampus kuda**
Apart from the fascination of its unusual body shape, with its equine appearance, and amusing activity among the coral branches, the Seahorse also displays a very different method of reproduction – the male incubating the fertilized eggs in his abdominal pouch.

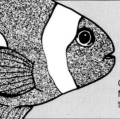

Common Clown (*Amphiprion ocellaris*)
Mature at 80mm (3.2in) and shown as a guide
to the maximum wild size of each species.

Family: TETRAODONTIDAE
Puffers

Family characteristics

Puffers are generally smaller than Porcupinefishes and smooth scaled. Their jaws are fused, but a divided bone serves as front teeth. 'Tetraodon' means four toothed (two teeth at the top and two at the bottom), whereas 'Diodon' means two teeth (one at the top and one at the bottom). These fishes use their pectoral fins to achieve highly manoeuvrable propulsion, but the pelvic fins are absent. Their inflating capabilities vary from species to species; *Tetraodon* sp. – among which are some freshwater members – are 'fully-inflatable', but members of the genus *Canthigaster* can only manage partial inflation. The flesh is poisonous.

Diet and feeding

Puffers will eat readily in the aquarium, taking finely chopped meat foods. They have a bold feeding manner.

Aquarium behaviour

Generally peaceful but occasionally may be aggressive towards other fishes. Do not keep with invertebrates.

Arothron hispidus

White-spotted Blow fish
● **Distribution :** Indo-Pacfic, Red Sea.
● **Length:** 500mm/20in (wild).
● **Diet and feeding:** Finely chopped meat foods. Cruncher.
● **Aquarium behaviour:** Peaceful. Do not keep with invertebrates.

The distinctive features of this species are the number of bluish white spots over the patchy grey body. These spots are not so pronounced in adult fishes. Just behind the gill cover, and at the base of the pectoral fins, there is a dark patch surrounded by a circular yellow pattern. Like most Puffers, the flesh is poisonous.

Below: **Arothron meleagris**
Like all Puffers, the Spotted Puffer will inflate its body when disturbed or frightened, but do not provoke it.

Left: **Arothron hispidus**
As members of the Tetraodontidae, *Pufferfish have their teeth fused together to form four powerful teeth (Tetra= four, odon= toothed) at the front of the mouth, which they use to crunch up molluscs and crustaceans. Just in front of the white-rimmed eyes, two tentacle-like nostrils are visible.*

Arothron meleagris

Spotted Puffer; Guinea Fowl Puffer; Golden Puffer
● **Distribution:** Indo Pacific, Red Sea.
● **Length:** 300mm/12in (wild).
● **Diet and feeding:** Finely chopped meat foods. Cruncher.
● **Aquarium behaviour:** Peaceful, but do not keep with invertebrates.

Although a plain yellow colour phase occurs, normally the brown-grey body is densely covered with white spots, very similar to the female *Ostracion meleagris* (see page 140), although the mouth is clearly different in structure. When kept in a spacious aquarium, it will be less likely to release its poison under stress from other fishes.

Canthigaster margaritatus (C. solandri)

Sharpnosed Puffer
● **Distribution:** Indo-Pacific, Red Sea.
● **Length:** 120mm/4.7in (wild), 50mm/2in (aquarium).
● **Diet and feeding:** Finely chopped meat foods. Bold cruncher.
● **Aquarium behaviour:** Peaceful, except towards members of its own kind.

This spectacularly patterned fish has a gold-brown body and a caudal fin covered with pale spots. A blue wavy line replaces the spots on the upper part of the body and a large white-edged black spot appears at the base of the dorsal fin. The fish swims with its caudal fin folded. The pelvic fins are absent. Some authorities place this genus in a separate group, the Canthigasteridae.

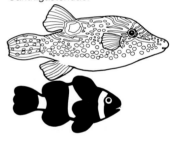

Canthigaster valentini

Black-saddled Puffer
● **Distribution:** Indo-Pacific.
● **Length:** 200mm/8in (wild), 75mm/3in (aquarium).
● **Diet and feeding:** Finely chopped meaty foods. Bold cruncher.
● **Aquarium behaviour:** Peaceful, although it has a reputation for nipping the fins of species with long fins, and may not tolerate its own kind.

The lower half of the body is cream in colour and covered with small brown dots. The upper part has four saddle-shaped dark areas; the one covering the forehead also has blue lines. These blue lines also occur on the two narrow vertical bars that reach three-quarters of the way down the sides of the fish between the head and dorsal fin. There is a final plain patch on the top of the caudal peduncle. A black spot at the base of the dorsal fin may merge with the other dark markings. The fins are red, but for the caudal fin, which is yellow. The pelvic fins are absent. This species is considered by some to be synonymous with *Canthigaster cinctus*.

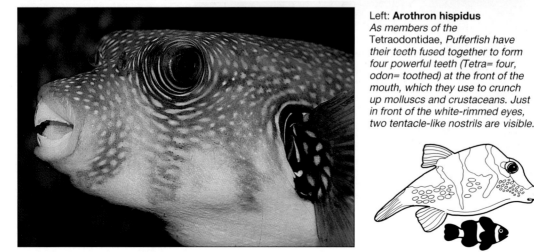

A practical reminder
Breeding marine fishes is news! If you attempt to breed your fishes (or they oblige anyway), do keep records of successes, failures, methods used, to benefit the less experienced among us.

Above:
Canthigaster margaritatus
This Sharpnosed Puffer is decorated with a most attractive spotted pattern, with bright radiating stripes around the eyes and top of the body. The clamped caudal fin is a characteristic of this fish's swimming action. They make good scavengers around the aquarium, usually adopting a head-down attitude, always on the lookout for meaty foods, particularly relishing snails. This wide-ranging species has, not surprisingly, also earned alternative names of C.solandri *and* C.papua, *presumably from different discoverers.*

Left: **Canthigaster valentini**
The Black-saddled Puffer has strong jaws with which it can crunch coral in its search for food. A nip from its teeth can be very painful. Although its slow swimming actions presumably make it an excellent target, its poisonous skin secretions give it a good defence against predators.

183

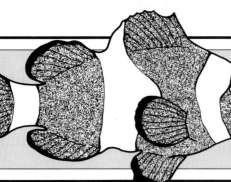

Common Clown (*Amphiprion ocellaris*)
Mature at 80mm (3.2in) and shown as a guide
to the maximum wild size of each species.

Family: THERAPONIDAE
Tigerfishes

Family characteristics
The most familiar species in this Serranid-related Family, the
Target Fish, is not confined to the marine aquarium, as it can be
kept in brackish and even freshwater tanks. It is a common inshore
fish, entering bays and estuaries. The dorsal fin appears to be
divided, the front spiny part being separated by a notch from the
softer rayed rear half.

The adhesive eggs are deposited in hollows or under stones
and guarded by the male until they hatch.

Diet and feeding
These are carnivorous fishes that need meaty animal foods.

Aquarium behaviour
Can be quarrelsome with their own species if kept in overcrowded
conditions, so allow plenty of space in the aquarium.

Therapon jarbua
Target Fish; Crescent Bass;
Tiger Bass
● **Distribution:** Indo-Pacific.
● **Length:** 250mm/10in (wild),
150mm/6in (aquarium).
● **Diet and feeding:** Animal foods.
Predatory.
● **Aquarium behaviour:** A
constantly moving fish, possibly
too lively (and too fast-growing) for
other species in the same
aquarium. It does well in brackish
water aquariums with species such
as *Monodactylus* (page 136) and
Scatophagus (page 166).

This species is easily recognizable
by the dark horizontal markings on
the body, which appear concentric
around the dorsal fin – and thus
target-shaped when viewed from
above. The two dorsal fins and
each lobe of the striped caudal fin
have dark tips.

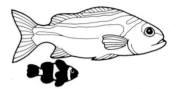

Below: **Therapon jarbua**
Fishkeepers fortunate enough to
take their vacation in the tropics
and taking their morning
constitutional walk along the
beach, can often see the Target
Fish as it cruises into the shallows
almost around their feet.

Family: ZANCLIDAE
Tobies

Family characteristics
The single species of this Family, *Zanclus canescens*, is a shoaling fish found throughout the Indo-Pacific Ocean. Scientifically, it is more closely related to the Acanthuridae (through the Suborder Acanthuroidea), particularly because of the physical form of the young fish, although it is difficult to see any resemblance at first glance in the adult. Other authorities feel that it is superficially nearer to the Chaetodontidae Family, especially to the similar genus *Heniochus*. The common name of Moorish Idol is derived from the high esteem in which the fish is held by some Moslem populations. When caught by them it is returned to the water with some ceremony.

Diet and feeding
Small crustaceans, chopped meat foods and plenty of greenstuff.

Aquarium behaviour
Since it may quarrel with others of the same species, it is best to keep only a single Moorish Idol in the aquarium.

Below: **Zanclus canescens**
Although the Moorish Idol is more closely related to Surgeonfishes than to Butterflyfishes, it lacks scalpels on the caudal peduncle, but does have hornlike projections in front of the eyes. There is often some debate about the validity of the scientific name or the often quoted Z. cornutus.

Zanclus canescens
Moorish Idol
● **Distribution:** Indo-Pacific.
● **Length:** 250mm/10in (wild), 125mm/5in (aquarium).
● **Diet and feeding:** Small crustaceans, chopped meat foods and plenty of greenstuff. Bold grazer in nature but shy in the company of other fishes.
● **Aquarium behaviour:** A sensitive shoaling fish in the wild that is difficult to acclimatize to aquarium life, especially feeding, and also may be intolerant of disease remedies. In the close confines of the aquarium, these fishes may quarrel among themselves. The ploy of keeping a number of youngsters together does not always turn out for the best either, as the dominant fish often bullies the rest into submission and eventual decline. On balance, therefore, it is best to keep only one of these fishes in the aquarium.

Three black vertical bands cross the body: one from the pelvic fins to the beginning of dorsal fin, another midway along the anal and dorsal fins, the third across the caudal fin. Behind the first black band, the body is yellow. Immediately in front of the eyes, across the beaklike snout, is a yellow saddle marking. The dorsal fin is extremely elongated, often trailing well past the caudal fin. Adult fishes have hornlike protruberances in front of the eyes.

This is not really a fish for beginners. However, if you obtain a healthy specimen and the water conditions are good, with low nitrate levels, a Moorish Idol will eat virtually anything and thrive in the aquarium.

Right: *The Banded Coral Shrimp,* Stenopus hispidus *makes a very colourful addition to the aquarium. When other shrimps become rivals, it lives up to its alternative common name of Boxing Shrimp. It also performs cleaning actions, removing parasites from fishes.*

The attraction of the marine aquarium is not limited to the fishes. The decorative corals, for example, add almost as much beauty to the underwater scene. Anyone who has travelled extensively under the sea – even if only as a television viewer – will vouch for this. However, these corals are usually dead skeletons and can only be brought to some simulation of real life by adding other living creatures that live on or around them in nature.

These animals include the sea anemones – which play host to the anemonefishes – the very colourful crabs, shrimps and prawns, tubeworms and featherdusters, starfishes, sea cucumbers, sea slugs and sea urchins. Providing sufficient care is taken to choose compatible tankmates, many of these animals can be kept alongside the fishes to present a truly complete underwater scene. Alternatively, you may want to set up a completely independent invertebrate collection, in which case you can progress to the stunningly colourful and fascinating soft corals, which open and close during the day like underwater flowers in the moving water currents.

To keep invertebrates you will need to learn different skills: many are normally sedentary, hardly moving from their coral or rockbound sites. Feeding can be a collective affair for filter feeding species – use a liquidizer to blend normal aquarium foods into a more acceptable form – but you will need to feed sea anemones by hand, placing morsels of food into their tentacles with tweezers. Any food that is missed will be taken by the scavenging crabs, shrimps or starfishes, but do not include these animals in the collection simply for this scavenging purpose.

Invertebrates will reproduce in the aquarium; sea anemones, for example, will simply divide, or expel young forms to increase their numbers. Hermit crabs make fascinating subjects for observation, especially when they are 'house hunting' for larger premises as they outgrow their former dwellings. Even at night there is activity in the aquarium; many of the soft corals and similar animals emit small points of light in the darkness.

Left: *The multitudinous tentacles of* Radianthus ritteri *make it an ideal safe 'home' for Clownfishes of the* Amphiprion *genus. Several fishes may take up tenancy in a large sea anemone such as this.*

187

The invertebrates kept in the marine aquarium range from the sedentary tubeworms and fanworms to the more mobile sea anemones, shrimps, hermit crabs, starfish and sea slugs. (The care of live corals and 'living rock' is a specialist subject and beyond the scope of this encyclopedia.) In this section, we look at the general care of invertebrates and the range of specimens available for the marine aquarium.

General care

As a rule, only if you are an experienced fishkeeper with sufficient information about the compatibility (or otherwise) of fishes and invertebrates should you try to keep both in the same aquarium. Some combinations are easier than others. It is clear, for example, that the 'inoffensive' seahorses could be safely kept together with invertebrates to create a compatible underwater marine community.

Obviously, if you decide to keep invertebrates you will have to make special provision for feeding them. Many invertebrates are not mobile enough to chase, catch or even reach their food before it is snapped up by fast-moving fishes. Others require much finer foods than fish and, again, the food usually has to be brought to them and not the other way round.

Feeding methods vary too, and many invertebrates need to be fed individually. Sometimes the presentation of the food is important. For instance, it is normal practice to put finely liquidized fish meat in the aquarium for filter feeders. This emulsion of food will be taken in by filter feeders and, in addition, may help to spur the proliferation of microorganisms in the water, which will also be taken as food later on. Obviously, it will be very hard to judge how much has been taken, so after about an hour use an efficient power filter to clear the water of uneaten food.

It is not necessary to feed invertebrates as frequently as fish; every two days is usually quite sufficient for sea anemones, for example. However, you may well enjoy hand feeding creatures such as shrimps and crabs at more regular intervals – always taking care not to overfeed them of course! Useful clearing up operations are also performed by bottom-scavenging shrimps and crabs, as well as sea cucumbers.

Invertebrates appreciate water movement much more than fishes, because they rely on the water currents to bring food circulating near to them. A reverse-flow biological filtration system fulfils this purpose very adequately. It keeps the floor of the aquarium clear of packed-down debris and brings water currents up around the more sedentary life forms. It is also a good idea to vary the water direction around the aquarium from time to time; strategically placed airstones operated at intervals are ideal for this.

Like fishes, many invertebrates appreciate algae growths. These help to absorb nitrogenous wastes and also provide browsing material and hiding places. Accordingly, a well-lit aquarium should be the order of the day, a fact that is often borne out by the way in which some invertebrates bask in areas lit by strong spotlights.

A top layer of soft coral sand will benefit species that burrow into it at night and those that constantly sift the substrate for food, such as sea cucumbers.

Invertebrates are very susceptible to changes in water conditions; they cannot tolerate any metal pollution – particularly by copper. This can be a problem if you have to treat the mixed aquarium with proprietary copper-based medicines, and this is another good reason for keeping invertebrates in a separate tank.

Some invertebrates are more nitrite tolerant than others, which makes them ideal for introducing into an almost mature aquarium. Generally you should play safe and not introduce invertebrates into a brand new set up.

Selecting healthy specimens

As relatively little is known about invertebrates, it is not easy to be sure that you are buying a healthy specimen. Always try to carry out a thorough visual inspection before making a final choice.

Even if they are not moving around, most invertebrates show signs of life, constantly twitching their tentacles, for example. Make sure that creatures are complete, although it is true that a missing limb sometimes regenerates. Starfish and sea anemones should be firm to the touch and not hanging limp and 'empty'. Examine tubeworms to see if their tentacles retract when touched. When disturbed, most molluscs and other life forms shut or retract their tentacles. Avoid any specimens where the tentacles are hanging half in or half out of the tube and any where the tube is obviously empty or damaged.

Introducing invertebrates

The same general guide lines that apply to fishes should be observed when introducing invertebrates to the aquarium (see pages 44-45). Quarantine new additions in an *unmedicated* isolation tank before introducing them into the main collection. This isolation tank should closely resemble a permanently set-up tank and be complete with a good growth of algae. Here, the new additions can be screened for disease, although they cannot be treated with proprietary remedies, due to their intolerance of copper.

Below: *The fascination of watching life in an invertebrate aquarium is never ending. Many of the animals are so small that you may be unaware of their activities. They are only seen occasionally and then not always in the same place twice. More mobile invertebrates, such as shrimps or nudibranchs, constantly disappear and reappear amid the luxuriant growths of corals.*

A SELECTION OF SPECIES

Clams

The genus *Tridacna* includes the Giant Clams (*T.gigas*) that are featured in all good underwater thriller movies. As well as obtaining food by filter feeding, the clam also digests the algae within its mantle. *T.elegans* is a smaller species. One problem with clams is that their normal activity is at such a low level that the fishkeeper does not always notice when they die. On the other hand, empty clam shells make excellent refuges and aquarium decorations.

Corals

Not all corals are hard, skeletal remains to be used simply as marine aquarium decorations. Living soft corals range in shape and form from delightfully delicate lace-like growths to the huge 'dining-table' configurations, topped with horizontal slabs. All are covered with millions of tiny tentacles that constantly wave in the water, both to breathe and to seize any passing planktonic foods. When tentacles retract, the surface of the coral becomes almost skin-like in its smoothness. At night, or under ultraviolet light, it is not unusual for the corals to emit tiny points of light. Obviously, such diverse forms of coral are not all suited for inclusion in the general bustle of the community aquarium, but a separate tank housing a self perpetuating number of soft corals and a few of the more mobile invertebrate life-forms will prove to be every bit as attractive as a marine aquarium stocked with fishes. A selection of corals suitable for inclusion in the marine aquarium are shown on this page.

Above: **Tridacna elegans**
The fringes of the shell are mirror images of one other, and form a tight fit when the Clam shuts.

Above:
Gorgonarie acanthomuricea
Gorgonarians take their name from their similarity to Medusa.

Above: **Tubipora musica**
The white tips on this piece of red Organ Pipe Coral – a favourite decoration – are the live polyps.

Below: **Dendronephthya sp.**
This soft coral makes its home either on rock surfaces or buried partially in the sand.

Left: **Euphyllia picteti**
This coral's skeleton has radiating ridges, but these are hidden by the mass of waving tentacles.

Above: **Xenia sp.**
The tentacles of this species of soft coral regularly open and close several times each minute.

Crabs

Many tropical crabs are ideal for the aquarium as they are smaller and usually more colourful than their relatives from cooler waters. However, the Anemone Crab, *Neopetrolisthes oshimai*, from the Indo-Pacific, is more closely related to the squat lobsters, since it has a tail, longer antennae and smaller back legs. As its common name suggests, it lives in close association with sea anemones, such as *Stoichactis*. It is tiny, barely reaching a length of more than 10mm (0.4in), even when mature. However, *Dardanus megistos*, the Hairy Red Hermit Crab (also from the Indo-Pacific) grows up to 200mm (8in). Hermit crabs are predatory scavengers and, while their lifestyles have a certain fascinating appeal, it is important to exercise care when choosing suitable tankmates for them – larger fishes and no small invertebrates.

Hermit crabs are particularly interesting because they carry their homes around with them in the shape of empty seashells; they have a soft abdomen which they can twist around in a spiral, thus enabling them to fit exactly into any chosen vacant shell of suitable size. As they grow, they are forced to come out of their shells and change their accommodation for larger premises; at this 'moving' stage, they are very vulnerable to predators, since their soft bodies no longer have the protection of the hard shell in which they previously lived. In an aquarium for hermit crabs, it is good policy to have a selection of various sized shells so that the crab can progress to more comfortable dwellings as it grows.

Lobsters

The highly coloured and intriguing *Enoplometopus occidentalis* is one species suitable for the aquarium. It is native to the Indo-Pacific and can reach a length of 200mm (8in). The large claws are covered with spines and the lobster does most of its feeding at night.

Nudibranchs

Sometimes it seems that these sea slugs achieve the impossible; at one and the same time they are incredibly ugly in shape and exceptionally beautiful in colour. They creep around the aquarium much like terrestrial slugs, but can also swim through the water with amazing convulsive actions. If handled, they can irritate the skin and may give off a poison to other animals as a defence mechanism. *Glossodoris* and *Casella* are just two striking examples of nudibranchs available to the marine fishkeeper.

Right: **Glossodoris sp.**
These slow-moving, brilliantly coloured sea slugs may take some time to find their way around the entire aquarium, but they are bound to brighten up the area wherever they eventually turn up.

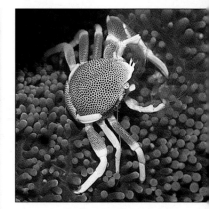

Above: **Neopetrolisthes oshimai**
This Anemone Crab is far shorter than its scientific name!

Left: **Dardanus megistos**
The rest of the Hairy Red Hermit is hidden deep inside its host shell.

Below:
Enoplometopus occidentalis
A colourful nocturnal lobster.

Above: *The multi-jointed legs of this invertebrate make for agile movement across the aquarium floor in search of food. The high-set eyes are ideal for locating food and the claws are used to collect it, and as a first line of defence.*

Sea anemones

Many fishkeepers will wish to keep a sea anemone in the aquarium, if only for the benefit of the Anemonefishes. The different species of sea anemone are not necessarily compatible, and one group often succumbs to the poisonous discharges of another. Many sea anemones have a low nitrite tolerance and you should seek advice on this point before buying any specimens for the aquarium. *Radianthus* species are a good choice, as they are more nitrite-tolerant than others, and are usually readily accepted by Anemonefishes. Other species also adopted by Anemonefishes include *Stoichactis* and *Discosoma*. A familiar sight in most aquatic stores is *Condylactis passiflora*, the Florida Sea Anemone, which has variously coloured tentacles that are more often than not tipped with violet.

Depending on their size, sea anemones have different feeding requirements. The smaller species need small particles of food – proprietary planktonic foods, cultured rotifers, brineshrimp, small freshwater *Daphnia*, *Cyclops* and maybe *Tubifex* can all be used. The larger species will be able to cope with morsels of suitable food placed within their tentacles. Crab, shrimp, mussel meat and frozen sea foods are readily taken, with the addition of pieces of liver, beef heart, and also proprietary aquarium granular and tablet foods.

Feeding twice a week is usually sufficient for large species, but smaller species can be fed with, say, brineshrimp a little more often. Needless to say, sea anemones should be offered food only when their tentacles are fully expanded. Be sure to remove any partially digested foods, ejected after a few hours or the next day, to prevent tank pollution.

Several sea anemones, although somewhat less brightly coloured, are also suitable for the coldwater marine aquarium, and are described on page 199.

Above: **Antheopsis koseiren**
The marine aquarium can be furnished just as artistically as a well-planted freshwater aquarium using contrasting colours of sea anemones and clumps of Caulerpa.

Left: **Stoichactis giganteum**
As its scientific name suggests, this short-tentacled sea anemone grows to a large size and can accommodate several clownfishes.

Sea apples

Sea apples belong to the Cucumariidae family, which includes the sea cucumbers. These strange animals are often quite brilliantly coloured. A favourite aquarium species is *Paracucumaria*, whose blue body has longitudinal yellow bars topped with bright red tentacles. Sea apples move across the aquarium floor, sifting the sand. There is generally enough food in an established aquarium for these animals, although they will take the extra foods provided for the benefit of other filter feeders.

Sea urchins

Sea urchins have a downward-facing mouth and vary in shape from roughly spherical to a flattened disc. Five rows of feet provide motive power; sometimes, the defensive spines that cover the body also assist movement. Despite being spine-covered, sea urchins are often preyed upon by large fishes such as Triggerfishes, although Cardinalfishes often use a sea urchin's spines as a convenient sanctuary from danger.

Do not take sea urchins out of water and always handle them extremely carefully; the spines are often venomous. Plant-eating sea urchins appreciate an aquarium where algae is plentiful but they may also eat morsels of meat or tablet food. The Long-spined Urchin, *Diadema antillarum*, from the tropical western Atlantic has particularly long black spines.

Above: *Spiny sea urchins make good subjects for the invertebrate aquarium, but be sure to handle them with the utmost care!*

Left: *Shrimps and sea apples help keep the aquarium clean by active scavenging; one picks up pieces, the other sifts the substrate.*

Shrimps

Many of the tropical shrimps are highly coloured and provide cleaner services to fishes. Shrimps and crabs shed their shells as they grow, so do not be alarmed if you find two identical bodies in the aquarium from time to time!

Stenopus hispidus, the Banded Coral Shrimp, is found in all warm seas and is easily recognized by the alternate red and white bands on its body and limbs. It grows to about 75mm (3in) and sets up a 'cleaning station', to which other fishes will come for its services. Because of its territorial behaviour, it is regarded as aggressive towards its own kind and has earned the alternative common name of Boxing Shrimp. Keep only single specimens or matched pairs. Sexing the shrimps is reasonably easy as the underside of the female is blue.

Hippolysmata grabhami, a Cleaner Shrimp from the western Atlantic, is easily identified by its red-topped yellow body and the white line that runs through the centre of the back. A feature of this genus is its ability to change sex over a period of time, from male to fully functioning female. Sperm can be stored in the female for long periods, enabling fertilized eggs to be produced in the absence of the male. You can keep these shrimps singly or in groups of any size.

Lysmata wurdemanni, another Cleaner Shrimp from the western Atlantic, has red and white longitudinal markings reminiscent of those on the Squirrelfish. (A Mediterranean species, *L.seticaudata*, is similarly marked.) *L.debelius* is a rich dark red with one or two white spots. *Rhynchochinetes uritae*, the Dancing Shrimp from Sri Lanka also has red and white stripes.

Hymenocera picta, the Indo-Pacific Harlequin Prawn, or Clown Shrimp, has a white body with blue ringed markings. It lives in association with sea anemones but

it feeds exclusively on starfishes, so do not keep it with these echinoderms. Indeed, you should buy it only if you have a ready supply of native starfish on which it can feed.

The Anemone Shrimps *Periclimenes* species (*P.brevicarpalis* and *P.pedersoni*) have transparent bodies with brightly coloured 'patch' markings that help to camouflage them should they clamber among the growths of *Caulerpa* in the aquarium. However, they rarely leave their chosen anemone.

Odontodactylus scyllarus, the Mantis Shrimp, is a highly aggressive creature that should only be kept with large fishes in spacious aquariums. It lives in caves or burrows waiting to pounce on anything edible that happens to be passing. Small specimens inadvertently introduced into the aquarium soon grow up to terrorize other inmates of the tank, and their repeated clubbing actions have even been known to shatter the glass.

Above left:
Hippolysmata grabhami
The central white line along the red back makes this Cleaner Shrimp easy to identify. As you can see, it gets along well with its own kind.

Above: **Saron marmoratus**
This bristly-backed Indo-Pacific species has a banded, or ringed, pattern to its legs. Males can be distinguished from females by their greatly enlarged front legs.

Left: **Lysmata debelius**
The white-spotted, port-wine red coloration of this defiant-looking shrimp shows up well against any background in the aquarium.

Below: **Stenopus hispidus**
You will need a large tank to accommodate these shrimps; they are always willing to pick a quarrel with intruding neighbours.

Starfishes

Starfishes are quite suitable for inclusion in the invertebrate aquarium, where they fare much better than when they are forced to compete with fishes for food. They are excellent scavengers, but do not leave them to forage for themselves in the belief that they will always find as much food as they require. They need green foods in their diet and, if the algae growth in the aquarium is insufficient, you should provide them with supplementary rations of lettuce or spinach.

Remarkably, starfishes are able to regenerate their entire body even when only the smallest part of it remains.

Not all starfishes conform to the standard shape; *Culcita schmideliana* (the Pin-cushion Star), for example, becomes less obviously 'star-shaped' when adult. If overturned, it can right itself by inflating its body until the feet grip again. It grows up to 100mm (4in) across.

From the Indo-Pacific Oceans come the following species of starfish: *Fromia elegans*, which grows up to 80mm (3.2in) across (young specimens have black tips to the arms); *Linckia laevigata*, a bright blue starfish that may reach up to 400mm (16in); and the *Protoreaster* species, brilliantly coloured starfish that may be green, purple or bright red.

Oreaster nodosus is from the Caribbean, where it roams the sea-grass beds (rather than coral reefs) feeding on sponges.

Above: **Protoreaster lincki**
The stunning colours of this starfish are almost too vivid.

Below: **Fromia elegans**
Juvenile forms eventually lose the black tips to their legs with age.

Top: **Spirobranchus giganteus**
The long body of this tubeworm allows it to grow from deep within the corals yet still present its tentacles into clear water.

Above: **Sabella sp.**
The feathery tentacles of fanworms are very delicately constructed and well worth a closer look using a powerful magnifying glass.

Above right:
Spirographis spallanzani
The retractable tentacles of this fanworm are arranged spirally and may be white, red and brown. The length of the body may reach 200mm(8in), ideal for its habitat of soft mud in the Mediterranean and adjacent Atlantic Ocean. Keep this fanworm in the warmer waters of the tropical marine aquarium.

Tubeworms

The most commonly imported genera are *Sabellastarte* (Fanworms), and *Spirobranchus* and *Spirographis* (Tubeworms). All have tentacles – or, more accurately, gills – that perform the dual functions of respiration and the collection of food. The outer tube of *Sabellastarte* is mud-covered, while those of *Spirobranchus* and *Spirographis* are calcium based. These tubeworms will accept suspension foods and newly hatched brineshrimp. Fanworms and tubeworms are very sensitive to abrupt changes of light, and may damage their tentacles by retracting them suddenly when the lights are switched off or on. (See page 19 for stress avoidance.)

COLDWATER FISHES AND INVERTEBRATES

Right: Corynactis viridis, *the Jewel Anemone, often produces masses of small growths, usually of the same colour, by simple asexual reproduction. Each typically has three rings of tentacles. It is found below the low water mark, in the northeastern Atlantic Ocean.*

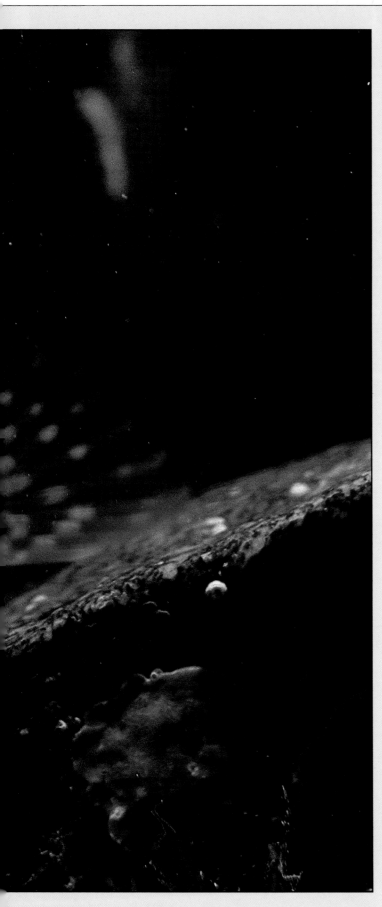

Since sea water extends outside the tropical zones to all regions of the world, you should not overlook the possibility of keeping fishes from cooler waters.

It may seem paradoxical, but it is safe to assume that the greatest numbers of tropical fishes are kept by hobbyists in temperate regions far removed from the fishes' wild origins. If this is so, then shouldn't we try to redress the balance a little by turning our attention to the varied aquatic life around our own shores?

Because the sun shines less brightly at higher latitudes, less light penetrates the water in temperate regions. And the water is often less clear, due to pollution and the heavy concentration of silt and mud constantly stirred up by coastal traffic. Understandably, fishes from these waters are not as brilliantly coloured as their tropical relatives, but they do offer one very real advantage for the hobbyist – they are far less expensive to obtain. In fact, if you live relatively near to the seashore you can collect your own specimens absolutely free! A further bonus is that collecting the fishes will bring you enjoyment in terms of personal involvement and you will soon appreciate the conservationist's point of view, perhaps more fully than you did before.

Just as in a tropical collection, the coldwater aquarium can be further expanded by collecting invertebrate life as well as fishes, but again the same precautions apply about keeping only compatible species together. Many of the sea anemones are very colourful, bearing in mind their murky origins, and there is also the advantage that should any species outgrow the tank, or outstay its welcome by more antisocial adult behaviour, you can just as easily return it to the wild to continue its natural lifespan.

Despite the apparent convenience of keeping local species, you may find problems arising during the summer months; as you enjoy the warm sun, the water temperature in the aquarium may rise uncomfortably high for its occupants and you may need to take steps to cool it down.

Left: *The commonly found Tompot Blenny,* Blennius gattorugine, *often adopts this typical pose; perched on the top of a rock, or peering out from an underwater cave, it watches for a passing smaller fish as a potential meal. It is a belligerent-looking creature, with the almost threatening crests (cirri) above the eyes.*

General care

Coldwater species require the same aquarium conditions as those described for tropical species (see page 16-31), with the obvious omission of heating equipment. Although substrate biological filtration is adequate, you should provide some extra water movement to create surface turbulence and to ensure well-oxygenated water.

As most of the species collected from the wild are likely to be rockpool inhabitants, you should furnish the aquarium with numerous retreats to recreate their natural habitat.

The biggest problem will be temperature regulation; in summer the average water temperature in the aquarium will be higher than you might expect to find in nature. Provide extra aeration at these times and improvise some kind of cooling system. Bags of ice cubes floated in the tank may help, and the serious hobbyist may even consider fitting a cooling plant, or using a second refrigerator to cool water in an outside filter system.

Feeding is not usually difficult as most fishes are more than willing to accept fish and shellfish meats. Only the fishes with the smallest mouths, such as Pipefishes and Sea Sticklebacks, will require copious amounts of tiny live food.

Regular monthly water changes will stabilize the water conditions. If you check the specific gravity, remember that it will give a higher reading at the lower water temperatures, probably about 1.025 at 15°C (59°F).

Collecting specimens

If you prepare the aquarium before you collect your fish, try to make sure that the water is the same specific gravity as the natural sea water in the rockpools. Otherwise, bring back as much natural water as you need to fill the tank or to reduce any differences in the specific gravity of the two bodies of water.

You must be well prepared to transport the livestock that you capture. Large plastic buckets with clip-on lids are ideal, although a double thickness of plastic film may be an adequate substitute for a lid. You will find that a battery-operated air pump, supplying air to an airstone in the water, will give the fish a better chance of surviving a long journey home. This is especially important during the summer months, when the journey may take longer. It is a good idea to take some extra sealable containers in which to collect some sea water, but make sure that it comes from an unpolluted or offshore site.

Collect specimens with care; rocks surrounding the rockpools are usually covered in very slippery seaweeds, so wear suitable footwear. Consult the tide timetables in advance to ensure that you get the maximum collecting time. DO NOT FORGET THE INCOMING TIDE. Remember also to leave the rockpool in a fit state for the animals left behind: if you collect invertebrates, such as sea anemones or starfishes, collect site and animal together, replacing any rocks that you remove with others to restore the number of hiding places in the pool. Transport anemones and other invertebrates separately from the fish; anemones will sting the fish in the close confines of a bucket, and fish may eat small invertebrates, such as shrimps, during transit.

NEVER OVER COLLECT. Not only is this bad practice from the conservation point of view, but it is also false insurance; it is better for the majority of specimens in a small collection to survive than to arrive home with none at all.

Family: BLENNIIDAE
Blennies

These are most common in rockpools, where they are found hiding under overhanging rocks. They are often confused with Gobies, but they lack the 'suction cup' formed by the fusion of the pelvic fins. Most Blennies have tentacles or a crest, described as 'cirri', positioned over the eye, giving them a distinctive appearance.

Above: **Blennius gattorugine**
The Tompot Blenny has some six attractive dark bars crossing its body vertically, easily seen once the fish comes out of its retreat.

Below: **Liophrys pholis**
The male Shanny's colours change from blotchy to very dark during the spawning period, but the mouth remains pale in contrast.

Aidablennius sphinx
Sphinx Blenny
● **Habitat:** Adriatic and Mediterranean.
● **Length:** 80mm (3.2in).
● **Diet:** All meaty worm foods.
● **Feeding manner:** Bottom feeder.
● **Aquarium compatibility:** May be territorial.

Once this fish leaves the security of its favourite bolt-hole, you can see that it is a most attractively coloured fish with dark bands crossing the body. It usually swims with the dorsal fin lowered, but raises it when alarmed. It spawns in caves, males physically covering any passing female inside.

Blennius gattorugine
Tompot Blenny
● **Habitat:** Mediterranean, Eastern Atlantic from West Africa to Scotland.
● **Length:** 200mm (8in).
● **Diet:** Live foods, meat and worm foods.
● **Feeding manner:** Bottom feeder.
● **Aquarium compatibility:** Can be territorial and may worry smaller fishes – and be themselves worried by larger ones.

These fishes prefer a tank decorated with medium-sized stones, under which they can hide. They can become tame, quite happy to make friends with you.

Blennius nigriceps
Black-headed Blenny
- **Habitat:** Mediterranean.
- **Length:** 40mm (1.6in).
- **Diet:** All meaty, worm foods.
- **Feeding manner:** Bottom feeder.
- **Aquarium compatibility:** May be territorial.

Whoever gave this fish its common name seems to have disregarded the predominant red of the body, concentrating instead on the darker reticulated patterning of the head region. *B.nigriceps* shares its habitat with the almost identical *Trypterygion minor*, from which it may be distinguished by the absence of a small extra dorsal fin in front of the main dorsal fins.

Lipophrys (Blennius) pholis
Shanny
- **Habitat:** Mediterranean, Eastern Atlantic from West Africa to Scotland.
- **Length:** 160mm (6.3in).
- **Diet:** Live foods, meat and worm foods.
- **Feeding manner:** Bottom feeder.
- **Aquarium compatibility:** Gregarious, but can be hard to please when it comes to a choice of hiding places; whelk shells are often acceptable.

Like all Blennies, these fish prefer a tank with plenty of hideaways. However, they also like to bask in the light, sometimes emerging from the water to do so. There are no cirri on the head.

Parablennius rouxi
Striped Blenny
- **Habitat:** Mediterranean.
- **Length:** 70mm (2.75in).
- **Diet:** All meaty, worm foods.
- **Feeding manner:** Bottom feeder.
- **Aquarium compatibility:** May be territorial.

A distinctive fish with a horizontal dark stripe from head to tail. The fins are colourless.

Salaria (Blennius) pavo
Peacock Blenny
- **Habitat:** Mediterranean.
- **Length:** 100mm (4in).
- **Diet:** Worm foods.
- **Feeding manner:** Bottom feeder.
- **Aquarium compatibility:** Territorial; needs plenty of retreats in which to hide.

Two obvious characteristics identify this species: the helmet-shaped hump above the eye in mature males and the blue-edged black spot just behind the eye. Blue-edged dark bands cross the green-yellow body.

Below: **Salaria pavo**
The Peacock Blenny tolerates wide extremes of temperature and salinities, and sometimes it will even enter fresh water.

Bottom: **Gobius jozo**
The somewhat misleadingly named Black Goby also tolerates brackish water. Mediterranean species spawn in the springtime.

Sticklebacks

Although freshwater Sticklebacks (*Gasterosteus* spp.) are able to tolerate some degree of salinity, there is one species within the family – *Spinachia spinachia* – that spends its entire life in marine conditions. Like its freshwater relatives, it also builds a nest in which to spawn, fabricating the structure from plant fragments stuck together with a secreted fluid.

Spinachia spinachia
Fifteen-spined Stickleback
- **Habitat:** Northeastern Atlantic.
- **Length:** 200mm (8in).
- **Diet:** Very small animal life.
- **Feeding manner:** Midwater feeder.
- **Aquarium compatibility:** Fin nipper; keep separately.

Gobies

Gobies have no lateral line system along the flanks of the body; instead, sensory pores connected to the nervous system appear on the head and over the body. They can live quite a long time; records show they have survived for up to ten years. A very large Family, Gobies inhabit many types of water – tropical and temperate, freshwater, brackish and full salt water.

Gobius cruentatus
Red mouthed Goby
- **Habitat:** Eastern Atlantic, North Africa to southern Ireland.
- **Length:** 180mm (7in).
- **Diet:** Crustaceans, worms, shellfish meats, small fishes.
- **Feeding manner:** Bottom feeder.
- **Aquarium compatibility:** Territorial at times.

Gobies are found on both sandy and rocky shores. Sand-dwelling species are naturally camouflaged, whereas rock-dwellers can be much more colourful.

Gobius jozo
Black Goby
- **Habitat:** Mediterranean, Black Sea and eastern Atlantic.
- **Length:** 150mm (6in).
- **Diet:** Worm foods, small crustaceans.
- **Feeding manner:** Bottom feeder.
- **Aquarium compatibility:** Territorial at times.

A generally dark blotched fish, but how it 'colours up' in captivity depends a great deal on the colour of its surroundings. It is very rarely black! Another scientific name for this fish is *Gobius niger*.

This species must have frequent meals of tiny live foods; brineshrimp are probably the most useful food for this purpose. The Stickleback lives for only about two years in the wild, and its life expectancy in the aquarium will be even shorter unless the feeding problem is solved.

Lepadogaster candollei
Connemara Clingfish
- **Habitat:** Eastern Atlantic, Mediterranean, Black Sea.
- **Length:** 75mm (3in).
- **Diet:** Worm foods.
- **Feeding manner:** Bottom feeder.
- **Aquarium compatibility:** Not known.

The common name refers to the ability of the fish to cling to rocks and other surfaces by means of a suction disc formed by the pelvic fins. Colours may vary but generally include reds, browns and greens; males have red dots on the head and on the lower part of the long-based dorsal fin.

Pomatoschistus minutus
Sand Goby
- **Habitat:** Eastern Atlantic, Mediterranean and Black Sea.
- **Length:** 95mm (3.7in).
- **Diet:** Worm foods.
- **Feeding manner:** Bottom feeder.
- **Aquarium compatibility:** Probably shy and likely to be predated upon by other fish. This species is best kept in a tank with its own kind.

Its natural camouflage colouring makes this fish difficult to see when you are collecting it. Being a sand colour, it will 'feel at home' with a similarly coloured covering on the aquarium floor.

Left: **Lepadogaster candollei**
The Connemara Clingfish has a variable coloration, mainly based on browns, reds and greens with some dotted markings. Male fish have red spots on the cheeks and at the base of the dorsal fin.

Family: LABRIDAE
Wrasses

Like their tropical relatives, Wrasses from temperate waters can also be brightly coloured. In fact, their colour can lead to identification and sexing problems; colour varies not only between the sexes (that of the male also changing at breeding time) but also depending on the mood of the fish and on the colour of the substrate! Sex reversals are also not uncommon. Young fishes act as cleanerfishes to other fishes, and many species hide away in crevices or bury themselves in the sand at night.

Family: PHOLIDIDAE
Gunnells

Often seen in the same areas as Blennies, members of the Pholididae are slender cylindrical fishes with a dorsal fin running the entire length of the back. The anal fin is also long based, occupying almost the rear half of the body. Both the dorsal and anal fins join with the caudal fin. The pectoral fins are small and the pelvic fins are limited to just one ray. Species are found on both sides of the North Atlantic Ocean and also on the northern Pacific coast of America.

Coris julis
Rainbow Wrasse
● **Habitat:** Mediterranean, eastern Atlantic.
● **Length:** 250mm (10in).
● **Diet:** Small marine animals, live foods.
● **Feeding manner:** Bottom feeder, although it will take surface plankton.
● **Aquarium compatibility:** Peaceful.

The long, slender, green-brown body has a horizontal white-red stripe. The eyes are red. These fishes are hermaphrodites, the females turning into fully functional males. Aquarium specimens are active during the day, but bury themselves in the substrate at night. This behaviour has not been observed in this species in the wild. Like their tropical relatives, juveniles act as cleaner fishes.

Pholis gunnellus
Butterfish; Gunnell
● **Habitat:** Eastern and Western Atlantic.
● **Length:** 250mm (10in).
● **Diet:** Crustaceans, worms, molluscs, shellfish meats.
● **Feeding manner:** Bottom feeder.
● **Aquarium compatibility:** Do not keep with small invertebrates.

The eel-like body has a long-based dorsal fin that is twice as long as the anal fin. It may have transverse dark bands on the body and white-edged markings along the base of the dorsal fin. This species is found under stones.

Left: **Coris julis**
The Rainbow Wrasse has colour variants depending on location and sex. Those from deeper water are red-brown; females have a pale spot on the gill cover base.

Below left: **Anthias anthias**
For a fish that has such appealing coloration, it is quite surprising that collectors have not yet endowed it with a popular name.

Bottom left: **Serranus hepatus**
The Brown Comber frequents fairly shallow waters, where it feeds on small fish and crustaceans.

Anthias anthias
● **Habitat:** Mediterranean, eastern Atlantic as far north as Biscay.
● **Length:** 240mm (9.5in).
● **Diet:** A varied selection of animal and meaty foods.
● **Feeding manner:** Bold.
● **Aquarium compatibility:** Peaceful.

The body is golden brown with blue speckling and the facial markings are blue. The long pelvic fins are yellow and blue. In the wild, the coloration may appear different because part of the colour spectrum of light is lost in deep waters due to absorption.

Serranus hepatus
Brown Comber
● **Habitat:** Mediterranean, eastern Atlantic (Senegal to Portugal).
● **Length:** 130mm (5in).
● **Diet:** Animal and meaty foods.
● **Feeding manner:** Bold.
● **Aquarium compatibility:** No reliable information is available, but do not keep with smaller fishes.

The reddish brown body has four or five vertical dark bars across it. The undersides of the body are pale. There is a black blotch on the dorsal fin at the junction of the hard and soft rays.

Family: SCORPAENIDAE
Scorpionfishes

Although they lack the ornate finnage of the tropical Scorpionfishes, species from temperate waters are just as dangerous. The spines on the head, which serve as positive species identifiers, are very venomous. When disturbed during the day, these sedentary nocturnal fishes swim only a short distance before settling down again to await any passing prey.

Scorpaena porcus
Scorpionfish
● **Habitat:** Mediterranean and eastern Atlantic (Biscay and further south).
● **Length:** 250mm (10in).
● **Diet:** Small fishes.
● **Feeding manner:** Lies in wait for prey.
● **Aquarium compatibility:** Distinctly unsociable; nocturnal. Keep in a separate tank.

The reddish brown mottled coloration makes this fish hard to see as it lies on the seabed. Not only is it a danger to other fishes, but also to swimmers who may inadvertently step on it. Use very hot water to bathe any wound, which may turn septic.

Above: **Scorpaena porcus**
Plume-like growths on the head, together with venomous spines on dorsal fin and gill covers make an attractive, but dangerous species.

Rockpools hold an extra fascination: they sustain a large number of life forms other than fish, and these, too, are well worth collecting. While it is true that temperate zone fishes and invertebrates do not match the brilliance of their tropical relatives, these animals will add colour and variety to the more subtle shades of the coldwater marine aquarium. The following is a representative selection.

Crabs
Although crabs seem to be endearing little creatures, the majority of 'free-swimming' species grow too large and become a disruptive influence in the aquarium. A better choice would be the smaller Hermit Crabs (*Pagurus* spp.), which interestingly shed their adopted shell for larger premises as they increase in size.

Nudibranchs
Relatively colourful species occur in the Mediterranean and northeastern Atlantic. *Chromodoris* and *Hypselodoris* are typical genera of these molluses.

Prawns and shrimps
It is easy to capture species of *Palaemon*, *Crangon* and *Hippolyte* - small shrimps and prawns – from rockpools in the northeastern and northwestern Atlantic and the Mediterranean. *Lysmata* is an interesting Mediterranean species, *L.seticaudata* being very similarly marked to the Indo-Pacific species *Rhynchonectes uritae*. Prawns and shrimps are excellent scavengers and often act as cleaners to other fishes. (See page 192 for tropical equivalents.) Egg-carrying females may provide extra numbers for the coldwater marine aquarium.

Above: **Palaemon serratus**
The Common Prawn is easily caught in rockpools – but be quick!

Above: **Actinia equina**
Strawberry Beadlet Anemones retract to form jelly-like blobs.

Sea anemones
Beadlet anemones (*Actinia equina*) can be found in a variety of colours. The columns can be red, green or brown and the tentacles are usually the same colour, but not always. They move around the aquarium, providing splashes of colour in an ever-changing pattern.

Actinia equina has two sub-species. *A.equina var. mesembryanthemum*, the Beadlet Anemone from the North and South Atlantic and the Mediterranean, is a very common sight in coldwater rockpools. The body and tentacles are bright red, but the body contracts to a dull red sphere just as you reach for it.

A.equina var. fragacea, the strawberry variant, is usually red with green spots – just like a strawberry. Its tentacles are usually red, but can be a paler pink. It is larger than the Beadlet and is found in the slightly deeper waters of the northeastern Atlantic and the Mediterranean.

The long tentacles of *Anemonia viridis (sulcata)*, the Snakelocks Anemone, are not fully retractable. Because it prefers strong light, it is found very close to the water surface in the northeastern Atlantic and Mediterranean. In the same waters you will find *Bunodactis verrucosa*, the Wartlet or Gem Anemone. It has tentacles with ringed markings and vertical rows of wartlike growths on its body, hence the common name.

Cerianthus membranaceus, the Cylinder Rose, is almost a cross between a sea anemone and a tubeworm, with a longer cylindrical body and less stocky in shape. The tube is often partially buried in the sand. It is a delicate animal that needs careful handling, although it may be able to regenerate a damaged tube fairly easily. Its tentacles vary in colour from species to species and are toxic to most fishes; for this reason, too, you should place other sea anemones beyond its reach. Unlike some sea anemones, *Cerianthus* does not move about the aquarium.

Although a fairly large anemone, *Condylactis aurantiaca* from the Mediterranean, has relatively short brown, white-ringed tentacles tipped with violet. Some *Epizoanthus* species are also native to the Mediterranean. They only grow to around 10mm (0.4in), but colonies can be found on rocks just below the waterline, where the constant water movement ensures a regular delivery of food.

Urticina (Tealia) felina var. coriacea, the Dahlia Anemone from the North Atlantic and northeastern Pacific, has a body covered with warts, sand and fragments of shell. Tentacles surround the patterned mouth disc. A similar species, *U.crassicornis*, occurs on the east coast of North America. *U.lofotensis* has white and pink tentacles on a red body and, with the larger *U.columbiana*, occurs in the northeastern Pacific. There is also a deepwater species known as *U.eques*.

Sea squirts
Sea squirts are vase-shaped bivalves that draw in water through one valve, trapping suspended minute food on a mucus-covered pharyngeal basket, and then exhale the water through the second siphon. *Halocynthia papillosa*, about 100mm (4in) tall, is red-orange in colour with many bristles around the siphons. It is common in the Mediterranean.

Sea urchins
Like their tropical relatives, sea urchins from temperate waters can also make interesting aquarium species. The Black Urchin, *Arbacia lixula*, from the Mediterranean is a purple-black in colour and looks like a short-spined version of the tropical *Diadema antillarum*.

Shellfish
When you are collecting from rockpools, do not forget that there are some surprisingly active shellfish that will add extra interest to the aquarium. Species of limpet (*Patella*) and winkle (*Littorina*) are quite suitable. Do not ignore empty shells; a collection of shells of various sizes make ideal homes for a growing hermit crab.

Above: **Crossaster papposus**
The Sun Star has more than twice as many 'arms' as other starfishes.

Sponges
Sponges are usually difficult to keep in the aquarium as they are very sensitive to adverse water conditions. They must have well-oxygenated, crystal-clear water and are not at all compatible with sea anemones. They attach themselves to shells, even those that contain hermit crabs. If this happens, they will devour the shell and in turn become the home of the crab. *Suberites domuncula* is a common Mediterranean and Atlantic species.

Starfishes
The following species are among the wide range of starfishes found in temperate waters.

Asterias rubens is commonly found in the northeastern Atlantic, where it feeds on mussels and scallops, prising them apart with its feet and introducing its stomach into the shell. The skin is covered with many tubercles.

Astropecten aranciacus, the Red Comb Star from the Mediterranean and northeastern Atlantic, is a large predatory starfish (up to 500mm/20in) with comblike teeth along the edges of its arms.

Echinaster sepositus, a Mediterranean species, grows to 300mm(12in). Fertilized eggs develop directly into small starfishes.

Ophidiaster ophidianus, another red starfish from the Mediterranean, grows to 200mm (8in). The long arms issuing from an almost non-existent central 'body' of this starfish are cylindrical in section rather than flat, with sharply tapering ends.

Above:
Cerianthus membranaceus
Elegant, but delicate in the tank.

Above: *A whelk shell hosts anemones and a hermit crab.*

Glossary

Activated carbon Material used in mechanical/chemical filtration systems (external 'power filter' canister types) to remove, by adsorption, dissolved matter.

Aeration Act of introducing compressed air to the aquarium; to ventilate the water to facilitate the intake of oxygen and to expel carbon dioxide.

Airstone Small block of porous wood (better than ceramic types) through which air is passed to produce air bubbles in the water for aeration purposes, or to draw water through filters or protein skimmers.

Airline (Tubing) Neoprene tubing to convey compressed air from an airpump to aquarium equipment such as airstones, filters, ozonizers, and protein skimmers.

Algae Primitive unicellular plants; marine plants such as *Caulerpa* are strictly algae rather than proper plants. Bright lighting is needed for algae growth. Much appreciated by herbivorous fishes.

All-glass tanks Aquariums made by bonding five otherwise unsupported panels of glass directly together with aquarium silicone sealant to form an aquarium.

Ammonia (NH₃) First byproduct of decaying organic material; also excreted by the fishes' gills. Toxic to fishes and invertebrates.

Anal fin Single fin mounted vertically below the fish.

Artemia salina Scientific name of brineshrimp.

Barbel Whisker-like growth around the mouth or head; used for detecting food by taste.

Benedenia Trematode parasite similar to *Dactylogyrus* gill fluke.

Biological filtration Means of water filtration using bacteria, *Nitrosomonas* and *Nitrobacter*, to reduce otherwise toxic ammonium-based compounds to safer substances such as nitrates.

Bivalve A mollusc or shell-dwelling animal with two respiratory valves.

Brackish water Water containing approximately 10% sea water; found in estuaries where fresh water rivers enter the sea.

Brineshrimp Saltwater crustacean, *Artemia salina*, whose dry-stored eggs can be hatched to provide live food for fish or invertebrates.

Buffering action Ability of a liquid to maintain its pH value, i.e. to resist pH changes. Calcareous substrates may assist in this respect.

Calcareous Formed of, or containing, calcium carbonate, a substance that may help to maintain a high pH in the aquarium.

Carnivore Will eat meat foods.

Caudal fin Single fin mounted vertically at the rear of the fish, the tail.

Caudal peduncle Part of fish's body joining the caudal fin to the main body.

Cirri Crestlike growths found above the eyes in some species, such as *Blennius*.

Coelenterates Family to which corals, jellyfish and sea anemones belong.

Commensalism Living practical partnership, where one party derives more benefit than the other.

Copper Metal used in copper sulphate form as the basis for many marine aquarium remedies. Poisonous to fishes in excess, and even more so, at much lower levels, to invertebrates.

Coral (hard) Natural growths of polyps whose external calcareous skeleton form coral reefs in warm waters.

Coral (soft) Live, more flowerlike, corals with retractable tentacles, kept for their colours, fantastic shapes and decorative beauty.

Coral sand Sand for the marine aquarium made from crushed coral.

Counter-current More efficient design of protein skimmer where the water flows against the main current of air, giving a longer exposure time for sterilization.

Cover glass Panel of glass or plastic to form an anti-condensation, anti-evaporation protection placed on top of the aquarium immediately below the hood.

Crustacean Type of aquatic animal with a jointed 'body shell', such as the shrimp.

Cryptocaryon Parasitic infection, often referred to as the marine equivalent of the freshwater whitespot disease *Ichthyophthirius*.

Daphnia Freshwater crustacean, the water flea, used as food in the marine aquarium.

Demersal Term usually applied to eggs or to spawning action of fishes. Demersal eggs are heavier than water and are laid in prepared spawning sites on the sea bed. The fertilized eggs are then guarded by one or both adult fishes until hatching occurs.

Diffuser An alternative name for airstones.

Direct-current Design of protein skimmer where the water flows with the main current of ozonized air. May provide too short an exposure time for efficient sterilization.

Dorsal fin Single fin mounted vertically on top of the fish; some species have two dorsal fins, one behind the other. Many marine species have poisonous rays in the dorsal fin.

Dropsy Disease, where body fluids build up and produce a swollen body.

Enchytraeids Small terrestrial worms (whiteworms, grindalworms, etc.) that can be cultured by the hobbyist for food. Very fatty foods; do not give them in excessive amounts as they can cause internal disorders.

Estuarine Fishes that frequent estuaries, able to tolerate changing salinities.

Euryhaline Ability of some species, such as eels and salmon, to enter both fresh water and salt water.

Filter Device for cleaning the aquarium water. May be biological, chemical or mechanical in form, internally or externally mounted. High rate of water flow recommended for marine aquariums.

Filter feeder Animal (fish or invertebrate) that sifts water for microscopic food, e.g. pipefishes, tubeworms.

Filter medium Materials used in filtration systems to remove suspended or dissolved materials from the water.

Fin rot Bacterial ailment; the tissue between the rays of the fin rots away.

Fins Collapsible, erectile membranes attached to the fish's body: used to produce propulsion or provide manoeuvrability.

Fluorescent Type of lighting; glass tube filled with fluorescing material that produces light under the influence of an electric discharge. Cool running and recommended for aquarium use; several tubes will be needed if luxuriant algae growth is required.

Foam fractionation Method of separating out proteins from water by foaming action. Also known as protein skimming.

Fry Very young fish.

Fungus Parasitic infection, causing cotton-wool-like growths on the body.

Gallon (Imperial) Measure of liquid volume (1 Imperial gallon = 1.2 US gallons = 4.54 litres.)

Gallon (U.S.) Measure of liquid volume (1 US gallon = 0.83 Imp gallons = 3.8 litres.)

Gill flukes Trematode parasites, such as *Dactylogyrus*, that in severe infestation cause rapid breathing and gaping gills.

Gills Membranes through which fish absorb dissolved oxygen from the water and release carbon dioxide into the water during respiration.

Grolux Brand name of fluorescent lighting with emphasized red and blue wavelengths; ideal for encouraging plant growth.

Heater Submersible device for heating the aquarium water; must be controlled by a thermostat, which is usually built in to make a heaterstat.

Herbivore Vegetable or plant eater.

Hood Cover of aquarium containing the light fittings, also known as the reflector.

Hydrometer Device for measuring the specific gravity (S.G.) of the salt water, especially useful when making up synthetic mixes for use in the aquarium. May be either a free-floating or swing-needle type.

Impeller Electrically driven propeller that produces water flow through filters.
Invertebrate Literally 'animals without backbones', such as sea anemones, corals, shrimps, etc.
Irradiation Method of exposing food to gamma rays to sterilize it.

Lateral line Line of perforated scales along the flanks that lead to a pressure-sensitive nervous system. Enables fish to detect vibrations in surrounding water caused by other fishes, or reflected vibrations of their own movement from obstacles.
Length (standard) Length of fish (SL) measured from snout to end of main body; excludes caudal fin.
Litre Measure of liquid volume (1 litre = 0.22 Imp gallons = 0.26 US gallons).
Lymphocystis Viral ailment that causes cauliflower-like growths on the skin and fins.

Marine Pertaining to the sea.
Mercury vapour Type of high-intensity lamp.
Mimicry The close resemblance of one creature to another. Specifically, the resemblance of predatory fishes to 'safe' fishes, allowing them to gain 'unfair' advantage over other animals.
Mollusc Group of animals that includes shellfish and nudibranchs.
Mouthbrooder Fishes that incubate fertilized eggs in the mouth until they hatch. The fry also shelter in the mouth for safety.
Mysis Commercially available marine shrimp used as live food.

Nauplius Term used generally for the newly hatched form of brineshrimp.
Nitrate (NO$_3$) Less toxic nitrogenous compound produced by *Nitrobacter* bacteria from nitrite.
Nitrite (NO$_2$) Toxic nitrogenous compound produced by *Nitrosomonas* bacteria from ammonia. Toxic to fishes, and even more so to invertebrates.

Omnivore Eats all foods.
Oodinium Single-celled parasite causing coral fish disease. Highly infectious, but curable with proprietary remedies.
Osmosis Passage of liquid through a semi-permeable membrane to dilute a more concentrated solution. Accounts for water losses through the skin of marine fishes.
Ozone (O$_3$) Three-atom, unstable form of oxygen used as a disinfectant. Best used in conjunction with a protein skimmer.
Ozonizer Device that produces ozone from air by high-voltage electrical discharge.

Pectoral fins Paired fins, one on each side of the body immediately behind the gill cover.
Pelagic Strictly meaning 'of the open sea', this term is also applied to eggs and spawning methods. Pelagic eggs are lighter than water and are scattered after an ascending spawning action between a pair of fishes in open water.
Pelvic fins Paired fins on the ventral (lower) surface, usually immediately below the gill covers. Not all marine fishes have pelvic fins; often only a rudimentary stub is present, or perhaps a flap of skin.
pH Measure of water acidity or alkalinity; the scale ranges from 1 (extremely acid) through 7 (neutral) to 14 (extremely alkaline). Seawater is normally pH 8.3.
Polyps Living filter-feeding animals whose accumulated dead skeletons produce decorative coral.
Power filters External canister-type filtration devices, usually fitted with an electric impeller to drive aquarium water through the enclosed filter media.
Powerhead Electric impeller system fitted to filters or used on their own to create water movement.
Protein skimmer Device that removes protein material from the water by foaming: may be air-operated or electrically powered. Also used in conjunction with ozonized air for further water sterilization purposes.

Quarantine Period of separation for new fishes to screen them from any latent diseases.

Rays Bony supports in fins.
Reaction tube Part of protein skimmer where foaming occurs. When used with ozonized air, the reaction tube effectively isolates fishes from harmful ozone.
Reef Outcrop of coral growths in the sea, often large enough to protect the shore from wave action. May form lagoons, atolls or larger offshore formations, e.g. Australia's Great Barrier Reef.

Salinity Measure of saltiness of the water. Quoted in terms of gm/litre. Natural sea water has a salinity of about 33.7 gm/litre.
Salt Sodium chloride, but more usually the salt mix to make synthetic seawater.
Salt mix Materials to make synthetic seawater, available in standard packs to make up specific quantities of water.
Scales Bony overlapping plates covering the fish's skin, for protection and streamlining.
Shimmying Condition of shivering; usually the result of a chill.
Shoal Group of fishes of the same species.
Silicone sealant Adhesive used to bond glass, stop leaks and build up rock formations.
Siphon A length of tube with which to remove water from the aquarium by siphonic action; may also refer to inhalant

organ of molluscs.
Spawning Act of reproduction involving the fertilization of the eggs.
Specific gravity (S.G.) Ratio of density of measured liquid to that of pure water. Seawater has an S.G. of around 1.025.
Starter Circuit necessary to initialize ('start') the discharge in fluorescent lighting.
Substrate Aquarium base covering.
Swimbladder Hydrostatic organ enabling fish to maintain chosen depth and position in the water column.
Symbiosis Relationship between two parties, each deriving mutual benefit, such as cleanerfish and their 'customers'.

Tail Caudal fin
Temperate Non-tropical areas; in this encyclopedia, the term 'coldwater marines' refers to fishes and invertebrates from these cooler locations.
Territory Area chosen by a fish as its own.
Thermometer Device for measuring temperature. Floating, stick-on or electronic versions available.
Thermostat Device for controlling the supply of electricity to a heater, usually mounted with the heater in a combined unit.
Total system Term given to aquariums with built-in filtration and other management systems providing full water treatment.
Trickle filter Slow filter, often involving inert granules, sand or algal system. Anaerobic types convert nitrates back to free nitrogen.
Tropical Warm-water areas, applied to fishes and invertebrates from such locations.
Tubifex Freshwater aquatic worm used as food. Often suspected of carrying disease.

Ultraviolet (UV) High-energy, small-wavelength type of light used as disinfectant, produced by a special tube usually enclosed in a surrounding water jacket through which aquarium water is passed.

Ventral Undersurface of a fish. May be flattened in bottom-dwelling species.
Ventral fins Alternative name for pelvic fins.

Water change Regular replacement of a proportion (usually 20-25%) of aquarium water with new synthetic seawater.
Water flea Common name for *Daphnia*, a freshwater crustacean used as a food.
Water turnover Water flow rate through a filter. For marine aquariums a high water turnover is recommended.
Wattage Unit of electrical consumption used to classify power of aquarium heaters or brightness of lamps.

General index

Page numbers in **bold** indicate major references including accompanying photographs or diagrams. Page numbers in *italics* indicate captions to other illustrations. Less important text entries are shown in normal type.

Species index

Page numbers in **bold** indicate major references including accompanying photographs or diagrams. Page numbers in *italics* indicate captions to other illustrations. Less important text entries are shown in normal type.

Picture Credits

Artists
Copyright of the artwork illustrations on the pages following the artist's name is the property of Interpet Publishing

Stonecastle Graphics: Line artwork on pages 64-185
Phil Holmes: 22, 24, 27, 29
Stuart Watkinson 9, 16(B), 17(B), 18(T), 20(BR), 28(R), 30(T), 34, 45(T), 48, 53(BL), 55(B), 56

Photographs
The publishers wish to thank the following photographers and agencies who have supplied photographs for this book. The photographs have been credited by page number and position on the page: (B)Bottom, (T)Top, (C)Centre, (BL)Bottom left etc.

David Allison: 47(BR), 63(T), 72(B), 73, 77, 78, 80(B), 99(T), 103, 110(B), 118(B), 123(B), 127(B), 129(T), 130, 134, 138(B), 147, 165, 170, 191(BR)
Ardea (London): 10(CR, Jim Zipp), 16(TC, Kurt Amsler)
Peter Biller: 74, 84, 98, 116(T), 118(T), 131(T), 141(BR), 146(T), 154(B), 164(B), 167(T), 168, 178(B), 189(TR), 190(BR), 191(BL), 192(C)
Bioquatic Photo - Alf J Nilsen (ajnilsen@online.no): Half-title (RC), Title page (R), Contents page (B), Copyright page (B), 6-7, 13, 15(C), 17, 19, 43(BR)
Dieter Brockmann: 150, 173(B), 193(CR)
Bruce Coleman: 20(BL, Pacific Stock), 55(Jeff Foott), 67(T, Jane Burton), 71(TR, Alan Power), 108(B, H. Rivarola), 114(Jane Burton), 137(B, Alain Compost), 145(T, Bill Wood), 149(T, H. Rivarola)
Joachim Grosskopf: Half-title (R), 83(TL), 92, 95(T), 97(B), 99(B), 101(T), 105(B), 107(B), 117(T), 120, 121(T), 123(T), 127(T), 154-155(TL), 171, 187(T), 189(CL, BR), 190(TL, BL)
Les Holliday: 53(BR)
Andy Horton: 11
Jan-Eric Larsson: 33(BC), 62-63, 68(B), 70(B), 72(T), 80(T), 96,100(B), 106(T), 119, 121(C), 128(B), 156-157(T), 177(TR), 183(T), 184, 185
Dick Mills: 93(B), 100(T), 108(T), 126, 133(B), 138(T), 151(B)
Heather Angel/Natural Visions: Title page (L), 60-61(Ian Took), 104(T), 106(B), 111(T), 115(T, K. Sagar), 133(T), 142, 143, 151(T), 167(B, Ian Took), 180, 194-5, 195, 196, 199(TL,BL,TC,BR)
Arend van den Nieuwenhuizen: 64, 65,66, 67(B), 69, 71(TL,B),

75, 79(B), 81, 82, 83(TR), 85, 86(B), 87, 88-9(T), 93(T), 95(B), 97(T), 101(BL), 102, 107(T), 109, 112, 113(T), 115(B), 116(B), 124, 125, 129(B), 131(B), 132(B), 139, 140(T), 144, 145(B), 149(B), 152, 155(B), 157(B), 159(B), 162, 172, 174, 175, 177(B), 181, 182(T), 189(CR,BL), 191(C), 193(T)
Photomax (Max Gibbs): Half-title (L, RB), Copyright-Contents page (C), Contents page (TR), 8, 9, 10(TR), 24-25, 52, 54, 59, 76(T), 88(B), 91, 104(B), 117(B), 122, 137(T), 140-1(BL), 153, 158, 159(T), 160, 161, 163(T), 164(T), 176(B), 179(B), 180(B), 183(B)
Geoff Rogers © Interpet Publishing: 12, 14, 15(TC, BL), 16(TR), 18(B), 21, 23, 26, 28(L), 30(B), 31, 32, 33(T), 35, 36, 37, 38, 39, 40, 41, 42, 44, 45(B), 47(CB), 49, 50, 51, 57
Mike Sandford: 121(B), 132(T), 148, 156(B), 163(B), 166, 173(T), 179(T), 182(B), 190(TR, C), 198(T,C)
David Sands: 70(T), 128(T), 135
Gunther Spies: 89(B), 169
William A. Tomey: Endpapers, 33(BR), 68(T), 79(T), 86(T), 90, 94, 110(T), 111(B), 113(B), 136, 155(T), 186-7, 188, 189(TL), 191(T), 192(TL, TR, B), 193(CL, BL, BR), 197, 198(BL, BR), 199(TR), 207
F. L. Trutnau: 76(B), 101(BR), 176(T)
Uwe Werner: 146(B), 177(TL), 178(T)

Acknowledgments
The publishers wish to thank the following individuals and organizations for their help in the preparation of this book:

Arcadia, Croydon, Surrey; Aquaworld, Warrington, Cheshire; Heaver Tropics, Ash, Sevenoaks, Kent; NT Laboratories Ltd., Wateringbury, Kent; Swallow Aquatics, Southfleet, Kent; Tropical Marine Centre, Chorleywood, Herts.

The information and recommendations in this book are given without any guarantees on the part of the author and publisher, who disclaim any liability with the use of this material.